QuickBooks® Online

FOR DUMMIES®
A Wiley Brand

2nd Edition

P9-CJK-356

QuickBooks® Online

FOR DUMMIES®

A Wiley Brand

2nd Edition

by Elaine Marmel

QuickBooks® Online For Dummies®, 2nd Edition

Published by: **John Wiley & Sons, Inc.,** 111 River Street, Hoboken, NJ 07030-5774, www.wiley.com

Copyright © 2016 by John Wiley & Sons, Inc., Hoboken, New Jersey

Published simultaneously in Canada

For general information on our other products and services, please contact our Customer Care Department within the U.S. at 877-762-2974, outside the U.S. at 317-572-3993, or fax 317-572-4002. For technical support, please visit www.wiley.com/techsupport.

Wiley publishes in a variety of print and electronic formats and by print-on-demand. Some material included with standard print versions of this book may not be included in e-books or in print-on-demand. If this book refers to media such as a CD or DVD that is not included in the version you purchased, you may download this material at http://booksupport.wiley.com. For more information about Wiley products, visit www.wiley.com.

Library of Congress Control Number: 2015960528

ISBN 978-1-119-12733-8 (pbk); ISBN 978-1-119-12735-2 (ebk); ISBN 978-1-119-12734-5 (ebk)

Manufactured in the United States of America

10 9 8 7 6 5 4 3 2 1

Contents at a Glance

Table of Contents

Introduction

*H*ave you been thinking about moving your accounting into a web-based product? Are you a QuickBooks desktop user who wants to stick with something you know but wants the flexibility of a web-based product? Are you interested in finding out more about Intuit's web-based product, QuickBooks Online (QBO)? Are you an accountant who is considering beginning to support your QuickBooks clients via QuickBooks Online Accountant (QBOA)? If you answered yes to any of these questions, this book is for you.

QuickBooks Online and QuickBooks Online Accountant are web-based accounting solutions from Intuit. Don't be fooled; they are *not* the desktop product migrated to the web. They've been built from the ground up to function on the Internet.

About This Book

Intuit's web-based accounting product is really almost two products: end users who want to do their accounting on the web use QBO, whereas accountants use QBOA, which enables the accountant to log in to a client's books and make changes and queries as needed. Although much of QBO and QBOA look and behave alike, QBOA incorporates tools that an accountant needs while working on a client's books. And accountants need to manage multiple client companies, whereas end-user clients do not.

QBO and QBOA are not for everyone. Before you commit to Intuit's web-based solution, you need to explore the available editions and examine the requirements for the products.

In the first part of the book, I examine what QBO and QBOA are — and what they aren't — and I describe what you need to be able to use QBO and QBOA. I explain the various editions available and the product costs at the time I wrote this book, and I describe the features available. And in Chapter 1, you'll find some information about the available interfaces for QBO and QBOA (you can work with the products using a browser or using an app).

The second part of the book focuses on using QBO and is aimed at the end user; but, the accountant who opens a client's company via QBOA will be able to use the same tools that the end user uses to manage lists, enter transactions, and print reports.

The third part of the book is aimed at the accountant and covers using QBOA.

I don't pretend to cover every detail of every feature in QBO or QBOA. Instead, I've focused on covering the tools I think most users will need as they navigate QBO and QBOA.

As I discuss in Chapter 2, there are different versions of QBO; I used QBO Plus as I wrote this book because it contains the most features. Users of other versions might find references in this book to features they don't have because they aren't using the Plus version.

Before we dive in, let's get a few technical convention details out of the way:

- ✔ Text that you're meant to type as it appears in the book is **bold.** The exception is when you're working through a steps list: Because each step is bold, the text to type is not bold.

- ✔ Web addresses and programming code appear in monofont. If you're reading a digital version of this book on a device connected to the Internet, note that you can tap or click a web address to visit that website, like this: www.dummies.com.

- ✔ You can use QBO and QBOA from the Windows app for QBO and QBOA or from any of the major browsers (Chrome, Firefox, Safari, or Internet Explorer). In my experience, QBO and QBOA function best in Chrome. For that reason, I've devoted The Part of Tens chapters in this book to Chrome so that, if you aren't familiar with Chrome, you can get up and running more quickly.

- ✔ When I discuss a command to choose, I separate the elements of the sequence with a command arrow that looks like this: ➪. For example, when you see Chrome Menu ➪ Settings, that means you should click the Chrome Menu button (on the right side of the Chrome screen — see Chapter 16 for a description of Chrome's screen elements) and, from the drop-down menu that appears, click Settings.

Foolish Assumptions

I had to assume some things about you to write this book. Here are the assumptions I made:

- You know that you need to manage the accounts for your business, and you might even have some sort of setup in place to record this information. I *don't* assume that you know how to do all that on a computer.

- You have some interest in managing the accounts for your business using a web-based product.

- You are probably but not necessarily a QuickBooks desktop edition user.

- You have a personal computer (that you know how to turn on) running Microsoft Windows Vista, Windows 7, Windows 8.1 or Windows 10. I wrote this book using Windows 10.

- You might have purchased an edition of QuickBooks Online, but not necessarily.

Icons Used in This Book

Think of these icons as the fodder of advice columns. They offer (hopefully) wise advice or a bit more information about a topic under discussion.

This icon points out juicy tidbits that are likely to be repeatedly useful to you — so please don't forget them.

Danger, Will Robinson, danger! Well, okay, it's really not life-threatening. In this book, you see this icon when I'm trying to help you avoid mistakes that can cost money.

This icon signifies that you'll find additional relevant content at www. dummies.com/extras/quickbooksonline.

Beyond the Book

In addition to the content in this book, you'll find some extra content available at the www.dummies.com website:

- ✔ **The Cheat Sheet for this book at** www.dummies.com/cheatsheet/quickbooksonline.

- ✔ **Online articles covering additional topics at** www.dummies.com/extras/quickbooksonline.

  Here you'll find the articles referred to on the page that introduces each part of the book. So, feel free to visit www.dummies.con/extras/quickbooksonline. You'll feel at home there . . . find coffee and donuts . . . okay, maybe not the coffee and donuts (hard to deliver over the ether), but you can find information about setting up budgets in QBO and details on converting a desktop QuickBooks company to a QBO company.

- ✔ **Updates to this book, if any, at** www.dummies.com/extras/quickbooksonline.

Where to Go from Here

Simply turn the page. Seriously. You can dive in anywhere you want and come back as often as you like. You don't have to read through this book cover to cover, because each section stands alone and provides step-by-step instructions for common tasks. You should consider this book a reference that you use when you need it.

That said, if you're just getting started with QBO or QBOA, you might want to turn the page and follow, in order, the chapters in Part 1. Then feel free to explore any topic you like, using the table of contents or the index to help you find a topic.

Part I

Getting Started with QuickBooks Online

getting started

with

QuickBooks

Online

In this part . . .

- ✔ Examine what QBO is and what it isn't.
- ✔ Learn the requirements to use QBO.
- ✔ Meet the QBO interface.

Chapter 1

Introducing QBO and QBOA

In This Chapter

▶ Taking a first look at QuickBooks Online and QuickBooks Online Accountant

▶ Considering the cloud

▶ Meeting requirements to use QBO and QBOA

QuickBooks Online (QBO) and QuickBooks Online Accountant (QBOA) are web-based products you can use to manage your business's accounting. This chapter introduces these products and discusses whether you should move into the cloud to manage your accounting. It also examines the system requirements for these products.

QBO for the Client and QBOA for the Accountant

QuickBooks Online offers you the ability to manage your business's accounting in the cloud. The product is divided into two products: one for end users and the other for accountants. Interfaces for both products are available on multiple platforms.

QBO is the cloud-based product for end users who need to perform typical accounting tasks. QBO is based on the same principles as the QuickBooks desktop product — that is, it uses lists to, for example, manage customers and vendors, and it includes transactions similar to the ones found in the QuickBooks desktop product. But, QBO is *not* simply a "rewrite" of the QuickBooks desktop product for the web.

QBOA is the cloud-based portal that accountants use to access client QBO companies, work in them, and communicate with clients. QBOA also comes with one free company that accountants can use to track their own businesses.

Comparing interfaces

QBO and QBOA were initially written and optimized to be used in the major web browsers — Chrome, Firefox, Safari, and Internet Explorer. Later, Intuit added QBO apps that you can use for Windows, the Mac, and mobile devices. In this section, you explore what QBO and QBOA look like in a browser and in the Windows app.

In a browser, an open company in QBO looks similar to the one shown in Figure 1-1. I cover the interface in more detail in Chapter 3, but for the time being, the most important thing to notice is the Navigation bar that runs down the left side of the screen. If you've been a QuickBooks desktop user and you've used the Left Icon Bar in that product, you might find the Navigation bar a familiar tool. The Left Icon Bar and the Navigation bar work the same way; you click a link in either of them to navigate to a portion of the program.

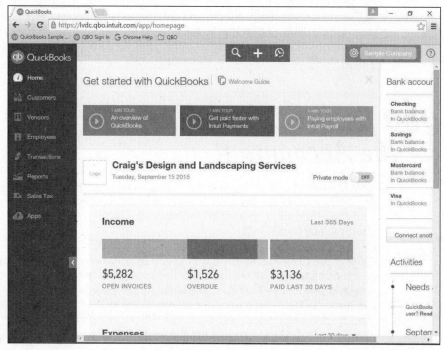

Figure 1-1:
An open company in QBO.

The arrow in the Navigation bar enables you to collapse the Navigation bar to view just the icons (and expand it back to the view in Figure 1-1). When you collapse the Navigation bar (you see an example of it collapsed in Chapter 3), you have more screen real estate to view the right side of the QBO interface.

REMEMBER

At the time I wrote this, the arrow feature was being tested in QuickBooks Labs. I include this feature in some of the figures because I want to give you an idea of things making their way into the software. You, too, can turn on features being tested in the lab; see Chapter 3 for details.

At the top of the screen, you see tools that help QBO users create transactions, search for existing transactions, and view recent transactions.

Now compare Figure 1-1 with Figure 1-2, which shows what an accountant sees after opening a client's company using QBOA in a browser. The accountant's view of a QBO company looks a bit different from a client QBO user's view. First, the tools used to search for a transaction, go to a report, and view recent transactions are combined into one Search box. And second, the Accountant Tools menu (the briefcase icon) displays tools not found in QBO that help accountants manage client companies.

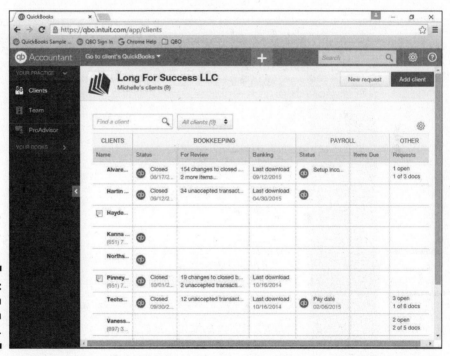

Figure 1-2:
An open company in QBOA.

Even though an open company looks a bit different depending on whether it is opened using QBO or QBOA, the basic functionality doesn't really change, other than accountants having more options than end users have.

Because QBOA contains functionality that QBO doesn't have, I've organized this book so that QBO users can focus on Part II when using the product, and QBOA users can use the information in both Parts II and III to work in a company online.

To browse or not to browse. . .

In addition to working in a browser, you also can work in QBO and QBOA apps, available on Windows and Macs. Figure 1-3 shows QBOA in the Windows app.

QBO apps are also available for mobile devices on the iPhone, the iPad, and Android devices.

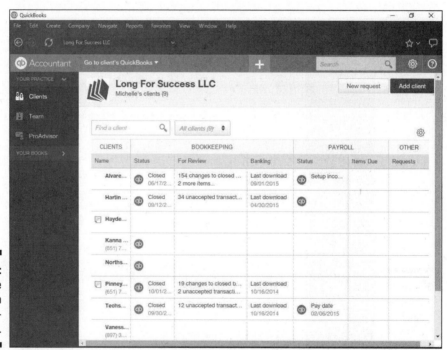

Figure 1-3: QBOA while working in the Windows app.

If you compare Figure 1-3 to Figure 1-2, you'll notice that, once again, QBOA users have the same additional options in the Windows app that they have in a browser. The biggest visual difference between QBO and QBOA in the Windows app and QBO and QBOA in a browser appears in the menus that appear at the top of the screen in the Windows app. If you've been a QuickBooks desktop product user, you know that you use the menus to navigate. Under the hood, the Windows app offers some options that you won't find readily available in a browser, such as the ability to work in multiple windows.

The same visual distinction holds true for QBO users working in a browser or in the Windows app; the only difference you'll notice in your working environment is the appearance of the menus in the Windows app. So, take your choice: Work in a browser, or work in the app, or work in both, depending on your needs at the moment! You're not limited; you don't have to choose between an app or a browser. Work in one or the other, as suits your needs at the moment.

At the time I wrote this book, Intuit was working on optimizing the Windows app, so it still functioned slowly. For that reason, I used QBO and QBOA in a browser predominantly.

Understanding the Cloud

Just to make sure we're on the same page here, I'm defining the *cloud* as software and data housed securely in data centers and accessed securely using the Internet. Working in the cloud can increase your efficiency by offering you the opportunity to work anywhere, communicate easily with others, and collaborate in real time.

Regardless of whether you use QBO or QBOA in a browser or in an app, both the software and the data are housed on servers controlled by Intuit and accessible via the Internet.

In the traditional model of software use, you buy software and install it on your desktop. Or you might buy the software and install it on a vendor's server. QBO and QBOA fall into the category of Software as a Service (SaaS). You typically don't buy SaaS software; instead, you rent it (that is, you purchase a subscription).

Because SaaS software is typically web-based software, you typically access SaaS software over the Internet using a browser. A *browser* is software installed on your local computer or mobile device that you use to browse the Internet — and to work with web-based software such as QBO and QBOA. In the case of QBO and QBOA, you can work with these web-based SaaS products using either a browser or an app you download to your computer.

Using web-based software can be attractive for a number of reasons. For example, using web-based software, you have access to that software's information anywhere, anytime, from any device — computer or mobile.

Some folks see the "anywhere, anytime" feature as a potential disadvantage because it makes information too readily available — and therefore a target for hackers. Intuit stores your data on servers that use bank-level security and encryption, and Intuit automatically backs up your data for you.

In addition, web-based software like QBO and QBOA promote collaboration and can help you save time. Using QBO and QBOA, accountants, bookkeepers, and clients can communicate about issues that arise, as described in Chapter 14.

Then there's the issue of keeping software up to date. Desktop software such as QuickBooks is updated typically once each year. Unlike their desktop cousin, QBO and QBOA are updated every two to four weeks.

Because updating occurs so frequently to QBO and QBOA, by the time this book is published, things (and screens) might have changed. Actually, make that "probably have changed."

Should You Move to the Cloud?

Before you make the move to the cloud, you should consider the needs of your business in the following areas:

- Invoicing, point of sale, electronic payment, and customer relationship management
- Financial and tax reporting
- Budgeting
- Time-tracking and payroll
- Inventory, job costing, and job scheduling
- Managing company expenses and vendor bills

Beyond the advantages described in the preceding section, the particular needs of a business might dictate whether you can use QBO. For example, QBO *won't* work for you if your business has industry-specific needs or is mid-sized and needs to use ODBC-compliant applications. In addition, QBO won't work for you if you need to

  ✔ Track your balance sheet by class

  ✔ Process more than 350,000 transactions annually

  ✔ Prepare international transactions

  ✔ Track labor costs

  ✔ Manage a robust inventory

  ✔ Prepare and track progress invoices

Robust inventory needs means that you make and sell goods instead of selling finished goods. If you sell finished goods, QBO will work for you.

In any of these cases, you would probably be better off with one of Intuit's desktop products.

When QBO and QBOA were first released, the US version didn't support multiple currencies. That feature has been added to both products.

System Requirements

Using a web-based software product typically doesn't require a lot of hardware and software; in fact, the demands of QBO and QBOA aren't extensive. In particular, you need

  ✔ An Internet connection — Intuit recommends a high-speed connection

  ✔ One of the four supported Internet browsers:

   • Chrome

   • Firefox

   • Internet Explorer 10 or higher

   • Safari 6.1 if your operating system is iOS 7 or higher

Although QBO and QBOA work in all the major browsers, they work best, in my experience, in Chrome, with Firefox coming in a close second. Therefore, I use Chrome throughout this book, and the Part of Tens chapters cover using Chrome so that you can get comfortable with that browser. If you're a Firefox user, give QBO and QBOA a try in Firefox.

You also can use the QuickBooks Online mobile app, which works with the iPhone and the iPad, and with Android phones and tablets. The requirements for the QuickBooks Online mobile app are the same as those outlined for the non-mobile versions: You need a browser on your device and an Internet connection, and your device needs to meet the basic requirements for the operating system installed on it. Be aware that mobile devices do not support all features of QBO and QBOA. In this book, I use a Windows 10 desktop computer and the Chrome browser.

Whether you work on a desktop computer or on a mobile device, the computer or device should meet the basic requirements of the operating system you use on that computer or device. For example, if you're using a Windows desktop computer, you need the amount of RAM (random access memory) specified by Microsoft to load Windows on the computer before you ever launch your browser. If you don't have sufficient RAM to run the computer software, you certainly won't be happy with the behavior of QBO and QBOA. You won't be happy with the behavior of the computer, either.

Basic requirements (and I stress the word *basic*) for a Windows 7, 8.1, and 10 computer, as specified by Microsoft, are

- 1-gigahertz (GHz) or faster 32-bit (x86) or 64-bit (x64) processor
- 1 gigabyte (GB) of RAM (32-bit) or 2GB of RAM (64-bit)
- 16GB of available hard disk space (32 bit) or 20GB (64 bit)
- A display that supports at least 800 x 600 dpi
- DirectX 9 graphics device with WDDM 1.0 or higher driver

These versions of Windows work with multi-core processors, and all 32-bit versions of Windows can support up to 32 processor cores, whereas 64-bit versions can support up to 256 processor cores.

And a word on the word *basic*. You'll be a whole lot happier if your desktop computer components have higher numbers than the ones listed above. If you have a computer that's fairly new — say, three to four years old — you might need only to add some RAM or possibly hard drive space. If your computer is older than three or four years, you should consider purchasing new equipment.

If you buy a new computer, you don't need to worry about much to meet more than the basic requirements. I'm pretty sure you can't buy a new computer containing a 1-gigahertz processor; most computers today come with at least 2.5-gigahertz processors and they support better graphics than the DirectX 9 graphics listed in the basic requirements. And most monitors available for purchase today don't support low resolutions such as 800 x 600; you most likely own a monitor that supports higher resolution. In my opinion, 1GB of RAM is insufficient; your desktop computer should have at least 2GB of RAM, and you'll be much happier if it has 4GB of RAM. On the hard drive requirement, if you don't have the 16GB or 20GB of available space specified, you probably should be considering a hard drive replacement for your computer.

Chapter 2

Embracing the QBO/QBOA Format

- -

In This Chapter

▶ Understanding available QBO subscriptions and their costs

▶ Examining ways to meet payroll needs

▶ Taking a tour of the App Center

- -

*Q*BO and QBOA are not traditional software that you buy and install on your local computer. In this chapter, you explore the QBO/QBOA software format, and I assume that you've read Chapter 1 and evaluated whether QBO can meet your needs.

It's All about Subscriptions

QBO and QBOA fall into the category of Software as a Subscription (SaaS). As such, you don't buy the software. Instead, you rent it; that is, you buy a subscription to use the software.

Traditionally, you buy a *license* to use software that you purchase and install on your computer, and typically, that license permits you to install the software on only one computer.

And, of course, a client can pay varying amounts for a subscription, depending on the subscription level purchased.

QBO is available at different subscription levels, and each subsequent subscription level costs more and contains more functionality. The QBO subscriptions available at this writing are

- ✔ Independent Contractors
- ✔ Simple Start
- ✔ Essentials
- ✔ Plus

All versions of QBO share three attributes in common. First, you can use a tablet, smartphone, or desktop computer to access your data. Second, your data is automatically backed up online. And third, all versions of QBO use 128-bit Secure Sockets Layer (SSL), the same security and encryption used by banks to secure data sent over the Internet.

Once you assess your needs as described in Chapter 1, use the following information to identify the lowest subscription level that will meet your requirements. At this point in time, you can upgrade to a higher level, but you cannot downgrade to a lower level.

Originally, accounting professionals signing up clients for QBO and creating client companies couldn't switch client companies from one version of QBO to another if the accounting professional created the client as part of the Intuit Wholesale Pricing program. That's no longer the case, so you no longer need to anticipate your client's requirements for more advanced features such as the ability to track inventory or prepare 1099s.

The Self-Employed version

This version of QBO is aimed at freelancers and self-employed individuals, basically, those who receive Federal Form 1099 to account for the money they've been paid. Using the Independent Contractors version, you can

- Separate business from personal spending
- Calculate and pay estimated quarterly taxes
- Track mileage and IRS Form 1040 Schedule C deductions
- Track your income and expenses
- Download transactions from your bank and credit card accounts

Like the other versions of QBO, you can use a tablet, smartphone, or desktop computer to access your data. In addition, the Self-Employed version uses the same security and encryption as banks, and your data is automatically backed up online. As you might expect, this version has the fewest reports available — only three — and only one person can access QBO.

The Simple Start version

The Simple Start version of QBO is great for a new business with basic bookkeeping needs. With Simple Start, you can

- ✔ Track your income and expenses
- ✔ Download transactions from your bank and credit card accounts
- ✔ Create an unlimited number of customers
- ✔ Send unlimited estimates and invoices
- ✔ Print checks and record transactions to track expenses
- ✔ Import data from Microsoft Excel or QuickBooks desktop
- ✔ Invite up to two accountants to access your data
- ✔ Integrate with available apps

You can't track bills due in the future in the Simple Start version because it doesn't include any Accounts Payable functions. One other important consideration: The Simple Start version also has no general ledger.

Although the Simple Start version allows two accountants to work in the client's company, Simple Start is still designed for a single user. Therefore, the accountant cannot create the client's company for the client. At the time the company is created in QBO, whoever creates the company becomes, in QBO parlance, the Master Administrator.

In addition to the single-user restriction, the Simple Start version offers more than 20 reports. And Simple Start users can memorize report settings and produce memorized reports.

For subscription levels that support multiple users, the accountant can create the company for the client and then transfer the Master Administrator role back to the client.

The Essentials version

The Essentials version of QBO includes all the features found in Simple Start. In addition, with the Essentials version, you can

- ✔ Set up invoices to automatically bill on a recurring schedule
- ✔ Take advantage of Accounts Payable functions, including entering vendor bills and scheduling their payment for later
- ✔ Compare your sales and profitability with industry trends
- ✔ Compare your sales and profitably with industry trends
- ✔ Create and post recurring transactions
- ✔ Control what your users can access

The Essentials version permits three simultaneous users and two accountant users. In addition, the Essentials version contains more than the reports found in Simple Start and ten additional reports.

The Plus version

The Plus version of QBO is the most full-featured version of QBO. It contains all the features found in the Essentials version. In addition, you can

- ✔ Create, send, and track purchase orders.
- ✔ Track inventory using the first in, first out (FIFO) inventory valuation method. QBO supports light inventory needs: If you sell finished goods, QBO should be able to manage your needs. But if you need to assemble finished goods to sell, QBO won't meet your needs on its own. You can look for an app to supplement your inventory needs; I talk about apps later in this chapter.
- ✔ Track, create, and send 1099-Misc forms.
- ✔ Categorize income and expenses using class tracking.
- ✔ Track sales and profitability by business location. You can assign only one location to a transaction, but you can assign multiple classes to a transaction.
- ✔ Give employees and subcontractors limited access to the QBO company to enter time worked.

- ✔ Track billable hours by customer.

    QBO supports light job-costing needs, but it does not allow you to automatically cost labor.

- ✔ Create budgets to estimate future income and expenses, and you can create multiple budgets per year, location, class, or customer.

I used QBO Plus as I wrote this book because it contains the most features; therefore, users of other versions might find references in this book to features they don't have. Accounting professionals: The company that comes with QBOA is a Plus company.

The Plus version supports five simultaneous users and two accountant users and can be scaled up to support 20 users. The Plus version also contains more than 65 reports: all the reports found in both the Simple Start and the Essentials versions, and some additional reports.

Essentials and Plus with Payroll

If an end user signs up for QBO Essentials or Plus on his own and creates his own company, he can create the company using the Plus Payroll option, or later, he can sign up for QBO Payroll (QBOP) separately. An accountant also can create the company that uses QBOP for a client. For details, see the section "Addressing Payroll Needs," later in this chapter.

What Does It Cost?

The big question: What does it cost? The price is dependent primarily on the QBO version you choose.

If you are an end user who signs up on your own for a QBO subscription, the annual pricing as of the date this book was written appears in Table 2-1.

The prices shown in Table 2-1 are for annual billing; monthly billing is more expensive. For example, the Plus subscription is $40/month.

Table 2-1	QBO Subscription Pricing
QBO Version	*Price*
Independent Contractor	$8/month
Simple Start	$10/month
Essentials	$20/month
Plus	$30/month

You'll receive a bill on a regular basis from Intuit. Intuit gives you a free 30-day trial that includes payroll processing along with the rest of the subscription's features. If you opt to continue QBO Payroll after the 30-day trial, your subscription fee increases. The free trial also includes the Payments app, which gives you the capability to process online and mobile payments with rates per use as low as 1.75 percent + 25 cents per swipe and 50 cents per bank payment/ACH.

If you are an accounting professional, you can sign up for the Wholesale Pricing program and use QBOA for free. If you create a client's company as part of the Wholesale Pricing program and you manage the client's subscription, Intuit sends you the bill for the client's subscription. It is your responsibility to bill the client for the QBO subscription. The bill you receive from Intuit is a single consolidated bill for all the QBO subscriptions you manage. For details on the Wholesale Pricing program, contact Intuit. Note that accounting professionals might be able to get QBO for their clients at a reduced price.

If an accounting professional creates a company through QBOA, the company does not come with a 30-day free trial. Instead, at the time the accounting professional creates the company, he must provide a payment method to ensure uninterrupted service.

If your client initially sets up QBO with her own subscription, you can move that existing QBO subscription to your consolidated bill at the discounted rate. And, if your arrangement with your client doesn't work out, you can remove the client from your consolidated bill, and the client can begin paying for his own subscription.

Addressing Payroll Needs

QBO can handle payroll regardless of whether an end user or an accountant creates the QBO company.

If an end user signs up for QBO Essentials or Plus on his own, he can create his own company using the Plus Payroll option or, after the fact, he can sign up for QBO Payroll from the Employees screen (see Figure 2-1).

QBO Payroll sports the following features:

- ✔ Paying employees with printed checks or by directly depositing paychecks

- ✔ Automatically calculating tax payments and paying them electronically

- ✔ Processing Federal and State quarterly and annual reports and preparing W-2 forms

- ✔ Processing payroll for employees in multiple states

- ✔ Keeping payroll tax tables up to date without having to install updates like you do with the QuickBooks desktop product

- ✔ Using the QBO Payroll mobile app to pay employees, view past paychecks, electronically pay taxes, and electronically file tax forms

For details on preparing payroll in QBO, see Chapter 9.

Click here to turn on payroll

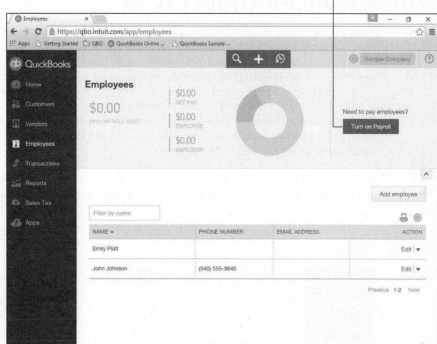

Figure 2-1:
If you sign
up for QBO
on your
own, you
can turn on
payroll from
the Employ-
ees screen.

If an accountant who is not enrolled in the Intuit Wholesale Pricing program creates a QBO Essentials or Plus company for a client, the client company can turn on QBO payroll (QBOP) from the Employees screen in the client's company (refer to Figure 2-1). If the accountant is enrolled in the Intuit Wholesale Pricing program and creates a QBO Essential or Plus company for a client as part of the program, the accountant can set up the QBO company to use QBO Payroll (QBOP).

Clients can prepare payroll for themselves or accounting professionals can manage all payroll functions for clients.

Last, you always have the option of subscribing to Intuit Full Service Payroll, where Intuit prepares payroll for you. Or your accountant can add an Intuit Full Service Payroll subscription to your company through QBOA, regardless of whether he or she is enrolled in the Wholesale Pricing Program.

Where Add-On Apps Fit In

QBO doesn't operate as a complete, stand-alone accounting solution. It has functional limitations. The preceding section highlights one such limitation — and shows how you can use Intuit add-ons to achieve more functionality in QBO. And, in this chapter I briefly mention Intuit's Payments app, which supports electronic customer payment processing and integrates with QBO.

But those aren't the only apps available for QBO; third-party developers have been creating apps to enhance the functionality of QBO. And, over time, you can expect more apps to be developed.

You can click the Apps link in the Navigation bar that runs down the left side of QBO to visit the App Center and explore available apps (see Figure 2-2).

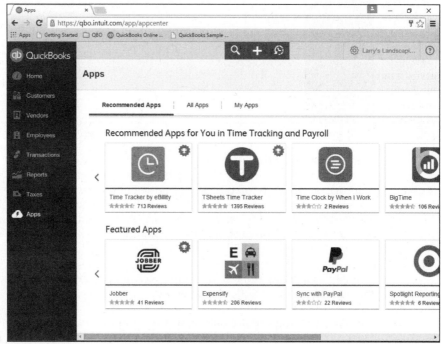

Figure 2-2:
Take a trip to the App Center to search for additional functionality for QBO.

Click any app to navigate to a page that describes the app, provides pricing information, and often provides a video about the app (see Figure 2-3).

Figure 2-3:
When you click an app in the App Center, you see details for the app.

Although add-on apps can provide additional functionality in QBO, some functionality is still missing; no doubt, that functionality will appear over time. For example, using QBO, you can't

- Track your balance sheet by class
- Process more than 350,000 transactions annually
- Prepare international transactions
- Track labor costs
- Manage a robust inventory
- Prepare and track progress invoices

But apps are making inroads to eliminating these limitations. For example, Lettuce, an app that provides advanced inventory management features for QBO, did such a fine job of handling inventory functions that Intuit acquired Lettuce for the purpose of integrating it into QBO.

Part II
Managing the Books for the End User

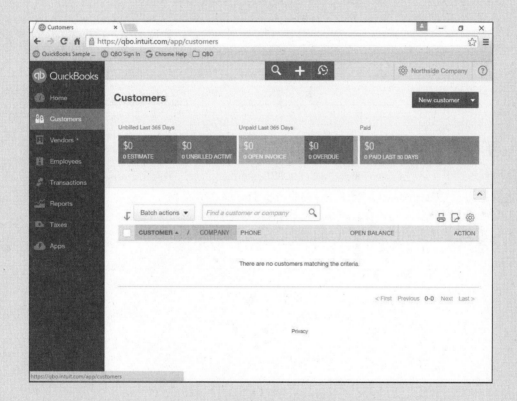

Check out the free article at www.dummies.com/extras/quickbooksonline to learn how to prepare budgets in QBO.

In this part . . .

- ✔ Become familiar with the QBO interface.
- ✔ Manage list information needed to use QBO.
- ✔ Enter transactions in QBO to update your company's books.
- ✔ Use reports to examine the condition of your company.

Chapter 3

Creating a Client Company in QBO

In This Chapter

▶ Signing up for a QBO account

▶ Setting up a new QBO company

▶ Understanding the interface

▶ Working with company settings

*A*fter you sign up for QBO, you log in. QBO then prompts you to set up your company. With certain limitations, you can import a company if you've been using a QuickBooks desktop product. Or, you can use the QBO Setup wizard, as shown in this chapter.

For details on importing a company, see Chapter 12 (or ask your accountant to help you with the import). And, don't worry, if you don't import your entire desktop company; you can import just the list information from that company, as described in Chapter 4.

Signing Up for QBO

After you complete the sign-up process for a QBO account, Intuit, by default, logs you into your account and walks you through the process of setting up your QBO company. The process is short — much shorter than the one you go through when setting up a QBO desktop product company — and you need the following information:

✔ Your company's name and address

✔ The industry in which your company operates

✔ Your company's legal organization (such as S-Corp or Limited Liability Partnership)

✔ Whether you want to import company information from a QuickBooks desktop product

✔ The types of payments you accept from your customers (that is, cash, checks, and credit cards)

✔ The way you want to handle payroll

To sign up for a QBO account, follow these steps:

1. **Visit** `quickbooks.intuit.com/online`.

2. **Scroll down the page until you find the three boxes describing each version of QBO.**

3. **Click the Free 30-Day Trial link, which appears in the box for the version of QBO you want to check out.**

   The Free 30-Day Trial link appears below the Buy Now button.

4. **Fill in your name, email address, and a password (see Figure 3-1).**

   If you already have an Intuit user ID, supply that user ID and password.

   Your password must be between 6 and 32 characters and consist of a mix of letters and numbers. The password can also contain some special characters; I included an exclamation point (!) in my password and it was accepted. The user ID and password you supply are the ones you use each time you log in to QBO.

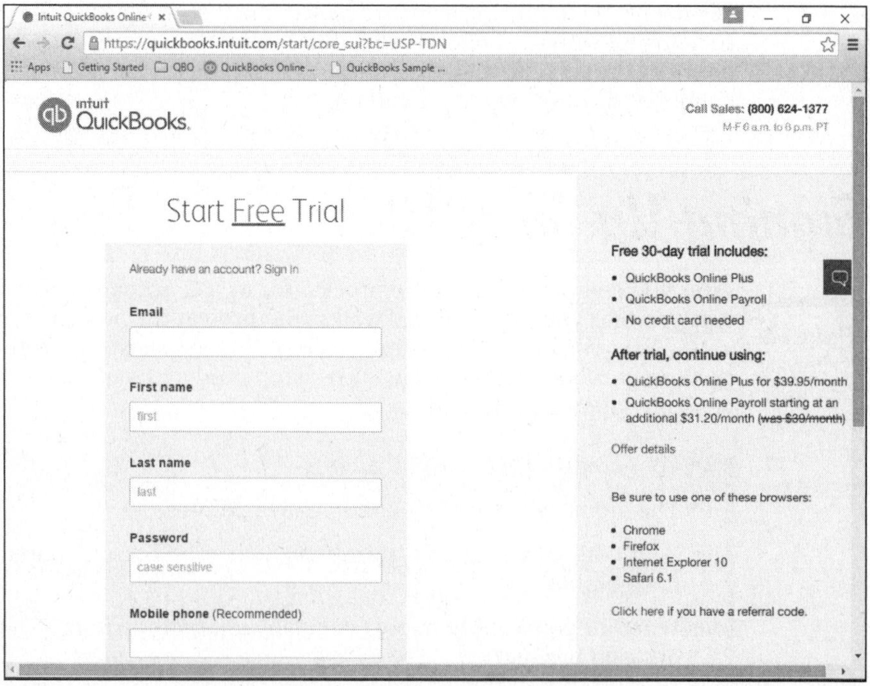

Figure 3-1: Fill in the information needed to start the free trial.

5. Click the Sign Up button below the boxes you completed in Step 4.

At the time that I wrote this, a window appeared that offered the option to skip the free trial and buy the product at a discounted rate. You can buy, but I opted to click the Continue to Trial button.

Your free trial is now set up, you're logged in to QBO, and the Setup wizard appears . . . read on.

Setting Up a New Company

When you first sign up for a QBO account, Intuit logs you in to your QBO account and, by default, displays the Setup wizard. The first screen of the wizard, shown in Figure 3-2, asks for basic company information.

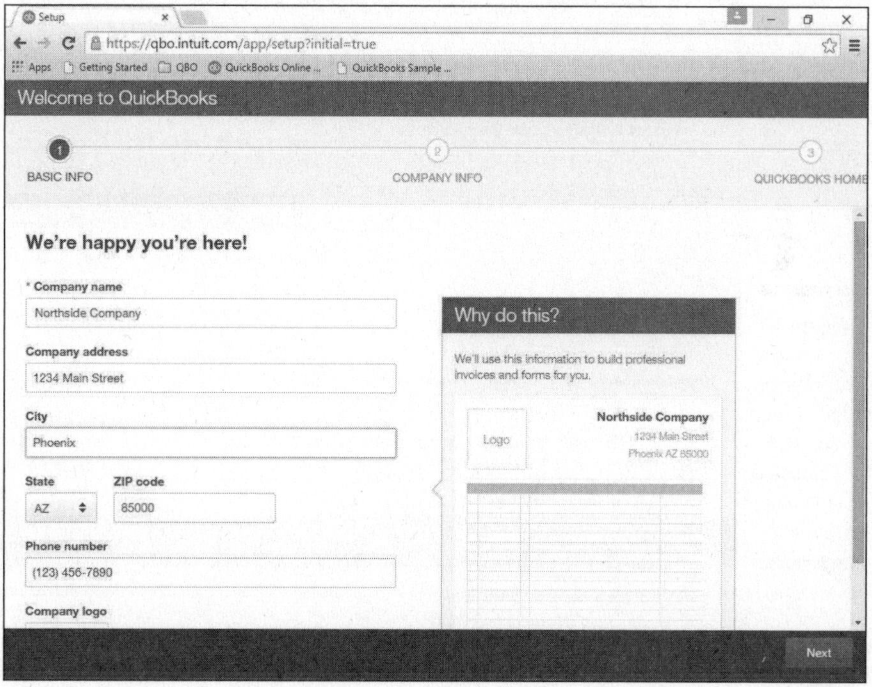

Figure 3-2: Provide basic company information.

As you supply address information, QBO automatically prepares an invoice form that contains the information; you'll use this form (or a variant of it) to prepare the invoices you send to customers.

If you have a basically square company logo in JPG, GIF, BMP, or PNG format, you can upload it to include it on your invoice. Just scroll down the page a bit and click the Browse button to navigate to your logo.

When you finish providing address information, click the Next button in the lower-right corner of the screen.

On the Set Up QuickBooks screen, shown in Figure 3-3, you provide more information about your company so that Intuit can customize QBO to suit your needs: Supply your industry and company type; answer questions about importing data from a desktop version of QuickBooks; and decide how you want to handle payroll and how you want your customers to pay you.

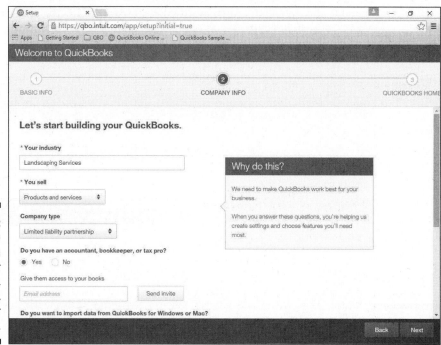

Figure 3-3: Provide information about your company, industry, and other preferences.

If you opt not to import desktop information, you can change your mind later, as long as you do so within 60 days of starting your QBO subscription. If you decide that you want to import data after 60 days, you must cancel your subscription and start a new one.

When you click Next, QBO searches online for businesses similar to yours and establishes appropriate options and settings; when QBO finishes the search, you see a screen like the one shown in Figure 3-4, which contains information on what QBO did while creating your QBO company.

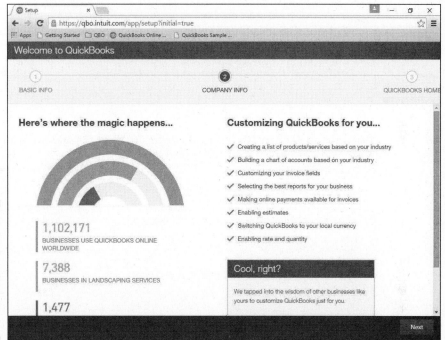

Figure 3-4: QBO customizes the interface using the information you provided.

When you click Next, QBO displays your company's Home page and opens the Create menu to make sure you know where it is — but I'm getting ahead of myself just a bit. We examine the Home page in the next section, but essentially you've just completed most of the initial setup work; I cover other program settings later in this chapter.

Understanding the Home Page

When you first see your QBO company, your Home page contains three links in the Get Started with QuickBooks box at the top of the screen (see Figure 3-5). The 1-Minute tour might interest you, although you'll probably already know most of what appears in the tour by the time you sign up for QBO. The other two links, also 1-minute tours, describe the basics of using

Intuit Payments (to accept electronic payments from customers) and Intuit Payroll. You can close the window containing the tours by clicking the X in the upper-right corner of the window.

Figure 3-5:
You can
watch these
optional
short
videos.

You also can click the Welcome Guide link to view 12 tasks you can complete to familiarize yourself with QBO (see Figure 3-6).

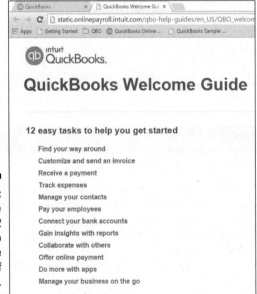

Figure 3-6:
Complete
these 12
tasks to
familiarize
yourself
with QBO.

Notice, at the top of the screen, that the Welcome Guide opens in its own browser tab; you can leave the tab open and redisplay QBO just by clicking the QuickBooks browser tab. You can also redisplay the Welcome Guide at any time; it's available on the Help menu.

Let's examine the Home page (see Figure 3-7). In the center of the screen, using most of the Home page real estate, you find information that changes depending on what you have clicked while using QBO. For example, when you initially open QBO, the information is overview company information. If you click an entry in the Navigation bar (on the left side of the screen), the information in the center of the Home page is related to the entry you clicked. If you select a setting on the Gear menu (discussed later in this section), the information is related to the setting you select.

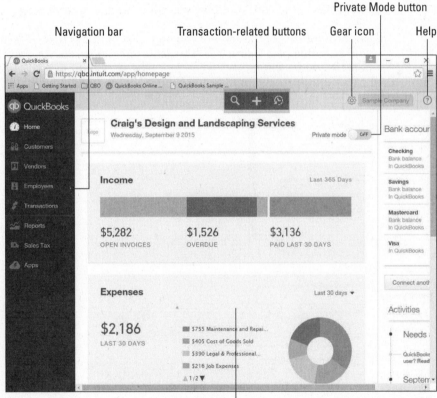

Figure 3-7:
Examining
Home
screen
elements.

Main portion of the Home page

You might have noticed the Private Mode button in Figure 3-7. This button appears after you have entered at least one transaction, and you can use it to temporarily hide financial information on your Home page. For example, you might want to turn Private Mode on if you're using QuickBooks in a public place or even in your office when you're not alone. Once you turn on Private Mode, it remains on until you turn it off again.

As I just mentioned, the Navigation bar runs down the left side of the screen. You use the Navigation bar the same way you'd use a menu; click an item in the Navigation bar to, well, navigate to that part of QBO. For example, you can click Transactions in the Navigation bar to see the available transactions in QBO and then click one to use that type of transaction.

The highlighted entry in the Navigation bar does not always change to match the information shown in the main portion of the Home page. You use the Navigation bar to navigate to a portion of the program, not to determine the portion of the program you are viewing. In other words, don't depend on the Navigation bar to "tell you" how you got to what you're viewing.

On the right side of the screen, you find a list of things that QBO thinks needs your attention (see Figure 3-8). The list is interactive, so, you can click an item to interact with it.

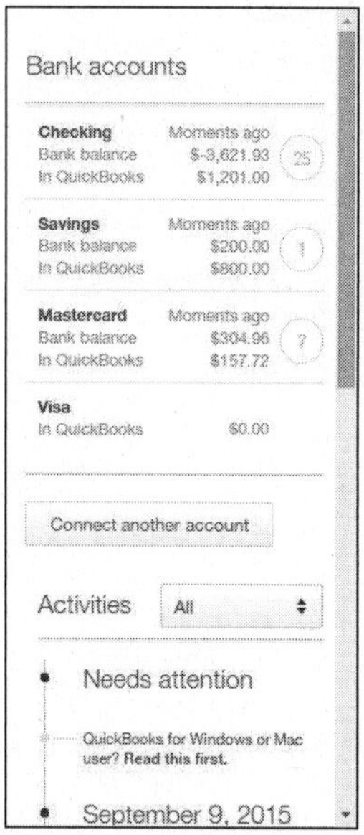

Figure 3-8:
A list of things that need your attention.

When you click the Help button, you see a menu of common topics related to the area of QBO you are currently viewing, and you can type in the Search box to find help on a particular topic (see Figure 3-9). For example, you can click Home Page Overview to display a Help window that contains a link to the Welcome Guide.

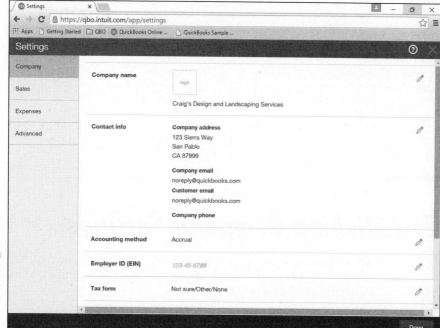

Figure 3-14:
Review
company
settings.

Setting sales preferences

To review the Sales preferences of your QBO company, choose Gear ⇨ Company Settings to display the Settings dialog box. Then, click Sales in the pane on the left.

At the top of the page that appears (see Figure 3-15), you can click the Customize Look and Feel button to customize the appearance of the invoice you send to customers. We return to the customization process at the end of this section; first, let's examine the settings available to you.

Examining sales settings

You can set a variety of options related to sales:

✔ In the Sales Form Content section, you can define the fields that appear on the form you complete to prepare invoices, sales receipts, and other sales forms.

✔ In the Products and Services section, you can make changes to the product- and service-related fields that appear on sales forms.

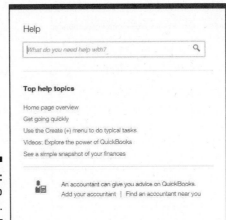

Figure 3-9:
The Help
menu.

In the center of the top of the screen, you see three transaction-related buttons that display lists you can use to work with transactions. Figure 3-10 shows what you see when you click the leftmost transaction button, the Search button.

Figure 3-10:
Click the
leftmost
button to
search for
past trans-
actions.

Figure 3-11 shows the Create menu that appears when you click the center transaction button.

The Create button appears as a plus sign (+) when the menu is closed and an X when the menu is open; compare Figures 3-7 and 3-11.

When you click the third transaction button — the one that looks like a clock — you see a list of recently entered transactions; you can click any transaction in the list to open that transaction (see Figure 3-12).

Create

Customers	Vendors	Employees	Other
Invoice	Expense	Payroll	Bank Deposit
Receive Payment	Check	Single Time Activity	Transfer
Estimate	Bill	Weekly Timesheet	Journal Entry
Credit Memo	Pay Bills		Statement
Sales Receipt	Purchase Order		
Refund Receipt	Vendor Credit		
Delayed Credit	Credit Card Credit		
Delayed Charge	Print Checks		

▶ Show less

Figure 3-11: Click the center button to create a new transaction.

Recent Transactions

Credit Card Expense	09/08/2015	$34.00	
Credit Card Expense	08/20/2015	$42.40	Hicks Hardware
Credit Card Expense Car Wash	08/26/2015	$19.99	Squeaky Kleen
Credit Card Expense Car Wash	08/19/2015	$19.99	Squeaky Kleen
Credit Card Expense Joint	08/19/2015	$18.97	Bob's Burger
Credit Card Credit	08/26/2015	$900.00	
Check No.Debit Car Wash	08/12/2015	$19.99	Squeaky Kleen
Cash Expense Joint	08/10/2015	$3.86	Bob's Burger
Cash Expense Car Wash	08/05/2015	$19.99	Squeaky Kleen
Cash Expense Joint	08/05/2015	$5.66	Bob's Burger

More...

Figure 3-12: Click the right button to display a list of recently entered transactions.

To the right of the three transaction-related buttons, you see the Gear icon followed by your company's name. If you click the Gear icon, you see the menu shown in Figure 3-13, which you use to look at and change QBO company settings; view lists; work with tools such as import and export, reconciliation, and budgeting tools; and view information about your QBO account. Note that the Gear menu is divided into four columns that organize related commands.

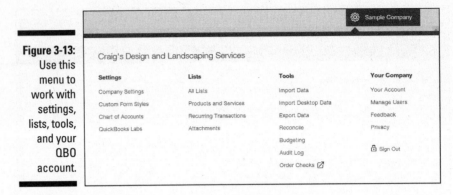

Figure 3-13: Use this menu to work with settings, lists, tools, and your QBO account.

Sample Company

Craig's Design and Landscaping Services

Settings	Lists	Tools	Your Company
Company Settings	All Lists	Import Data	Your Account
Custom Form Styles	Products and Services	Import Desktop Data	Manage Users
Chart of Accounts	Recurring Transactions	Export Data	Feedback
QuickBooks Labs	Attachments	Reconcile	Privacy
		Budgeting	
		Audit Log	Sign Out
		Order Checks	

Establishing Company Settings

After you set up your company, you should review the default settings Intuit established and make changes as appropriate. To examine and make changes to payroll settings, see Chapter 9.

Examining company preferences

To display the Company tab of the Settings dialog box (see Figure 3-14), choose Gear ⇨ Company Settings.

On this tab, you can make changes to your company name, address, federal ID number, legal organization, and accounting method. You also can opt, depending on the version of QBO you use, to track classes, locations, or both. Last, if you prefer to call your customers something other than Customer (such as Client, Patron, or Shopper), you can change the label you use to refer to those who make purchases from you.

To change any setting, click anywhere in the group where the setting appears. When you finish making changes, click the Save button that appears in the group of settings. You can then move on to other settings on the page.

If you make changes, click Done in the lower-right corner of the screen to save them.

✔ In the Messages section, you can control the default email message sent to customers with sales forms and the default message that appears on those sales forms.

✔ If you scroll down the Sales page, you can set, in the Online Delivery section, email delivery options for sales forms such as attaching the sales form as a PDF, showing a summary or details of the sales form in the email, and email formatting options for invoices.

✔ In the Statements section, you can specify whether to show the aging table at the bottom of the statement.

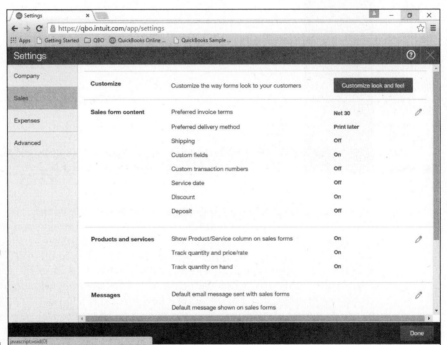

Figure 3-15:
The Sales
page of the
Settings
dialog box.

Customizing form appearance

To customize forms that your customers receive, click Customize Look and Feel at the top of the Sales page in the Settings dialog box to display the Custom Form Styles page shown in Figure 3-16.

The Custom Form Styles page lists any form styles you have already created. By default, QBO creates one form style for you when you sign up; that form style is named Standard and is used by default for invoices, estimates, and sales receipts.

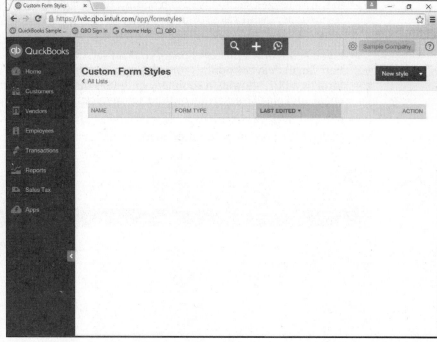

Figure 3-16:
Use this
page to edit
an existing
form style or
set up a
new form
style.

If you are satisfied with the appearance of the majority of the form style, you can edit it instead of creating a form style. Alternatively, you can create separate customized forms for invoices, estimates, and sales receipts. To do so, click New Style in the upper-right corner of the Custom Form Styles page. Whether you edit or a create a new form style, QBO displays the Customize Form Style dialog box, whose appearance varies only slightly, depending on whether you are editing or creating a new form style. In particular, if you opt to create a form style, the dialog box gives you the option to select the type of form style (see Figure 3-17).

You use the tabs that run down the left side of the dialog box to establish form style settings:

✔ From the Style tab, shown in Figure 3-17, you can select a style for the form: Airy, Modern, Fresh, Friendly, or Bold. The preview shown in Figure 3-17 is the Fresh form style.

✔ From the Appearance tab, you can modify the appearance and place-ment of your logo; set the form's font, line height, and page margins; and specify whether to print your form to fit in a standard window envelope. You also can specify whether to show an account summary table, which shows your customers how much past due they are in paying you.

✔ From the Header tab, you can define the names used for each form and the fields that appear in the header area of the form — such as your company name, address, contact information, payment terms, due date, and form number. You also can opt to show your customer's terms, due date, shipping and payment methods, as well as set up custom fields.

✔ From the Activity Table tab, you can control the appearance of the body of the invoice, determining whether to display, in columns, information such as the quantity, rate, and description for each item — and the order in which the elements appear. You also can specify whether to display billable time and markup on billable expenses (most people don't display markup on billable expenses).

Chapter 6 contains an example of customizing the Activity Table so that you can include subtotals on an invoice.

✔ From the Footer tab, you can control the information that appears in the footer portion of the form, along with messages to your customer.

You can click the Preview or Print button to preview your invoice in a browser window but in PDF format.

Click the Save button to save changes you make to the appearance of your forms.

Use this list to select the type of form style you want to create

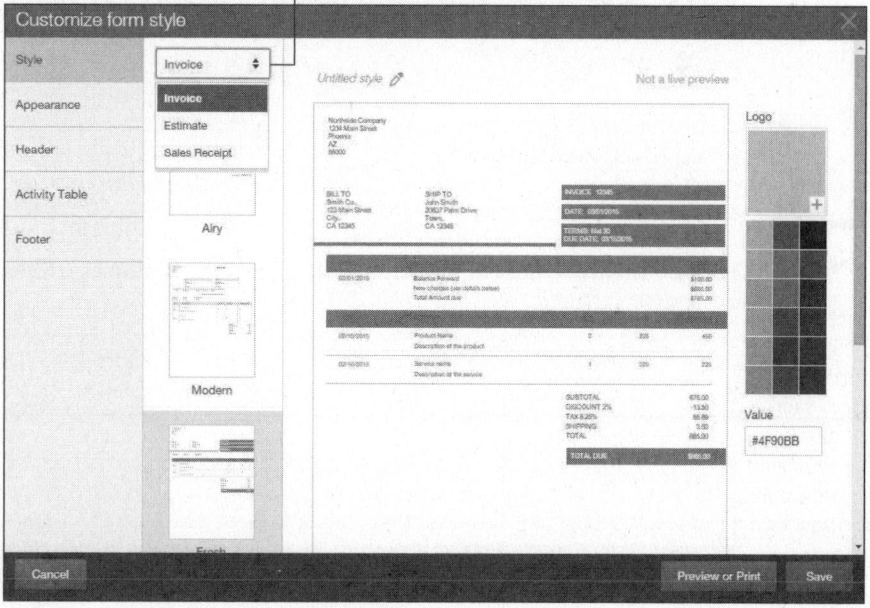

Figure 3-17:
The dialog box you use to customize sales forms.

Importing form styles

At the time I wrote this, importing form styles was a feature "under construction" in QBO and therefore not available unless you enable it using QuickBooks Labs. For details on using QuickBooks Labs, see "Working with QuickBooks Labs," later in this chapter. For purposes of this discussion, I have enabled the feature.

If the form templates supplied with QBO don't meet your needs, you can use Microsoft Word 2010 or later to create a form style and then upload it into QBO. As part of the import process, you map fields you've identified on your Word document form style to QBO fields.

The tricky part of this process is getting the form correctly designed in Word. But, luckily, Intuit anticipated the challenge and provides sample forms and instructions to simplify the process. To download the samples and instructions, you need to pretend you've already created your form style in Word. If this feels like I'm putting the cart in front of the horse, well . . . I am, sort of.

To get the sample information and instructions, click Gear ➪ Custom Form Styles. On the Custom Form Styles page, click the down arrow beside New Style, and choose Import Style. QBO displays the page shown in Figure 3-18.

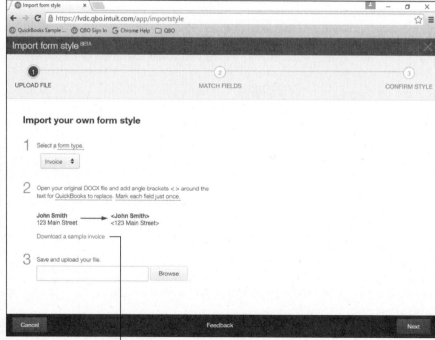

Figure 3-18: Use the Import Form Style page to download sample forms and instructions to create your own form style.

Click here to download sample files and instructions

To download the sample information, click the Download a Sample Invoice link. A zip file downloads, containing two sample forms you can use as starting points.

The zip file also contains detailed instructions that describe what to do and what not to do when creating a form style. For example, the instructions list the fonts QBO will recognize and also describe the best way to use Word tables. Suffice it to say, use these instructions and save yourself some pain.

Open either of the sample files to see how a customized form style should look in Word (see Figure 3-19). Note, for example, that you simply type information that won't change, but you place less than and greater than brackets around fields you want to replace with QBO data, such as your customer's billing and shipping addresses and item information.

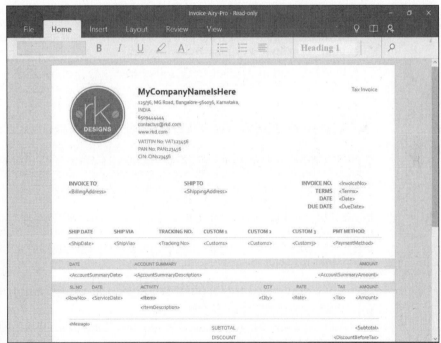

Figure 3-19: Place information that QBO should replace in brackets.

When you're ready to upload your form style, follow these steps:

1. **Choose Gear ⇨ Custom Form Style to display the Custom Form Style page.**

2. **Click the arrow beside the New Style button and choose Import Style to redisplay the page shown in Figure 3-18.**

3. **Click the Browse button and navigate to the Word document you created for your form style.**

4. **Click Next.**

   QBO uploads the document and scans it for fields you placed in brackets. If you successfully uploaded the Word document, you'll see a message telling you that you succeeded in uploading. If this process is not successful you will see errors; review the instruction document included with the sample files for details on errors and how to correct them.

5. **Assuming your document successfully uploaded, click Next.**

   A page appears where you can map the fields on your form style to fields in QBO.

6. **Match the fields on your form style to QBO fields; when you finish, click Next.**

   A preview of the new form style appears.

7. **If you're happy with what you see, click Save and supply a name for your form style. It's now ready to use.**

   If you're not happy, click Back and correct any problems.

Taking a look at expense preferences

From the Expenses tab of the Settings dialog box, you can control expenses related to purchase orders, bills, and payments you make to vendors (see Figure 3-20). Choose Gear ⇨ Company Settings ⇨ Expenses.

In the Bills and Expenses group of settings, you can opt to display a table on expense and purchase forms so that you can itemize and categorize the products and services you buy. If you purchase goods and services for your customers, you can

- ✔ Add a column to the table so that you can identify the customer for whom you made the purchase.
- ✔ Add a column where you identify expenses and items for which you want to bill customers.

You also can set default bill payment terms.

In the Purchase Orders group, you can opt to use purchase orders.

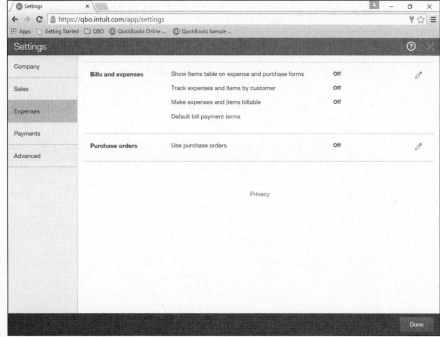

Examining options to receive customer payments

The Payments tab of the Settings dialog box offers you a way to connect with Intuit Merchant Services via a QuickBooks Payments account. If you don't have a QuickBooks Payments account with Intuit and you want one, click the Learn More button. If you already have a QuickBooks Payments account, you can click the Connect button to connect your QBO account with your QuickBooks Payments account.

QuickBooks Payments is the name Intuit uses to describe the service it offers that enables you to accept credit cards or bank transfers from your customers. You might also know this service as GoPayment or Merchant Services.

Reviewing advanced preferences

The Advanced tab of the Settings dialog box enables you to make changes to a variety of QBO settings (see Figure 3-21). Choose Gear ⇨ Company Settings ⇨ Advanced to view and update these settings:

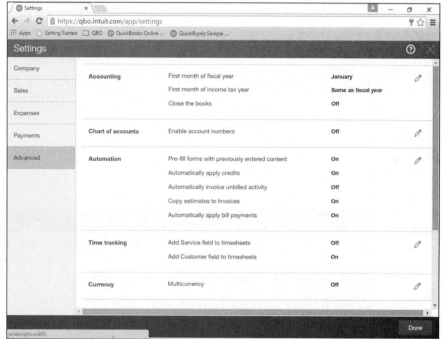

Figure 3-21: The Advanced tab of the Settings dialog box.

✔ In the Accounting group, you can control fiscal year settings.

✔ In the Chart of Accounts group, you can turn on account numbers — something most accountants prefer you do.

✔ In the Automation group, you can control some of QBO's automated behavior. For example, if you don't want QBO to prefill new forms with information from forms you entered previously, feel free to turn that setting off.

✔ In the Time Tracking section, you can control the appearance of timesheets. For example, you can opt to add a service field to timesheets so that you can select services performed for each time entry. By default, QBO includes a customer field on timesheets so that you can optionally charge work performed to a customer.

✔ Use the Currency section to turn on multi-currency tracking.

✔ In the Other Preferences group, you can make changes to a variety of settings, such as date and number formats, whether QBO warns you if you reuse a check number or bill number you used previously, and how long QBO should wait before signing you out because you haven't done any work.

Updating the Chart of Accounts

On the Advanced tab of the Settings dialog box, you saw that you could turn on account numbers for the accounts in your Chart of Accounts. To make changes to those accounts, choose Gear ⇨ Chart of Accounts. On the page that appears (see Figure 3-22), you can perform a variety of functions. For example, you can print a list of your accounts if you click the Run Report button, which is at the top of the page.

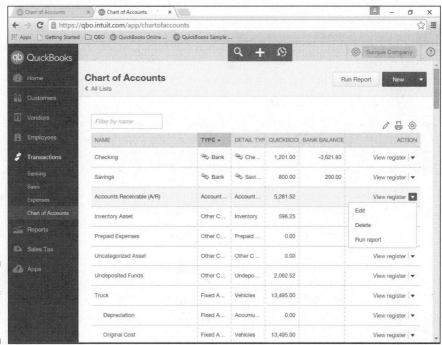

Figure 3-22:
The Chart of
Accounts
page.

For individual accounts, you can perform a few actions. Balance Sheet accounts have registers; you can view the transactions in the account by clicking View Register in the Action column. You can identify Balance Sheet accounts by looking in the Type column. Balance Sheet accounts display one of the following account types:

- ✔ Bank
- ✔ Accounts Receivable
- ✔ Other Current Assets
- ✔ Fixed Assets
- ✔ Other Assets
- ✔ Credit Card
- ✔ Other Current Liabilities
- ✔ Long Term Liabilities
- ✔ Accounts Payable
- ✔ Equity

For other accounts — the ones without registers — you can run reports for the account by clicking Run Report in the Action column.

You also can edit any account and you can delete an account you have not yet used. Click the down arrow in the Action column (at the right edge of the account's row) to display a short menu of the actions you can take for the account.

If you edit an account, don't change its type unless you're sure you know what you're doing. Consider consulting your accountant before you make a change to an account's category or detail type. You also can identify if the account is actually a sub-account of another account.

If you decided to turn on account numbers, you can click the Batch Edit icon (it looks like a pencil and appears just above the Action column). The appearance of the Chart of Accounts page changes to enable you to quickly assign account numbers (see Figure 3-23).

Type a number for each account; when you finish, click the Save button at the top of the page. QBO displays the account number as part of the account name on the Chart of Accounts screen.

You also can establish budgets for accounts; see "Budgeting in QBO," the online article at www.dummies.com/extras/quickbooksonline, for details.

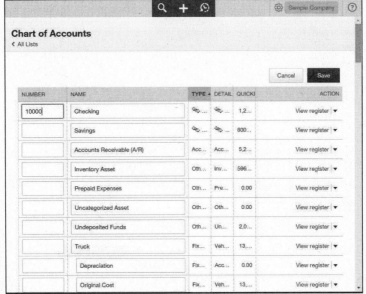

Figure 3-23:
The Chart of
Accounts
page in
Batch Edit
mode.

The screens you use to add or edit an account look almost exactly alike. Because you need a Bank account for your company, we examine the screens as you create your Bank account. If you plan to connect your QBO Bank account to its corresponding account at a financial institution, don't follow these steps; instead, see Chapter 8 for details on creating the account. And, if you decide now that you don't want to connect and later you decide that you *do* want to connect, all isn't lost. Once again, see Chapter 8 for details on merging the Bank account you create here with an online version.

Follow these steps to create an account in QBO:

To ensure an accurate bank balance in QBO, reconcile your bank account before you set up the account in QBO.

1. **Click the New button on the Chart of Accounts page to open the Account dialog box (see Figure 3-24).**

2. **Open the Category Type list and choose Bank.**

3. **Click the entry in the Detail Type list that most closely matches the type of account you want to add.**

   QBO uses the choice you make in the Detail Type list as the account's name, but you can change the name to something else. For my example, I chose Checking, changed the account name to Checking-Chase Bank, and supplied Chase Checking account as the description.

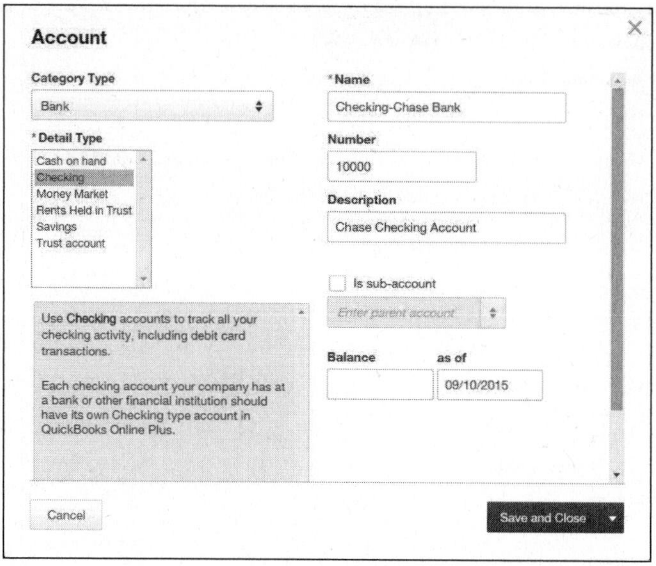

Figure 3-24:
The dialog
box you use
to create an
account.

Account

Category Type

Bank

*Detail Type

Cash on hand
Checking
Money Market
Rents Held in Trust
Savings
Trust account

Use **Checking** accounts to track all your
checking activity, including debit card
transactions.

Each checking account your company has at
a bank or other financial institution should
have its own Checking type account in
QuickBooks Online Plus.

*Name

Checking-Chase Bank

Number

10000

Description

Chase Checking Account

Is sub-account

Enter parent account

Balance   as of

09/10/2015

Cancel

Save and Close

4. **If you're using account numbers, supply a number for the new account.**

   You can, optionally, supply a description for the account.

5. **You can enter your account's balance as it appears on the last statement you received from your bank.**

   My example company is just starting out and has no opening balance yet, so I'm not entering an opening balance. See the sidebar, "Proper account balances," for details on what to do here.

6. **Click Save.**

   QBO redisplays the Chart of Accounts page and your new account appears in the list.

Working with QuickBooks Labs

You might be wondering about the QuickBooks Labs option on the Gear menu (you can see it if you refer back to Figure 3-13). Intuit calls QuickBooks Labs its "high-tech playground." If you're adventurous, check out the lab and turn on experimental features to see how they work.

In most cases, features you find in QuickBooks Labs eventually become part of QBO.

Proper account balances

If you've been in business for a while, transactions have occurred. To ensure accurate account balances, you need to account for these transactions in QBO.

To make sure that you start your work in QBO with correct account balances, begin by deciding on the first date you intend to use QBO. This date determines the "as of" date of historical information you need to collect. Try to start using QBO on the first day of an accounting period — either on the first day of your company's fiscal year or on the first day of a month. If you start using QBO Payroll (QBOP) on January 1, you do not need to enter any historical payroll information.

Although it might seem like more work, I suggest that the easiest way for you to ensure proper account balances is to enter $0 as your Bank account's opening balance in Step 5 in the preceding steps for creating a Bank account. Then, enter all transactions that have occurred so far this year.

If you've been in business since before the beginning of the year, enter $0 for your Bank account's balance and ask your accountant for opening amounts for your Balance Sheet accounts as of December 31 of last year. Enter these amounts by entering a journal entry: click the plus sign (+) icon at the top of QBO and choose Journal Entry from the Other column in the list.

The transactions you enter for the current year will ultimately affect your bank balance (for example, a customer eventually pays an invoice), and, when you finish entering the transactions, your QBO Bank account balance should agree with the one your financial institution has. So, I suggest that you enter transactions for *all* customer invoices (and corresponding payments customers made) and *all* vendor bills (and corresponding payments you made) during the current year.

If you choose to ignore my suggestion and enter an opening amount for your bank balance in Step 5, you need to then enter all transactions that have affected your bank account *since the last statement*.

QBO posts balances you enter while creating an account to the Opening Balance Equity (Equity) account, an account created by QuickBooks. Most accountants don't like this account and will want to create journal entries to move the balances to proper accounts.

That second approach sounds like a lot less work and, if you don't use payroll, or you make payroll payments from a separate bank account, you can safely ignore my suggestion and enter an opening amount for your bank balance in Step 5 and then enter outstanding customer invoices and unpaid vendor bills.

But, if your company does prepare payroll, has prepared one or more payrolls so far this year, and you use only one bank account, I strongly urge you to take my suggestion because you need accurate *annual* information to successfully manage payroll. The easiest way to ensure that you have accurate annual payroll information is to enter all payrolls you've completed this year so far — and these payrolls will affect your Bank account, so, entering a Bank account balance in Step 5 will lead you into trouble. Yes, you can try to do a mix of both approaches and subtract payroll amounts from the bank balance you previously entered in Step 5, but that approach is seriously error-prone.

If you use one bank account for everything and you feel that entering all transactions that have occurred so far this year is just too much work, I suggest that you enter your bank account's balance as of your last bank statement, enter outstanding invoices and unpaid vendor bills, and then contact Intuit technical support for help entering historical payroll information.

For example, when I wrote this, the collapsible Navigation bar was a QuickBooks Labs feature and therefore didn't appear by default. Here's how you turn on a QuickBooks Labs feature:

1. **Log into your company.**

2. **Click Gear ⇨ QuickBooks Labs.**

   The QuickBooks Labs window appears (see Figure 3-25).

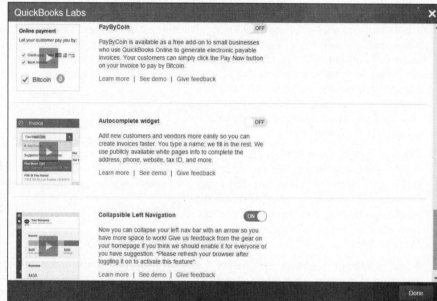

Figure 3-25:
Use this page to turn on features not yet available by default in QuickBooks.

Note that you can provide feedback on QuickBooks Labs features. The more positive feedback a feature receives, the more likely that feature will become a standard part of QBO.

3. **Check out the features available and, for any you want to try, click the Off button.**

   The Off button changes to the On button.

4. **When you finish turning on features, click Done.**

   Your QBO company reappears, with the features you selected enabled.

You might need to refresh the browser page to see the new features you chose to make available. Click your browser's Refresh button or press F5 on your keyboard.

For example, I enabled the Collapsible Left Navigation bar feature. I then clicked the arrow just below the commands on the Navigation bar, and the bar collapsed, as shown in Figure 3-26. To expand the bar, I clicked the arrow again.

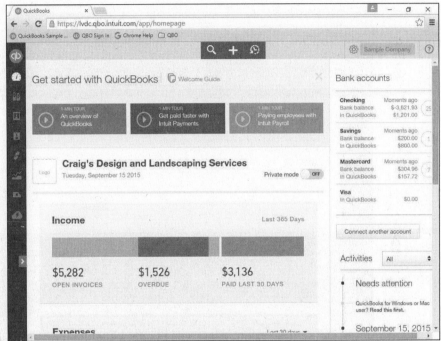

Figure 3-26: Using an experimental feature from QuickBooks Labs to collapse the Navigation bar.

Signing In to and Out of QBO

If you followed the process in this chapter to sign up for QBO, you're currently signed in to QBO. But, obviously, you don't sign up for QBO every time you want to use it. And then, of course, there's the question of how you sign out of QBO each time you finish using it.

To sign out of QBO, click the Gear icon and, from the menu shown earlier in Figure 3-13, click Sign Out (at the bottom of the list of commands under Your Company).

To sign in to QBO in the future, visit `https://qbo.intuit.com` (you get redirected to a long web address you don't need to type) and supply your username and password (see Figure 3-27). I suggest you bookmark this page to make signing in easy.

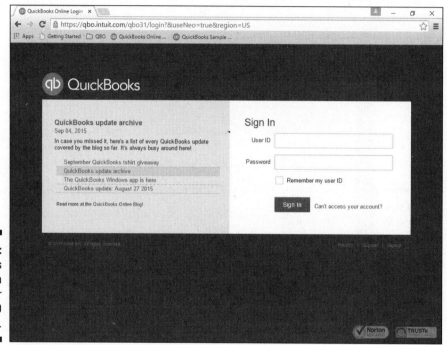

Figure 3-27:
Use this page to sign in to your QBO company.

Chapter 4

Managing List Information

In This Chapter

▶ Adding new list entries by typing or importing

▶ Searching lists for people

▶ Changing settings for lists

▶ Displaying other lists

*L*ike its cousin the QuickBooks desktop product, QBO relies on lists to help you store background information that you'll use again and again. For the most part, you enter information about the people you do business with: customers, vendors, and employees. But you also store other background information in lists, such as information about the stuff you sell. This chapter focuses on setting up people in their various lists, and, at the end of the chapter, you learn where to find other lists you might need.

If you have been using one of the QuickBooks desktop products and have all your lists set up, you can import the list information. And, you can import list information stored in Excel files; see the section "Importing People into a List," later in this chapter.

Adding New People to a List

You use the Customers, Vendors, and Employees links in the Navigation bar to work with, well, your customers, vendors, and employees. In this section, I show you how to set up a new customer. The steps are the same to set up a new vendor or a new employee; you just start by clicking the appropriate link in the Navigation bar. Follow these steps to set up a new customer in QBO:

1. **Click Customers in the Navigation bar to display the Customers page shown in Figure 4-1.**

   QBO displays the Customer Information dialog box shown in Figure 4-2.

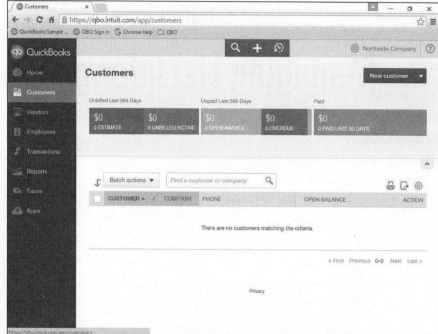

Figure 4-1:
Start from the appropriate page when you want to create a list entry for a new person.

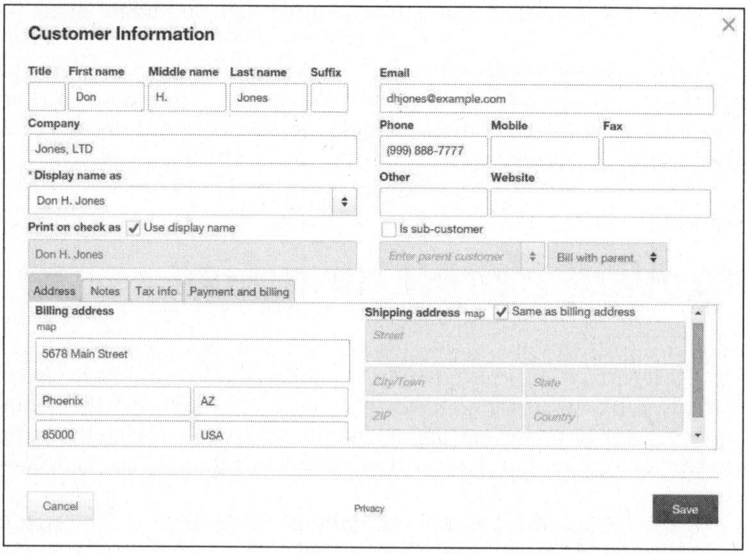

Figure 4-2:
Use this dialog box to enter information for a new customer.

2. **Click the New customer button in the upper-right corner of the screen.**

3. **Type the requested information.**

4. **Click Save.**

   QBO saves the customer and displays a page showing transactions for that customer. If you click Customers in the Navigation bar, the Customers list page reappears, and the new customer now appears in the list.

You can make any list entry inactive. Click that entry in the appropriate list, and then click the Action down arrow at the right edge of the list. In the list that opens, click Make Inactive.

Importing People into a List

Importing list information from QuickBooks desktop into a free trial of QBO can help you become accustomed to QBO while using list information you already recognize. And, importing that information into QBO can help you avoid retyping all the information for each list entry. You can import list information from a QuickBooks desktop company by using an Excel file or a CSV file. CSV stands for *comma-separated values;* most programs enable you to export information to a CSV format. Coincidentally, Excel can open and save CVS files. So, you can open a CSV file, edit it in Excel as needed, and then resave it as a CSV file. Or, after editing, you can save the file as an Excel 97-2003 workbook.

You can create a CSV file by saving an Excel file in CSV format. With the Excel file open, choose File ⇨ Save As. In the Save As dialog box, change the Save As Type list below the filename from Excel Workbook to CSV (Comma Delimited).

You use the same process to import customers or vendors from a QuickBooks desktop product; in this section, I import vendors.

Importing list information is not the same thing as importing a QuickBooks desktop company. For details on importing a company, see Chapter 12 in Part III.

To successfully import information into QBO from a CSV file or an Excel workbook, the information must conform to a specific format. And, luckily, QBO gives you the option to download a sample file in Excel format so that you can view the required format for importing list information; you can use this sample as a guideline for setting up the data in your own file.

To download and view the sample file for vendors, follow these steps:

1. **Click Vendors in the Navigation bar to display the Vendors page (see Figure 4-3).**

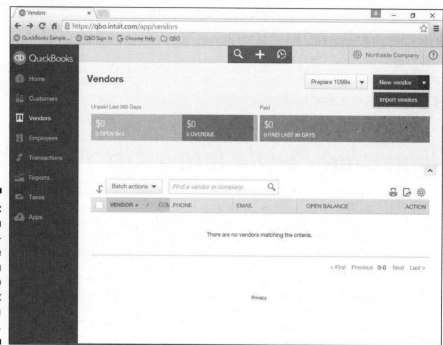

2. **Click the down arrow beside the New Vendor button in the upper-right corner of the screen.**

3. **Click Import Vendors.**

   QBO displays the Import Vendors page (see Figure 4-4).

4. **Click the Download a sample file link.**

   Once you click the link, QBO downloads the sample file and displays a button in the Windows taskbar for it.

5. **Click the sample file's button in the Windows taskbar.**

   The sample file opens in Excel (see Figure 4-5).

6. **Examine the file's content by scrolling to the right to see the information stored in each column.**

7. **Create your own file, modeling it on the sample file.**

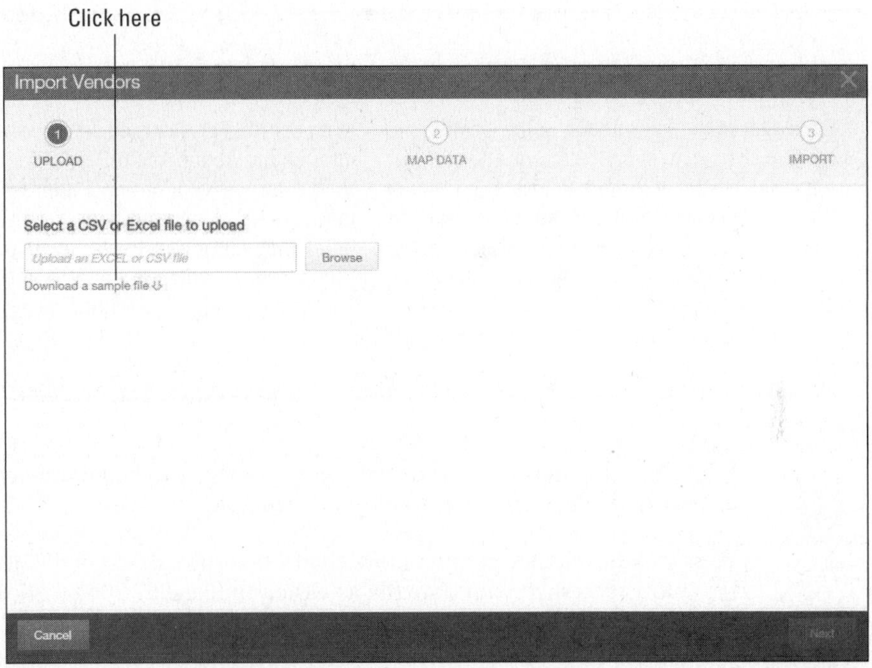

Click here

Figure 4-4:
The Import
Vendors
page.

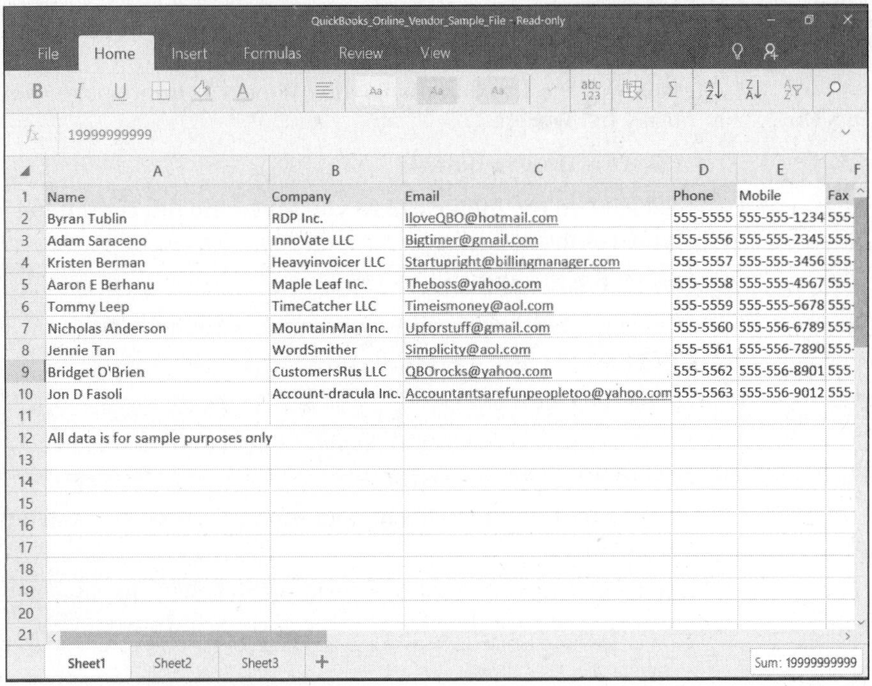

Import Vendors

① UPLOAD   ② MAP DATA   ③ IMPORT

Select a CSV or Excel file to upload

Upload an EXCEL or CSV file   Browse

Download a sample file ⊍

Cancel   Next

Figure 4-5:
A file
showing the
format you
need to
successfully
import list
information.

QuickBooks_Online_Vendor_Sample_File - Read-only

File   Home   Insert   Formulas   Review   View

fx   19999999999

	A	B	C	D	E	F
1	Name	Company	Email	Phone	Mobile	Fax
2	Byran Tublin	RDP Inc.	IloveQBO@hotmail.com	555-5555	555-555-1234	555-
3	Adam Saraceno	InnoVate LLC	Bigtimer@gmail.com	555-5556	555-555-2345	555-
4	Kristen Berman	Heavyinvoicer LLC	Startupright@billingmanager.com	555-5557	555-555-3456	555-
5	Aaron E Berhanu	Maple Leaf Inc.	Theboss@yahoo.com	555-5558	555-555-4567	555-
6	Tommy Leep	TimeCatcher LLC	Timeismoney@aol.com	555-5559	555-555-5678	555-
7	Nicholas Anderson	MountainMan Inc.	Upforstuff@gmail.com	555-5560	555-556-6789	555-
8	Jennie Tan	WordSmither LLC	Simplicity@aol.com	555-5561	555-556-7890	555-
9	Bridget O'Brien	CustomersRus LLC	QBOrocks@yahoo.com	555-5562	555-556-8901	555-
10	Jon D Fasoli	Account-dracula Inc.	Accountantsarefunpeopletoo@yahoo.com	555-5563	555-556-9012	555-
11						
12	All data is for sample purposes only					

Sheet1   Sheet2   Sheet3   +   Sum: 19999999999

The data file's layout in Excel

Excel stores the information in the sample file (and you'll need to store the information in your data file) in a table format, where each row in the Excel file contains all the information about a single vendor or customer (each row is referred to as a *record*), and each column contains the same piece of information for all customers and vendors (each column is referred to as one *field* in a record). For example, in Figure 4-5, all the information about Adam Saraceno appears in Row 3, and all vendor email addresses appear in Column C. Also note that Row 1 contains a label that identifies the type of information found in each column; don't forget to include identifying labels in your data file.

You'll find that importing your data works best if you can match the headings in your data file to the ones found in the sample data file.

Your data file cannot contain more than 1,000 rows or exceed 2MB in size. Don't forget to save your data file as either an Excel 97-2003 workbook or as a CSV (comma-delimited) file.

After you have created an Excel file or a CSV file containing your list information, you can import it. Follow these steps:

1. **Make sure your data file is not open.**

2. **Follow Steps 1 to 3 to display the Import Vendors page shown previously in Figure 4-4.**

3. **Click the Browse button.**

4. **Navigate to the folder where you saved the file containing your list information.**

5. **Select the file and choose Open.**

   QBO updates the Import Vendors page with the name of the file you selected.

6. **Click Next.**

   QBO uploads your file and displays the Map Data screen shown in Figure 4-6.

7. **Make sure that the fields in your data file correctly match fields in QBO.**

   As needed, open the list box beside each QBO field name and match it to the labels in your data file.

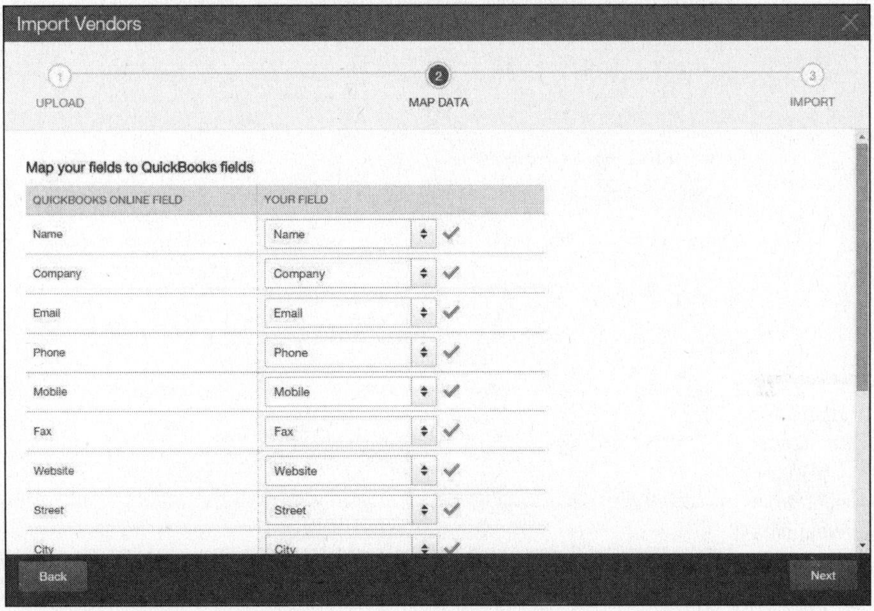

Figure 4-6:
Match the
fields in
your data
file to QBO
fields.

8. **Click Next.**

   QBO displays the records it has identified (see Figure 4-7).

9. **Review the records QBO proposes to import to make sure the information is correct.**

   You can make changes to the information in any field by clicking that field and typing. You also can uncheck any row to avoid importing the information in that row to QBO.

10. **When you are satisfied that the information is correct, click the Import button.**

    QBO imports the information and displays a message that identifies the number of records imported. When you click the Vendors link in the Navigation bar, the list displays the vendors you imported (see Figure 4-8).

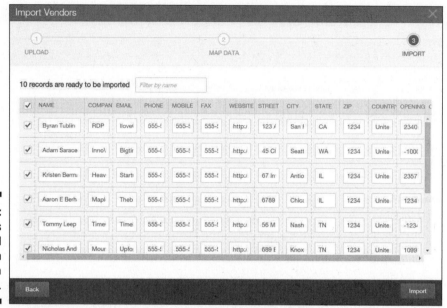

Figure 4-7:
The records
QBO will
import from
your data
file.

Figure 4-7:
The records
QBO will
import from
your data
file.

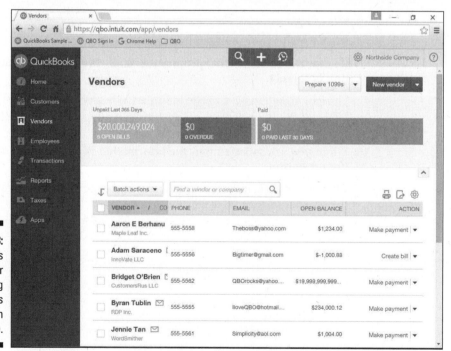

Figure 4-8:
The Vendors
page after
importing
vendors
using an
Excel file.

Searching Lists for People

You can use the Customers, Vendors, and Employees pages in a variety of ways. You can sort the people that appear in the list, export the list to Excel, and perform actions on a selected group of people on the list. You also can search for a specific person.

To search for a particular person, type some characters that match the customer or company name in the Search box that appears above the list of people.

Sorting a list

You can sort the lists on the Customers and Vendors page by name or open balance. By default, QBO sorts the entries on these pages alphabetically by name in ascending order.

To change the sort order for either of these lists, click the Customers or Vendors link in the Navigation bar to display the appropriate page; for this example, I use the Customers page.

Next, click the heading for the column by which you want to sort. If you click the Customer/Company column heading, QBO displays the customers in descending alphabetical order. If you click the Open Balance column heading, QBO sorts the list in Open Balance order, from lowest to highest.

Once you turn on payroll, you can sort the employees that appear in the payroll list alphabetically in ascending or descending order by clicking the Name column heading.

Exporting a list to Excel

You can export a list of your customers or vendors to Excel. Click the appropriate link in the Navigation bar to display either the Customers page or the Vendors page; I use the Customers page in this example. At the right edge of the page, just above the list, three buttons appear. Click the middle button, and QBO exports the list to an Excel file; a button for the file appears at the bottom of the screen (see Figure 4-9).

Click here to export the list

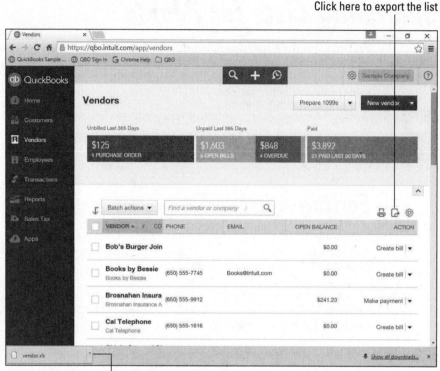

Figure 4-9:
Exporting a
customer
list to Excel.

Click here to open the Excel file

Click the button at the bottom of the screen, and Excel opens the file. You can edit the file if you click the Enable Editing button in the yellow bar at the top of the window.

Working with a batch of people

When you work with customers or vendors, you can take certain actions for a group of people at one time. For example, you can select specific vendors by clicking the check box beside each name and then send the same email to those vendors.

For customers, in addition to sending email, you can send statements to them.

To use one of these actions for a group of people, click the appropriate link in the Navigation bar to display the associated page. For this example, I used the Customers page.

Next, click the check box beside the names you want to include in your action and then click the Batch Actions button (see Figure 4-10). Select the action you want to take, and then follow the prompts onscreen to complete the action.

Click this gear

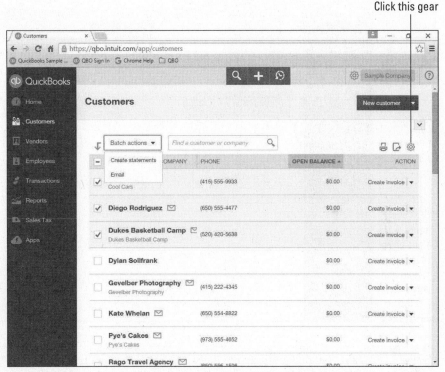

Figure 4-10:
Performing an action for several customers.

Changing Settings for People Lists

You can, to some extent, control the appearance of the lists on the Customers page, the Vendors page, and the Employees page. For example, you can opt to show or hide street address, email, and phone number information, and you can opt to include or exclude inactive entries in the list. You also can control the number of entries displayed on each page, as well as adjust those entries' column widths.

Click the appropriate link in the Navigation bar to display the associated page; for this section, I worked on the Vendors page.

To control the information displayed in the list, click the Gear icon at the right edge of the page just above the list's labels (see Figure 4-11). Then select or deselect check boxes to display or hide information. Click outside the list when you finish.

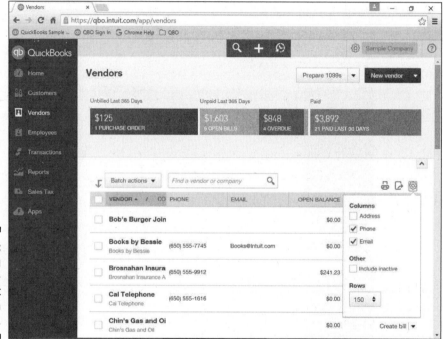

Figure 4-11:
Controlling the information that appears in the list.

When you click outside the list, I suggest that you click in the empty area at the bottom of the Navigation bar (below the Apps link) so that you don't accidentally navigate away from the current page.

To adjust the width of any column, slide the mouse pointer into the row of column heading labels above the list and place it over the right edge of the column you want to adjust. When the mouse pointer changes to a pair of vertical lines and a pair of horizontal arrows pointing outward, drag the mouse (see Figure 4-12). A vertical bar appears to guide you in resizing the column. Release the mouse button when you're satisfied with the column width.

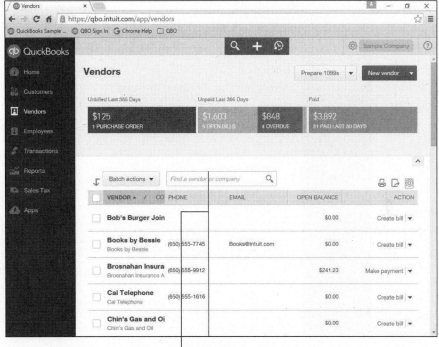

Figure 4-12: Adjusting the width allotted to the vendor's name on the Vendors page.

Use the vertical line to guide resizing a column

Displaying Information for Other Lists

Just as QuickBooks desktop has other lists besides lists of people, QBO also has other lists. To find them, click the Gear icon beside the company name and, from the menu that appears, click All Lists in the second column from the left. QBO displays the Lists page shown in Figure 4-13.

Click any list name to open that list and work with it. You can add new entries, select and edit existing entries, and select and delete entries that have never been used. I use the Products and Services list (see Figure 4-14) to show you how to create a new list element; the steps will be similar for any QBO lists.

The Products and Services list is the QBO equivalent of the QuickBooks desktop product's Items list. Be aware that I've removed some columns that appear by default to make this list page more readable.

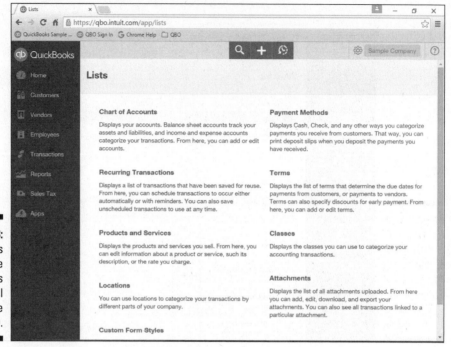

Figure 4-13:
The Lists page contains links to all available lists in QBO.

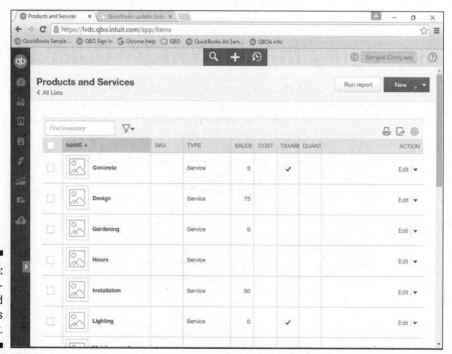

Figure 4-14:
The Products and Services list.

You can set up items in QBO, but remember that QBO doesn't have strong inventory capabilities. However, inventory has improved greatly since Lettuce was integrated into QBO.

Adding to a list

You can create non-inventory items as well as inventory and service items, and you can edit batches of items to change their type. I show you how to change an item's type after I show you how to add an item to the list.

1. Click the New button.

QBO displays a panel on the right side of your screen (see Figure 4-15), where you indicate whether you're creating an inventory item, a non-inventory item, or a service.

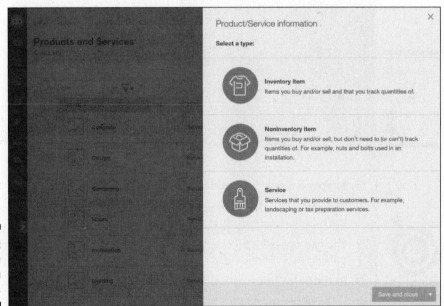

Figure 4-15:
Select a
type of item
to create.

2. Click a type to select it.

For this example, I chose Noninventory item. You create a service item the same way you create a non-inventory item, supplying the same kind of information shown in these steps. See the "Creating an inventory item" sidebar for details on the additional information you supply when creating an inventory item.

QBO displays the Product/Service Information panel shown in Figure 4-16.

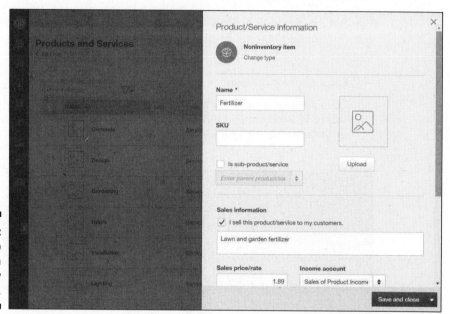

Figure 4-16: Use this to create an item you buy or sell.

3. **Supply a name for the item and, if appropriate, an SKU.**

You also can select the Is Sub-Product/Service box to specify whether the item is a sub-product or sub-service.

You can upload a picture of the item by clicking the Upload button and navigating to the location where you store the picture.

4. **In the Sales Information section, you can**

   a. **Select the I Sell This Product/Service to My Customers check box and supply a default description.**

   b. **Supply the price you charge when you sell this item.**

c. Select the income account associated with the item.

d. Select the Is Taxable check box if appropriate (scroll down in the panel to view this check box).

QBO uses this information when you select this item on sales transactions.

5. Scroll down in the panel and, in the Purchasing Information section, you can supply a default description, the cost you pay when you purchase the item, and the expense account associated with the item (see Figure 4-17).

QBO uses this information when you select this item on expense transactions.

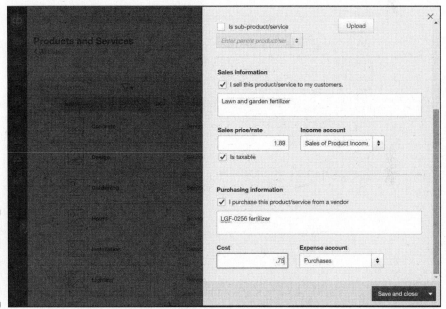

Figure 4-17: Add purchasing information for the item.

6. Click Save and Close.

QBO saves the item and redisplays the Products and Services list; the new item appears in the list.

Creating an inventory item

When creating an inventory, you need to supply a few additional types of information. For an inventory item, you supply quantity on hand information as well as the inventory asset account that tracks your inventory items, as shown in the figure.

Supply the quantity you have on hand and the date when you determine the quantity on hand.

Remember, before you can sell an item, you must own some of it. If you don't own any at the time you create the item, you'll probably buy some of it using an expense transaction, and that will update your quantities for you.

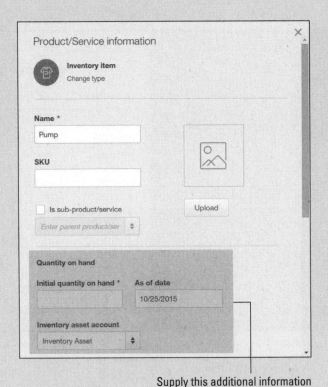

Supply this additional information

Item type changes you can make

Be aware that you can change item types with some limitations. First, you cannot change Inventory items to any other item types. You can make the following types of changes:

✔ Non-inventory and service items to inventory items

✔ Service items to non-inventory items

✔ Non-inventory items to service items

When changing item types, you change several items at one time only if you are changing non-inventory items to service items or service items to non-inventory items. If you need to change either a service item or a non-inventory item to an inventory item, you can make the change only one item at a time.

You also can print a basic report by clicking the Print button on any list page; the Print button appears just above the Action column. And, you can print a more detailed report for a list entry by selecting it and then clicking the Report button.

Changing item types

Originally, QBO offered only two types of items: inventory and service. With the introduction of a non-inventory item, users find that they need to change the type of existing service items to non-inventory items. You can change a service or non-inventory item's type individually or you can select several items and change their item types simultaneously.

To change any single item's type, edit that item by clicking Edit in the Action column of the Products and Services list. QBO displays the item in the Product/Service information panel (see Figure 4-18).

QBO displays the panel shown in Figure 4-19; the current item type contains a check mark. Click the new item type, and QBO redisplays the Product/Service Information panel using the new item type. Make any other necessary changes and then click Save and Close.

Changing the type of a single item using the method just described works well when you need to change only one item. But when you need to change

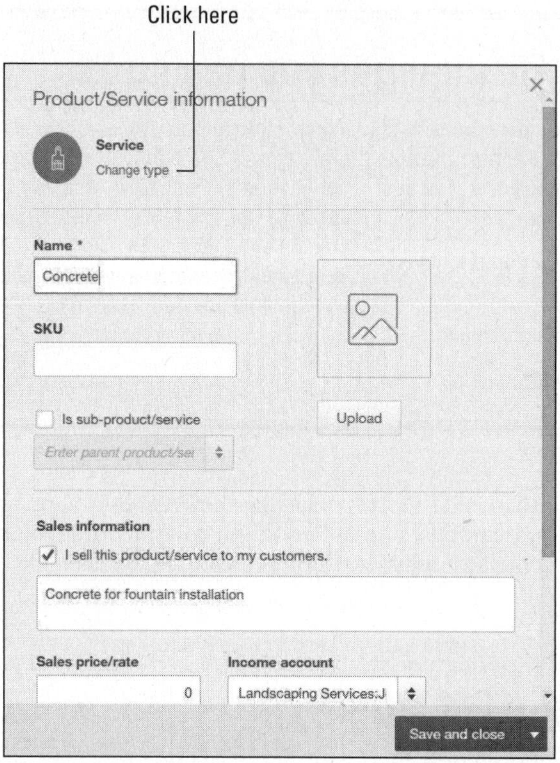

Click here

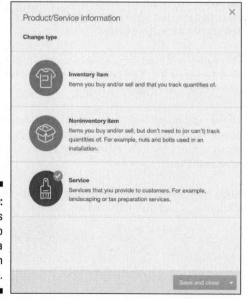

Figure 4-18:
Changing an
individual
item's type.

Figure 4-19:
Use this
panel to
select a
new item
type.

multiple items, use the following approach to change items of the same type to a different type:

1. **On the Products and Services page, select the check box that appears to the left of each item you want to change.**

    Make sure that you select either service items or non-inventory items, but not both.

    QBO displays two buttons above the table of items (see Figure 4-20).

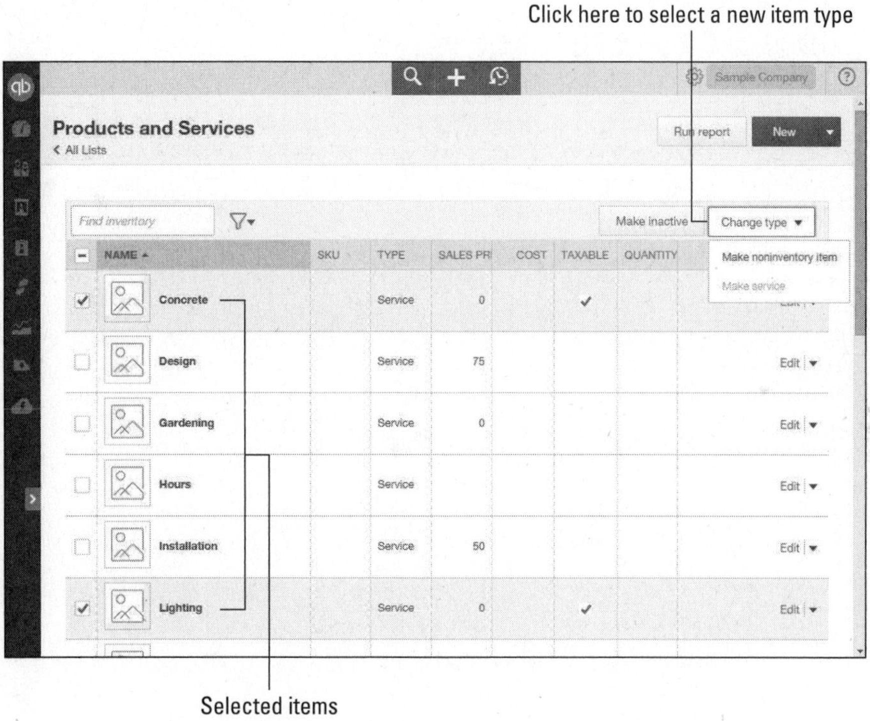

Click here to select a new item type

Figure 4-20: Changing the type of multiple items simultaneously.

Selected items

2. **Click the Change Type button and select the new type for the selected items.**

    QBO whirs a bit and then redisplays the Products and Services list, showing the new item types for the items you selected in Step 1.

Chapter 5

Dealing with the Outflow of Money

● ●

In This Chapter

▶ Writing checks

▶ Entering expenses

▶ Using purchase orders

▶ Entering and paying bills

● ●

*I*t's always more fun to make money than to spend it, but paying bills is part of life — unless you're living in *Star Trek: The Next Generation,* where they have no bills — but, I digress. This chapter explores the transactions you use in QBO to meet your financial obligations.

To record most expense-related transactions, you can choose Transactions ⇨ Expenses to display the Expense Transactions page shown in Figure 5-1. Click the New Transaction button to select a transaction type.

If the transaction type you want to record isn't available, click the Create plus sign (+) icon at the top of QBO and choose the type of transaction you want to record from the Create menu that appears; expense-related transactions show up in the Vendors column (see Figure 5-2).

The Create icon changes to an X when you open the menu.

Getting up and running

If you start using QBO after you've been in business for a while and have some outstanding bills you haven't yet paid, you can use those bills as a learning tool and enter them as described in this chapter. If you recorded an opening bank account balance back in Chapter 3, be sure to enter into QBO the checks you've written that haven't yet cleared your bank. If you didn't record an opening bank account balance back in Chapter 3, or you recorded a bank account balance as of December 31 of last year, be sure to enter into QBO all the checks you've written this year, even if they have cleared the bank.

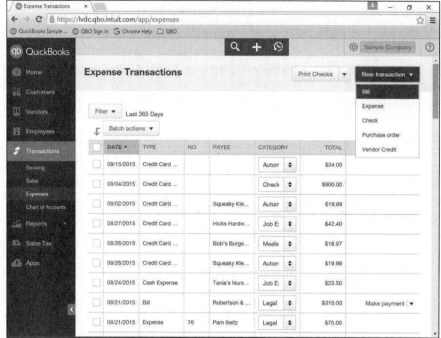

Figure 5-1:
The
Expense
Transac-
tions page.

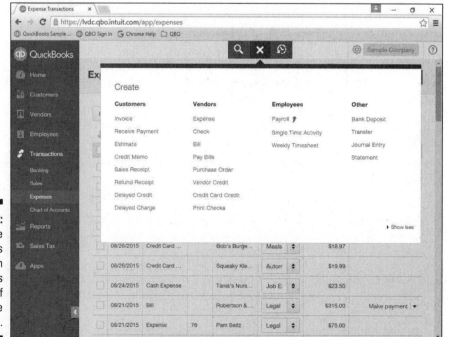

Figure 5-2:
Expense
transactions
appear in
the Vendors
column of
the Create
menu.

Writing a Check

Typically, you enter a check transaction when you intend to print a check to pay for an expense. Suppose that the UPS guy has just made a delivery for which you owe money and you want to give him a check: Use the Check transaction. You can print the check immediately or at a later time.

Assigning a check to accounts or items

When you write a check, you need to assign the expense for which you're writing the check to either an account or an item, and you can assign one check to both accounts and items. Follow these steps to enter and print a check:

1. **On the Expense Transactions page, click the New Transaction button.**

2. **From the list that appears, click Check.**

   QBO displays the Check window, which is divided into four sections:

   - **The Header section:** Shown in Figure 5-3, this section displays the balance in the selected checking account, the selected payee and the payee's mailing address, the payment date, the check amount and number, and the option to print the check later.

   - **The Account Details section:** You use this table when the expense is not related to an item you've defined.

   - **The Item Details section:** You use this table when you're writing a check to pay for a product or service you purchased. If you don't see this table, its preference isn't enabled. To display the table, choose Company Settings ⇨ Expenses ⇨ Bills and Expenses and edit the Show Items Table on Expense and Purchase Forms option.

   You typically write a check using *either* the Account Details section or the Item Details section, but not both. However, you can use both sections. If you won't be using a section, you can hide it by clicking the downward-pointing arrow beside the section name.

   - **The Footer section:** Contains the check total, the Memo box, and the box you use to attach an electronic document to the check.

Figure 5-3:
The Header
section of
the Check
window.

Check #75

| Hicks Hardware | Checking | Balance $1,201.00 | AMOUNT |
| 1 linked transaction | | | $228.75 |

Mailing address

Geoff Hicks
Hicks Hardware
42 Main St.
Middlefield, CA 94303

Payment date

08/21/2015

Check no.

75

Print later

3. **Choose a payee and an account from which to make the payment.**

   Along with the payee's address information, QBO displays information
   from previously entered transactions unless you haven't entered any
   transactions for that payee yet, or you have disabled the setting to display previously entered transaction information in Company Settings.

   If a pane appears on the right side, it displays transactions you might
   want to link to the check you're writing — and, if that's the case, see
   the next section, "Writing a check for an outstanding bill." On the other
   hand, if the check you're writing has nothing to do with any transaction that appears in the pane, just ignore the pane; you can hide it as
   described in the next section.

4. **Double-check the payment Date, and Check Number, and make an
   appropriate selection in the Print Later check box.**

5. **Assign part or all of the check to an expense account or an item using
   the Account Details section or the Item Details section (see Figure 5-4).**
   To assign a portion to an expense account:

   a. **Click in the Account column and select an appropriate expense
      account for the check you are recording.**

      You can type characters that appear in the account name and QBO
      will help you find the account.

   b. **In the Description column, type a description of the expense
      you're paying.**

   c. **In the Amount column, supply the amount of the check that you
      want to apply to the selected account.**

   d. **If you incurred the expense on behalf of a customer and you
      want to bill the customer for the expense, check the Billable
      box — and, if appropriate, the Tax box — and select the
      customer's name in the Customer column.**

   e. **Repeat Steps a to d to add more lines to the check.**

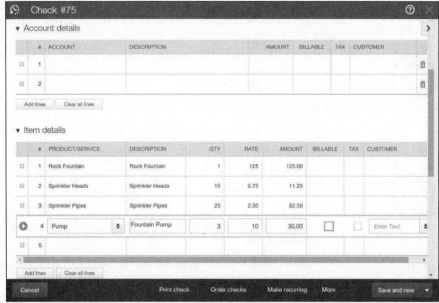

Figure 5-4:
The Account Details and Item Details sections of the Check window.

6. **To assign part or all of the check to items or services you have defined, use the Item Details section (also shown in Figure 5-4):**

   a. **Click in the Product/Service column and select an appropriate item for the check you are recording.**

   You can type characters in the Product/Service column and QBO will help you find the account.

   b. **Optionally, edit the Description column for the selected item.**

   c. **Use the Qty, Rate, and Amount columns to supply the quantity of the selected item you are purchasing, the rate you're paying for each item, and the amount you're paying.**

   When you supply any two of the Qty, Rate, and Amount values, QuickBooks calculates the third value.

   d. **If you purchased the item on behalf of a customer and you want to bill the customer for the item, check the Billable box — and, if appropriate, the Tax box — and select the customer's name in the Customer column.**

   e. **Repeat Steps a to d to add more items to the check.**

7. **You can scroll down in the Check window to the Footer section, type a message to the payee, and attach an electronic document (such as the payee's invoice) to the check.**

To attach an electronic document to the check, click in the Attachments box and navigate to the document or drag and drop the electronic copy into the Attachments box.

8. **At the bottom of the window, you can**

• **Cancel your action or clear the window and start again.**

• **Click Print Check to print the check.**

The first time you print checks, QBO walks you through the process of selecting the type of checks you use and aligning them for your printer.

• **Click Order Checks to visit the Intuit Marketplace and order check stock.**

• **Click Make Recurring to set up the check as a recurring payment you intend to make on a schedule you specify.**

• **Click More to see additional actions, such as voiding the check or viewing its audit history.**

• **Click Save and New to save the check and redisplay the Check window so that you can write another check.**

The Save and New button is a sticky preference. That is, if you click the dropdown arrow to the right of the button and select Save and Close, the next time you open the window to write a check, the default button will be the Save and Close button.

Writing a check for an outstanding bill

You can use the Check window to write a check to pay a bill you previously entered — something that you cannot do in the QuickBooks desktop product.

Don't use the Check transaction if you're planning on paying several bills. Instead, see the section "Paying bills," at the end of this chapter.

If you select a payee for whom an outstanding bill exists, QBO displays a pane at the right side of the Check window that shows transactions linked to the selected payee; each transaction appears as a separate entry (see Figure 5-5). If nothing in the pane applies to your transaction, you can hide the pane by clicking the button shown in Figure 5-5.

Click here to hide the pane

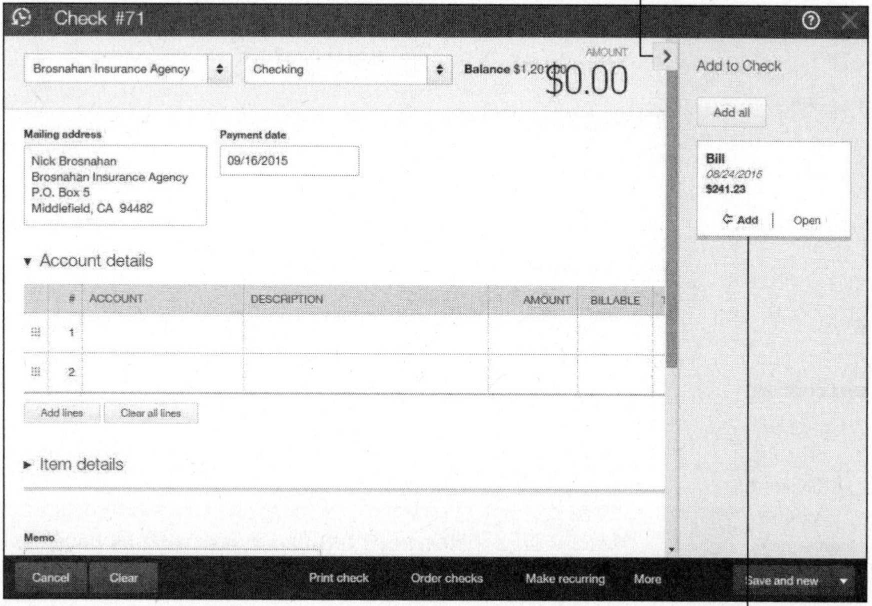

Figure 5-5:
If you select a payee for whom you previously entered a bill, the out-standing bill appears in the pane on the right side of the Check window.

Click here to use the check to pay an outstanding bill

If you're writing the check to pay a bill that appears in the pane, click Add in the bill transaction you want to pay. That way, QBO appropriately applies the check you're writing to the outstanding bill and correctly reduces your out-standing obligations.

If you write a check to pay a bill and you *don't* apply the check to the bill, your reports show that you continue to owe the bill amount to the payee, which really messes things up.

When you click Add, QBO adds that bill to the check and displays the Bill Payment window rather than the Check window, essentially converting the check to a bill payment transaction. In Figure 5-6, you see the Bill Payment window after I added an outstanding bill to a check in the Check window. If you compare Figures 5-5 and 5-6, you'll notice that the original check number was 71, and it's still 71 in the Bill Payment window.

Figure 5-6:
The Bill
Payment
window.

You complete the Bill Payment transaction the same way you complete a Check transaction; follow Steps 7 and 8 in the preceding section.

If you add the wrong bill to a check, you can cancel the Bill Payment transaction without saving it.

Creating an Expense

When you're trying to record an expense without printing a check — you might, for example, be using a credit or debit card to pay the expense, or you might have manually written a check that you now need to record in QBO without printing it — you can use the Expense transaction window. The major difference between the Expense transaction window and the Check transaction window is the lack of any tools to help you print an Expense transaction; compare Figures 5-4 and 5-7.

The Expense transaction window also contains a Payment Method list box that you don't find in the Check transaction window. Other than those two differences, the windows appear and function the same way.

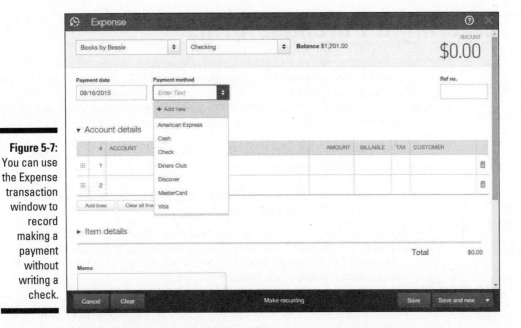

Figure 5-7:
You can use the Expense transaction window to record making a payment without writing a check.

QBO and credit card transactions

By default, QBO treats Credit Card account transactions as cash transactions, a conservative approach that recognizes expenses as they occur. You set up a Credit Card account in your Chart of Accounts and use Expense transactions to record credit card purchases to the account as you make each purchase. If you need to record a credit card return, use the Credit Card Credit transaction.

If you want to recognize credit card expenses when you pay your credit card bill (rather than when you make a purchase using your credit card), don't set up a Credit Card account in the Chart of Accounts, and don't enter Expense transactions or Credit Card Credit transactions in QBO for credit card transactions as they occur. Instead, when you receive your credit card statement, enter a Bill transaction, as described later in this chapter, and allocate each line on the credit card statement to the appropriate account or item. QBO then treats your Credit Card account as an Accounts Payable vendor. And when you're ready to pay the credit card bill, you can write a check or use the Pay Bills page to pay the credit card statement.

Entering a Purchase Order

Businesses that order lots of stuff from vendors often use purchase orders to keep track of the items on order. Purchase orders in QBO do not affect any of your accounts; instead, they simply help you keep track of what you order. And, when the order arrives, you can compare the goods that come in the door with the ones listed on the purchase order to make sure they match.

If you plan to use purchase orders, then your ordering process typically happens in the following way:

- ✔ You place an order with a vendor and you enter a purchase order in QBO that matches the order you placed.

- ✔ You receive the items you ordered, typically along with a bill for the items; you then match the items you receive to the purchase order and enter a bill for the items. Note that sometimes you receive the bill without out the items or the items without the bill.

- ✔ You pay the vendor's bill.

You enter a purchase order using the Purchase Order transaction window; you can open this window either from the Expense Transactions page or from the Create menu (the plus sign). A typical purchase order looks like the one shown in Figure 5-8, and you'll notice the window closely resembles the Check window shown earlier in Figure 5-4.

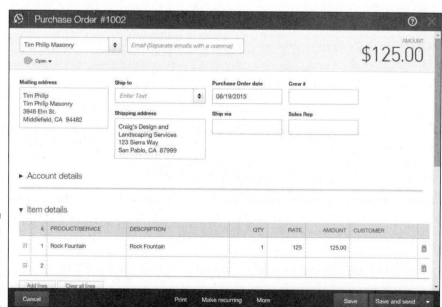

Figure 5-8: The Purchase Order window.

As you fill in the Purchase Order transaction window, QBO assigns a status of Open to the purchase order; the status appears just below the vendor's name in the upper-left corner of the transaction window.

When you receive the goods, the vendor's bill, or both, you record a bill as described in the next section, or a check, an expense transaction, or a credit card charge as described earlier in this chapter, showing what you paid (or what you owe) the vendor.

When you select a vendor who has open purchase orders on any of these types of transactions, a pane appears on the right side of the window, showing available purchase orders. You add a purchase order to the transaction the same way you added a bill to a Check transaction: by clicking the Add button. In Figure 5-9, I've opened a Check transaction and selected a vendor who has open purchase orders.

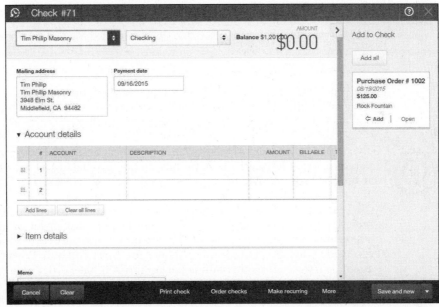

Figure 5-9: The Check window, with a vendor selected who has open purchase orders.

When I click Add to add the purchase order to my transaction, QBO adds the purchase order lines to the first available line in the Item Details section of my Check transaction. QBO also indicates, below the vendor name, that the Check transaction has one linked transaction (see Figure 5-10).

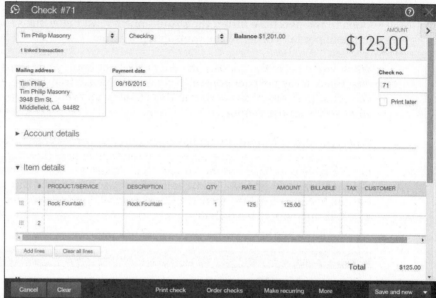

Figure 5-10:
A Check
transaction
after adding
a purchase
order to it.

If you save the Check transaction and then reopen the purchase order, QBO has changed the purchase orders status from open to closed so that you don't accidentally add the purchase order to another transaction.

If you add the wrong purchase order to a transaction, you can remove the purchase order line in the Item Details section by clicking the trash can icon at the right edge of the line.

QBO can't add only part of a purchase order to a transaction. So, if you receive only part of a purchase order, add the purchase order to your transaction and then record a payment for the part of the purchase order you received by deleting lines from the check for items you didn't receive. To continue to track the outstanding part of the purchase order, you can manually close the original purchase order and create a new purchase order that contains the remaining outstanding items; when you create the second purchase order — essentially a back order — try to assign a number to it that helps you track it in relation to the original purchase order.

You can use your own custom purchase order numbers if you choose Gear ⇨ Company Settings ⇨ Expenses. Then click the pencil beside Purchase Orders to edit purchase order settings, select the Custom Transaction Numbers check box, and then click Save.

When you need to identify open purchase orders, use the Open Purchase Order List report. For more on reports, see Chapter 10.

Entering and Paying Bills

You use QBO's Bill transaction to enter a bill from a vendor that you don't want to pay immediately. QBO tracks the bill as a *payable,* which is a liability of your business — money you owe but have not yet paid. Most companies that enter Bill transactions do so because they receive a fair number of bills and want to sit down and pay them at one time, but they don't want to lose track of the bills they receive. They also want to be able to easily determine how much they owe; if you enter Bill transactions, you can print the A/P Aging Summary and Details reports to find that information.

Depending on the version of QBO that you use, the Bill transaction might not be available to you; if that's the case, pay your bills using the Check or the Expense transaction.

Entering a bill

To enter a bill you receive from a vendor, you use QBO's Bill transaction. Follow these steps:

1. **Choose Transactions ➪ Expenses.**

2. **Click the New Transaction button and select Bill.**

   QBO displays the Bill transaction window shown in Figure 5-11.

Figure 5-11: The Bill transaction window.

3. **Select the vendor from whom you received the bill.**

   QBO fills in the vendor's mailing address information.

4. **Check and, if necessary, change the bill date and the due date.**

5. **Use the Account Details section, the Item Details section, or both to record information about the bill.**

   See the section "Writing a Check" for details on filling out the Account Details section and the Item Details section.

6. **Optionally, scroll down to the Footer section (which isn't shown in Figure 5-11) and enter information in the Memo field and attach electronic documents to the bill.**

7. **Click Save.**

Recording a vendor credit

You enter a vendor credit to record returns to vendors or refunds from vendors. A vendor might supply you with a credit document that indicates you no longer owe the amount stated on the document, or the vendor might issue a refund check to you.

If a vendor issues a credit document, you enter a vendor credit and then apply it when you pay the vendor's bill. If a vendor issues a refund check to you, you still enter a vendor credit, but you also enter a deposit and then link the deposit to the vendor credit.

Follow these steps to enter the vendor credit:

1. **On the Expense Transaction page, click New Transaction ⇨ Vendor Credit.**

   QBO displays the Vendor Credit window shown in Figure 5-12.

2. **Select the vendor who issued the credit.**

3. **Enter the date of the credit.**

4. **Enter the credit amount.**

5. **In the Account Details section, select the account used on the original bill.**

   If you received the credit because you returned items to the vendor, select the items you returned in the Item Details section.

6. **You can optionally scroll down and attach an electronic copy of the credit to the Vendor Credit transaction.**

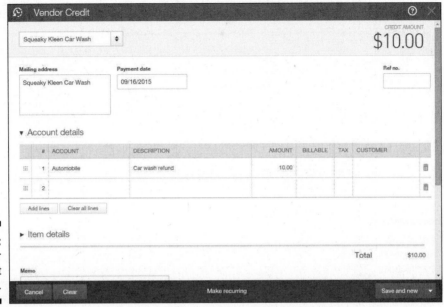

Figure 5-12:
A Vendor
Credit
transaction.

7. **Click the arrow beside Save and New and choose Save and Close.**

The Save option referenced in Step 7 is called a *sticky preference,* which means that after you select Save and Close, it will appear as the default Save option the next time you display this screen.

If the vendor issued only a credit document, read the section "Paying bills" to learn how to use the vendor credit you just entered to reduce the amount you owe the vendor when you pay the vendor's bill.

If the vendor issued a refund check to you, I assume you've completed the previous steps to enter a vendor credit. Now, enter a deposit for the refund check and link it to the vendor credit. Follow these steps:

1. **Click the Create plus (+) sign and, from the Other section of Create menu that appears, choose Bank Deposits.**

   QBO displays the Deposit transaction window shown in Figure 5-13.

2. **In the Add New Deposits section, enter the following information:**

   - **In the Received From column, select the vendor who issued the check.**

   - **In the Account column, select the Accounts Payable account.**

   - **In the Amount column, enter the amount of the check.**

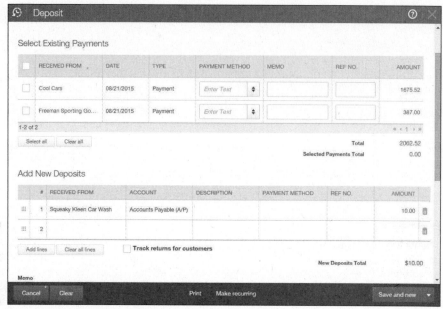

Figure 5-13:
The Deposit
transaction
window.

3. **Click the arrow beside Save and New and choose Save and Close.**

   The Save option functions as a sticky preference and you might not see Save and New because you previously made a different choice.

4. **Click the Create plus (+) sign and, from the Create menu that appears, choose Expense.**

5. **Select the vendor whose refund check you deposited.**

   QBO displays available deposits, credits, and bills (see Figure 5-14).

6. **Click Add in the outstanding Vendor Credit transaction.**

7. **Click Add in the Deposit transaction.**

   When you add these two transactions to the Expense, QBO creates a Bill Payment transaction with a net value of $0; Figure 5-15 focuses on the Details section of the transaction. QBO also applies the vendor credit to the deposit.

8. **Click the arrow beside Save and New and choose Save and Close.**

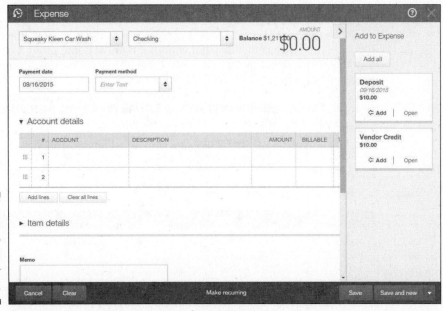

Figure 5-14:
Open trans-
actions for
the selected
vendor
appear.

Figure 5-15:
Adding the
vendor
credit and
the bank
deposit of
the vendor's
check
results in a
$0 bill
payment
transaction.

Paying bills

If you've been entering bills from vendors, then, at some point, you need to pay those bills. Most people sit down once or twice a month and pay outstanding bills. To pay bills in QBO, follow these steps:

1. **Click the Create plus (+) sign and, from the Create menu that appears, choose Pay Bills in the Vendors column.**

   QBO displays the Pay Bills page shown in Figure 5-16.

Overdue bills

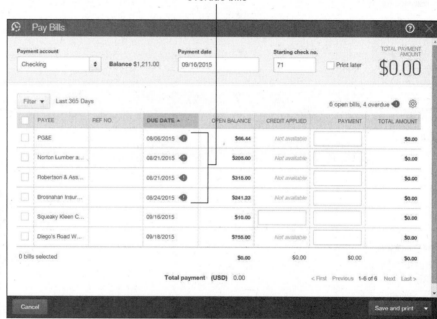

Figure 5-16: The Pay Bills page lists bills you owe but have not yet paid.

2. **In the Payment Account list, select an account to use to pay the bills.**

   QBO shows the balance in that account.

3. **Provide a payment date on the bottom-left side of the screen.**

4. **Enter the number of the first check you'll use to pay bills.**

   You can select the Print Later button to identify bills to pay and schedule them to print later; at the time you print the checks, QBO lets you establish the starting check number.

5. **In the Filter list, select an option to specify the outstanding bills you want to consider paying.**

   By default, QBO displays unpaid bills for the last year, but you can limit what appears onscreen for your consideration by a variety of dates and even for selected payees.

   Overdue bills display a red flag.

6. **By clicking the appropriate column heading, you can opt to sort the listed bills by Payee, Reference Number, Due Date, or Open Balance.**

7. **Select the check box in the column at the left side of each bill you want to pay.**

   As you select bills to pay, QBO updates the Payment column using the bill amount as the default payment amount (see Figure 5-17). You can change the payment amount of any bill by typing in the Payment column.

Figure 5-17: QBO uses the bill amount less any vendor credits to calculate a payment amount.

If a vendor credit exists, QBO assumes you want to apply outstanding vendor credits to reduce the amount you owe a particular vendor.

8. **Click Save and Print, or click the arrow beside Save and Print to choose either Save or Save and Close.**

   Click Save or Save and Close to mark the bills paid without printing any checks. Click Save and Print to print checks and mark the bills paid.

If you choose to pay the bills using a credit card instead of a bank account, no options appear related to printing checks, just as you'd expect.

If you opted, in Step 4, to print checks later, you can print those checks by choosing Create➪Print Checks. The Print Checks option appears in the Vendors column of the Create menu.

Chapter 6

Managing the Inflow of Money

*T*his is where the fun starts. "Why?" you ask. Because this chapter covers stuff related to bringing money into the business, which, from any businessperson's perspective, is the reason you started your business — and therefore the most fun part!

To record most sales-related transactions, you can choose Transactions ➪ Sales to display the Sales Transactions page shown in Figure 6-1; then click the New Transaction button. If the transaction type you want to record isn't available on the Sales Transactions page, click the Create button — the plus sign (+) icon at the top of QBO, which changes to an X after you click it — and choose the type of transaction you want to record from the Create menu that opens; sales-related transactions appear in the Customers column (see Figure 6-2).

Getting up and running

If you've been in business a while when you starting using QBO, and you have some invoices you've issued but customers haven't yet paid, you can use those invoices as a learning tool and enter them as described in this chapter. If you recorded an opening bank account balance back in Chapter 3, be sure to enter into QBO the deposits you've made since your last bank statement. If you didn't record an opening bank account balance back in Chapter 3, or you recorded a bank account balance as of December 31 of last year, be sure to enter into QBO all the deposits you've made this year, even if they have cleared the bank.

Click here to start a new sales transaction

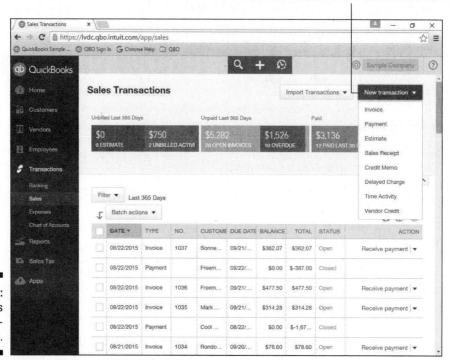

Figure 6-1:
The Sales
Transac-
tions page.

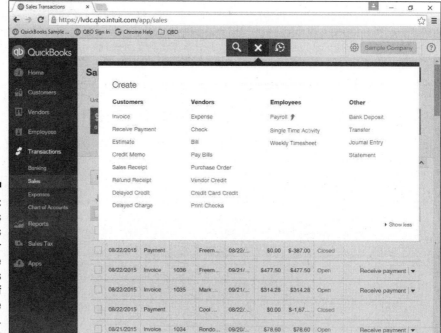

Figure 6-2:
Sales
transactions
appear
in the
Customers
column of
the Create
menu.

Customizing Forms to Handle Subtotals

Before we dive into preparing various types of forms, you should address a housekeeping task: setting up sales forms so that you can include subtotals on them. If you have no need to subtotal information on your sales forms, you can skip this section and move on to the next one.

You can subtotal lines on an invoice, an estimate, or a sales receipt. First, turn on the feature; for this example, I turned on the feature for the Invoice form. Follow these steps:

1. **Choose Gear⇨Custom Form Styles.**

2. **Select a form to customize, and then click Edit in the Action column.**

   The Customize Form Style dialog box appears.

3. **On the left side of the dialog box, click the Activity Table section.**

4. **In the More group, select the Group Activity By check box and make a selection from the list.**

   For my example, shown in Figure 6-3, I chose Type.

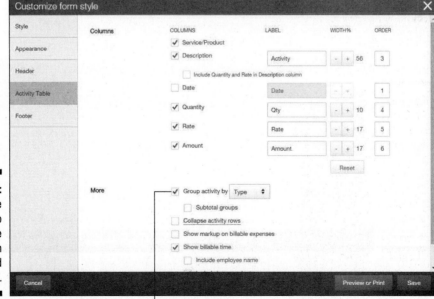

Figure 6-3:
Turn on the setting to enable grouping on the selected sales form.

Check this box to enable subtotaling

You can select Subtotal Groups if you want QBO to group specifically by the grouping type you select in Settings. Not selecting the option gives you more flexibility on the forms.

5. Save the settings.

You need to repeat the preceding steps for each type of form (invoice, estimate, and sales receipt) on which you want to be able to subtotal information.

Now you're ready to create an invoice and group lines on it. Using the steps in the next section, "Preparing an Invoice," add some lines to an invoice. To add the subtotal in the proper place on the invoice, click the last line on the invoice that should be subtotaled; in Figure 6-4, I clicked the third line of the invoice. Click the Add Subtotal button, which appears below the lines on the invoice, and QBO adds a line that subtotals the ones above it. You can continue adding lines to the invoice, and you can add more subtotals.

Click the last line to include in the subtotal   QBO adds the subtotal

Figure 6-4:
Click the
last line that
should be
part of the
subtotaled
group,
and then
click Add
Subtotal.

#	PRODUCT/SERVICE	DESCRIPTION	QTY	RATE	AMOUNT	TAX
1	Rock Fountain	Rock Fountain	1	275	275.00	✓
2	Pump	Fountain Pump	1	12.75	12.75	✓
3	Concrete	Concrete for fountain installation	5	9.50	47.50	✓
4					Subtotal: $335.25	
5	Design	Custom Design	3	75	225.00	
6						

Invoice #1037

Billing address: Russ Sonnenschein, Sonnenschein Family Store, 5647 Cypress Hill Ave., Middlefield, CA 94303

Terms: Net 30
Invoice date: 08/23/2015
Due date: 09/22/2015
Crew #: 102

Add lines | Clear all lines | Add subtotal

Subtotal $560.25
Taxable subtotal $335.25

Cancel | Revert | Print or Preview | Make recurring | Customize | More | Save | Save and send

Click here to add a subtotal

Preparing an Invoice

You enter invoices in QBO to inform customers that they owe you money for goods you sold them or services you performed for them. In QBO, you can prepare invoices and send them using email or using the U.S. Postal Service.

When you prepare an invoice, you include information about what you're selling to the customer by including items on the invoice. You create items for both services and products using the Products and Services list, as described at the end of Chapter 4. To enter an invoice, follow these steps:

1. **Choose Transactions⇨Sales to display the Sales Transactions page.**

2. **Click the New Transaction button and, from the list that appears, click Invoice.**

   QBO displays the Invoice window shown in Figure 6-5.

3. **Choose a customer.**

   QBO displays the customer's mailing address, payment terms, invoice date, due date, and Send Later option. Figure 6-5 also shows a Crew # field that appears because the invoice was customized. You can read more about customizing forms in Chapter 3.

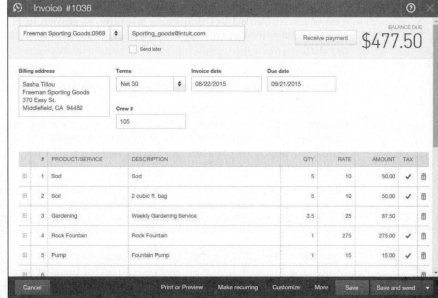

Figure 6-5: The header and the Details portion of the Invoice window.

If a pane appears on the right side, it displays transactions you might want to link to the invoice you're creating; you can see examples in the sections "Preparing an Estimate" and "Creating Billable Time Entries."

4. **Double-check the Invoice Date, Due Date, and Terms, and make an appropriate selection in the Send Later check box.**

   If you want to send invoices via email, you can set up your preferences in Company Settings; click the Gear icon beside your company name and choose Company Settings.

5. **Fill in the products and services the customer is buying:**

   a. **Click in the Product/Service column and select an appropriate item for the invoice you are creating.**

   You can type characters in the Product/Service column and QBO will help you find the item.

   b. **Optionally, edit the Description column for the selected item.**

   c. **Use the Qty, Rate, and Amount columns to supply the quantity of the selected item you are selling, the rate you're charging for each item, and the amount the customer should pay. When you supply any two of the Qty, Rate, and Amount values, QuickBooks calculates the third value.**

   d. **If appropriate, check the Tax box.**

   e. **Repeat Steps a to d to add more items to the invoice.**

6. **You can scroll down in the Invoice window, as shown in Figure 6-6, and select a sales tax rate and, if appropriate, a discount amount or percent.**

   You see the Sales Tax Rate option on invoices only if you have turned on the Sales Tax feature by choosing Sales Tax⇨Set Up Sales Tax Rates.

   You can also apply a discount to the invoice if you have turned on the company preference to display the Discount box; type a message to the customer; type information in the Statement Memo box, which QBO transfers directly to any statement you create in the future; and attach an electronic document to the invoice.

   If in the Company Settings dialog box, you turn on the preference to display the Deposit box at the bottom of the invoice, you can use it to reduce the amount of the invoice by the deposit amount paid by the customer.

   You can control whether the discount is a pre-tax or after-tax discount by clicking the switch that appears to the left of the Discount and Sales Tax Rate boxes. Clicking the switch swaps the position of the two boxes; when the Discount box appears on top, the discount is pre-tax.

Click here to control whether a discount is pre- or post-taxable

Figure 6-6:
Use the
bottom of
the Invoice
window to
handle
sales tax,
discount
information,
messages,
and attach-
ments.

7. **To attach an electronic document to the invoice, click in the Attachments box and navigate to the document or drag and drop the electronic copy into the Attachments box.**

8. **At the bottom of the window, you can**

   • **Cancel the invoice or clear the window and start again.**

   • **Click Print or Preview to print or preview the invoice.**

   • **Click Make Recurring to set up the invoice as a recurring invoice you intend to send on a schedule you specify.**

   • **Click Customize to customize the invoice form as described in Chapter 3.**

   • **Click Save to assign an invoice number and save the invoice in QBO.**

   • **Click Save and Send to assign an invoice number, save the invoice, and email a copy to the customer.**

   A window appears, in which you can write an email message and look at a preview of the invoice. After you send your invoice, the email time and date-stamp information appears in the header.

You can click the arrow beside Save and Send and then choose Save and New to save the invoice and start a new one, or choose Save and Close to save the invoice and close the Invoice window. The option you choose will appear the next time you display the Invoice window. In fact, in any transaction window, the choice you make appears the next time you open the window.

Recording a Customer Payment

When you receive a payment from a customer, you record it in QBO. You can display the Receive Payment window in the following ways:

- ✔ You can click the Create menu and select Receive Payment.
- ✔ You can click the New Transaction button on the Sales Transactions page and select Payment.
- ✔ In the Sales Transactions list, you can find the invoice for which you want to record a payment and click Receive Payment in the Action column.

If you use either of the first two methods, QBO displays an empty Receive Payment window. You then select a customer, and QBO displays all the customer's open invoices in the Outstanding Transactions section, at the bottom of the window (see Figure 6-7).

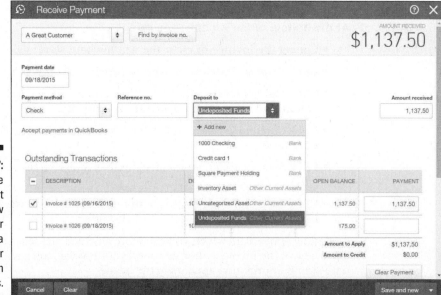

Figure 6-7: The Receive Payment window after selecting a customer with open invoices.

Using the Undeposited Funds account

If you receive more than one customer payment on any given day, you'll find the Undeposited Funds account a convenient way to handle the money that comes into your business. If you take several checks to your bank on a given day and deposit all of them as a single deposit, most banks typically don't record the individual checks as individual deposits. Instead, the bank records the sum of the checks as your deposit — pretty much the same way you sum the checks on the deposit ticket you give to the bank teller.

"And why is this important?" you ask. This fact is important because, when you receive your statement from your bank, you need to reconcile the bank's deposits and withdrawals with your own version of deposits and withdrawals. If you track each customer payment you receive as a deposit in the bank, then your deposits won't match the bank's deposits. And, if you don't use the Undeposited Funds account — and instead record customer payments directly into your QBO Bank account — your deposits definitely *won't* match the bank's version of your deposits.

Enter the Undeposited Funds account in QBO, which acts as a holding tank for customer payments before you've prepared a bank deposit slip. If you place customer payments in the Undeposited Funds account, you can then use the Bank Deposit feature in QBO to sum up the payments you receive and intend to deposit at your bank simultaneously — and, if you don't go to your bank daily to make deposits, there's no problem. QBO records, as the deposit amount in your QBO Bank account, the amount calculated in the Bank Deposit window, which will match the amount you actually deposit at your bank. Then, your bank reconciliation process becomes quick and easy — okay, maybe not quick and easy, but certainly quicker and easier than if you were trying to figure out which customer payments made up various bank deposits.

See Chapter 8 for details on preparing a bank deposit and reconciling a bank statement.

At the top of the screen, select a Payment Method and select the account in which you want QBO to place the customer's payment. In the Outstanding Transactions section, place a check beside each invoice being paid by the customer's payment.

At the bottom of the Receive Payment window, click Save and New to enter additional customer payments, or click the arrow beside Save and New and choose Save and Close.

So, what happens differently if you use the third method and opt to find the invoice on the Sales Transaction list, shown in Figure 6-8, and click the Receive Payment button in the Action column? If you work from the list, QBO automatically fills in the customer name, displays and selects in the Outstanding Transactions section the invoice you chose in the Sales Transaction list, and fills in a proposed payment amount. The window you see when you click the Receive Payment button looks just like the window shown previously in Figure 6-5.

Click here to open a blank Receive Payments window

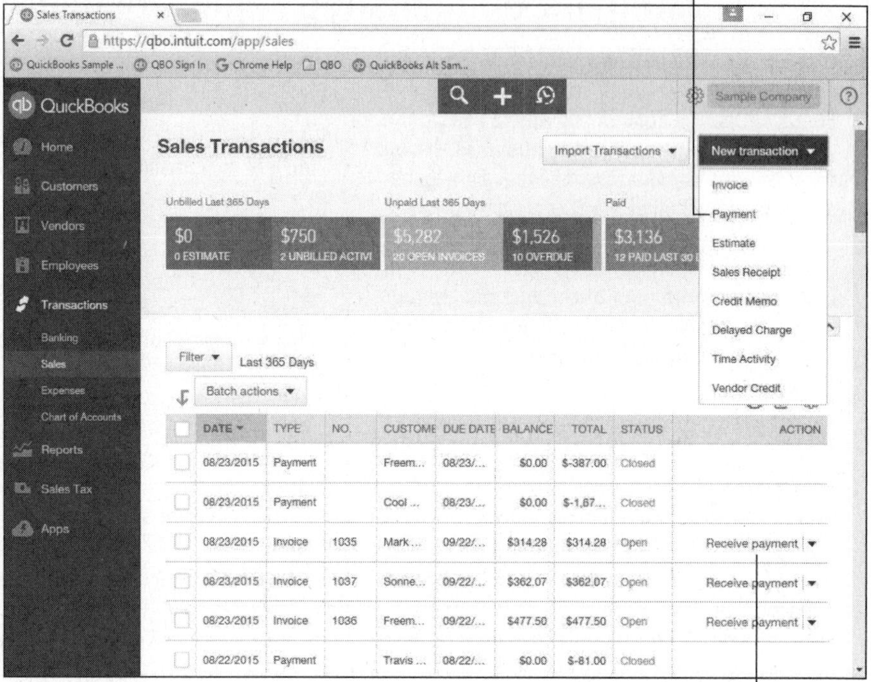

Figure 6-8:
You can
open the
Receive
Payments
window
from the
Sales Trans-
action list.

Click here to receive payment for a specific invoice

QBO interfaces with QuickBooks Payments, Intuit's online merchant service offering, so that you can accept ACH and credit card payments from your customers. Visit `http://payments.intuit.com/` or contact Intuit for details.

Preparing an Estimate

You can use estimates to prepare a document that estimates what you need to charge a client to complete a project; estimates don't update your QBO accounts but do enable you to keep track of proposals you make to customers. If a customer decides to buy, based on your estimate, you can convert the estimate to an invoice.

You prepare an estimate in much the same way you prepare an invoice. To display the Estimate window, click the Create menu and choose Estimate. Or, if you prefer to work from the Sales Transactions page, choose Transactions ➪ Sales, click the New Transaction button, and, from the menu that appears, click Estimate. QBO displays the Estimate window (see Figure 6-9).

	#	PRODUCT/SERVICE	DESCRIPTION	QTY	RATE	AMOUNT	TAX	
⠿	1	Rock Fountain	Rock Fountain	1	275	275.00	✓	🗑
⠿	2	Pump	Fountain Pump	1	15	15.00	✓	🗑
⠿	3	Concrete	Concrete for fountain installation	5	9.50	47.50	✓	🗑
⠿	4							🗑

Figure 6-9:
Creating an estimate.

Choose a customer, and QBO displays the customer's address information and the estimate date. You supply the estimate's expiration date and optionally select the Send Later option. Figure 6-7 also shows a Crew # field that appears because the estimate was customized. You can read more about customizing forms in Chapter 3.

As long as the estimate is open and has not expired or been converted to an invoice, the estimate's status is Pending, and the status appears just above the customer's billing address.

To fill in the products and services the customer is considering for purchase, click in the Product/Service column and select an item. You can type characters in the Product/Service column and QBO will help you find the item. QBO fills in any default information stored about the item. You can change the description, quantity, rate, amount, and taxable status of the item. Repeat this process to add more items to the estimate.

If you scroll down in the Estimate window, you see the additional fields shown in Figure 6-10.

Click here to control whether a discount is pre- or post-taxable

Estimate window showing:

Add lines	Clear all lines	Add subtotal

Subtotal $337.50

Taxable subtotal $337.50

Message displayed on estimate

Select a sales tax rate | 0.00

Discount percent | $0.00

Total $337.50

Memo

Estimate Total $337.50

Attachments Maximum size: 25MB

Drag/Drop files here or click the icon

Show existing

Privacy

Figure 6-10: The bottom of the Estimate window.

| Cancel | Clear | | Print or Preview | Make recurring | Customize | | Save | Save and send |

You can select a sales tax rate, apply a discount percentage or dollar amount to the estimate if you have the company preference turned on to display the Discount box, type a message to the customer, type information in the Memo box, and attach an electronic document to the estimate.

To attach an electronic document to the estimate, click in the Attachments box and navigate to the document or drag and drop the electronic copy into the Attachments box.

You can control whether the discount is a pre-tax or post-tax discount by clicking the switch that appears to the left of the Discount and Sales Tax Rate boxes. Clicking the switch swaps the position of the two boxes; when the Discount box appears on top, the discount is pre-tax.

At the bottom of the window, you can

- ✔ Cancel the estimate or clear the window and start again.
- ✔ Click Print or Preview to print or preview the estimate.
- ✔ Click Make Recurring to set up the estimate as a recurring estimate you intend to send on a schedule you specify.

> ✔ Click Customize to set up a custom form style for the estimate.
>
> ✔ Click Save to assign a number to the estimate and save it in QBO.
>
> ✔ Click Save and Send to assign a number to the estimate, save it, and email a copy to the customer. A window appears, in which you can write an email message and look at a preview of the estimate. After you send your invoice, the email time and date-stamp information appears in the header.

You can click the arrow beside Save and Send and then choose Save and New to save the estimate and start a new one, or choose Save and Close to save the estimate and close the Estimate window.

Converting an estimate to an invoice

So, you did a good job on your estimate, and now your customer wants to purchase based on the estimate you provided. You don't need to create an invoice from scratch; instead, you can copy the estimate's information to an invoice and, if necessary, make adjustments by adding or removing lines. You can copy an estimate's information to an invoice using any of several approaches.

Non-posting transactions

Non-posting transactions don't affect your accounts in any way, but they are helpful because they enable you to enter potential transaction information you don't want to forget. In addition to the estimate, QBO Essentials and Plus also enable you to record two other non-posting transactions: the Delayed Charge and the Delayed Credit.

You can use a Delayed Charge transaction pretty much the same way you use an estimate. The Delayed Charge transaction records potential future revenue, and you can convert a Delayed Charge to an invoice in the same way you convert an estimate to an invoice. For details, see the section "Converting an estimate to an invoice."

The Delayed Credit transaction enables you to record a potential future credit memo. When you prepare an invoice for a customer for whom you've entered a Delayed Credit transaction, QBO displays the Delayed Credit in the pane on the right side of the Invoice window, and you can add the credit to the invoice. A Delayed Credit transaction differs from a Credit Memo transaction because a Credit Memo transaction updates your accounts when you enter it, but a Delayed Credit transaction updates your accounts only when you include it on an invoice.

You fill out both forms the same way you create an invoice; for details, see the section "Preparing an Invoice."

First, you can open the Invoice window and select the customer with the open estimate. QBO displays available documents you can link to the invoice, including any estimates (see Figure 6-11). Click the Add button at the bottom of an estimate, and QBO automatically adds the estimate information to the Invoice window.

Click here to add estimate information to the invoice

Figure 6-11:
Converting an estimate to an invoice from the Invoice window.

Second, you can filter the Sales Transactions page to display only estimates, and click the Start Invoice link in the Action column beside the estimate you want to convert (see Figure 6-12). QBO displays an invoice that contains all the lines available on the estimate.

Third, from the Sales Transactions page, you can double-click the estimate to open it (and review its content, if you want). In the Estimate window of any estimate with a status of Pending, you'll find a Copy to Invoice button, as shown in Figure 6-13; click that button, and QBO displays the Invoice window containing all the information from the estimate.

After you have converted an estimate on an invoice, QBO changes the estimate's status from Pending to Closed. Be aware that QBO closes the estimate even if you don't invoice the customer for all lines on the estimate. Also be

Filtering to view only estimates

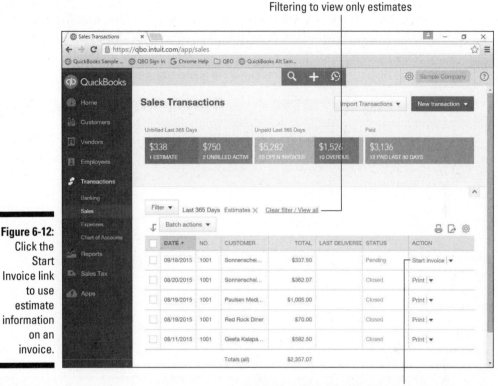

Figure 6-12:
Click the
Start
Invoice link
to use
estimate
information
on an
invoice.

Click this link to start an invoice based on an estimate

aware that you can change an estimate's status from Closed to Pending, but, if you do, you are making all lines on the estimate available for invoicing — and you could then accidentally invoice your customer twice for the same goods. So, if your customer buys only some lines on the estimate but intends to buy other lines at a later point in time, your best bet to ensure that you have the right information available for a future invoice is to let QBO close the original estimate and create another estimate for only the lines the customer didn't yet buy.

Copying an existing estimate

Suppose that you have an existing estimate — even one you've already converted to an invoice — and you want to create a new estimate using most of the information on the existing invoice. You can make a copy of the existing estimate, edit the copy as needed, and then save the new estimate. Making a copy saves you time because you don't need to reenter a lot of information.

On the Sales Transactions list, double-click the estimate you want to copy to open it in the Estimate window. Then, at the bottom of the window, click the More button and, from the menu that appears, click Copy (see Figure 6-14).

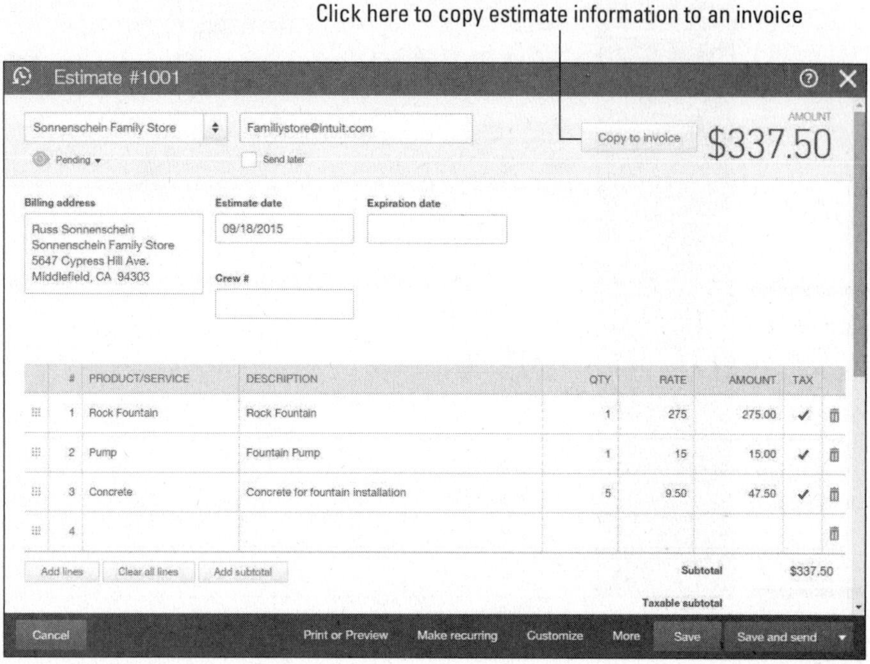

Click here to copy estimate information to an invoice

Figure 6-13: Click Copy to Invoice to display estimate information on an invoice.

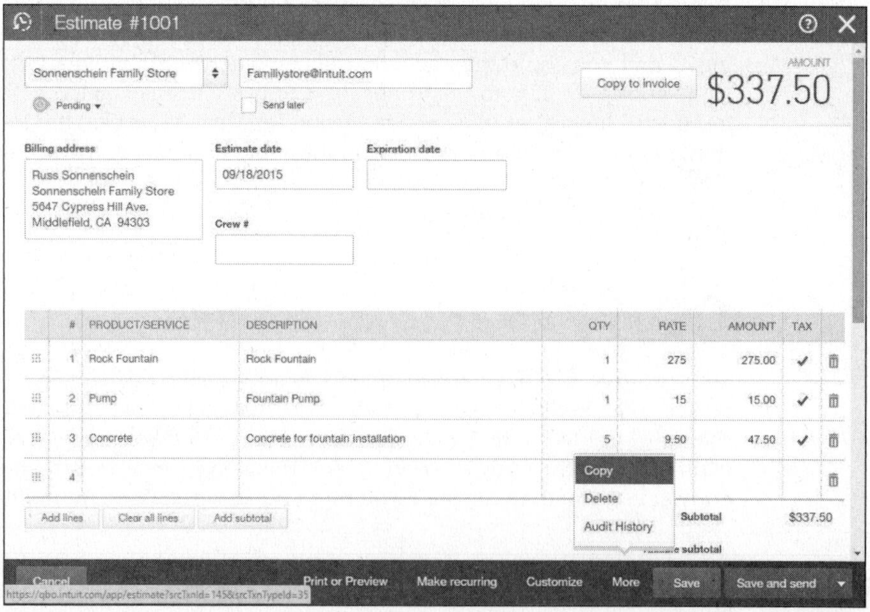

Figure 6-14: Click Copy to duplicate an estimate.

QBO opens a new estimate that already contains the information of the estimate you copied. Just above the Billing Address information, you see a message that explains that the estimate you're viewing is a copy and you should make any changes you need (see Figure 6-15). For example, change the customer, and QBO updates the Billing Address information. Feel free to add or delete lines as needed. When you finish making changes, click Save or Save and Send, as appropriate.

The message indicating you're working in a duplicate

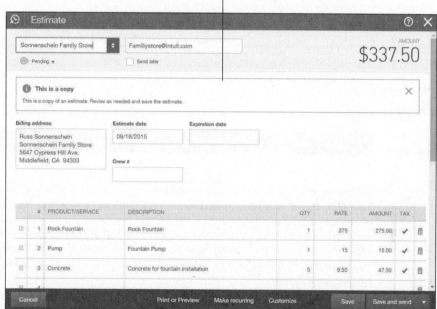

Figure 6-15: Edit the duplicated estimate and save it.

Entering a Sales Receipt

You use invoices when you need to track money that a customer owes you but hasn't yet paid. But suppose that your customer pays you at the time you sell goods or render services. In these situations, you don't need to enter an invoice; instead, you can enter a sales receipt.

From the Sales Transactions page or the Create menu, click Sales Receipt to display the window shown in Figure 6-16.

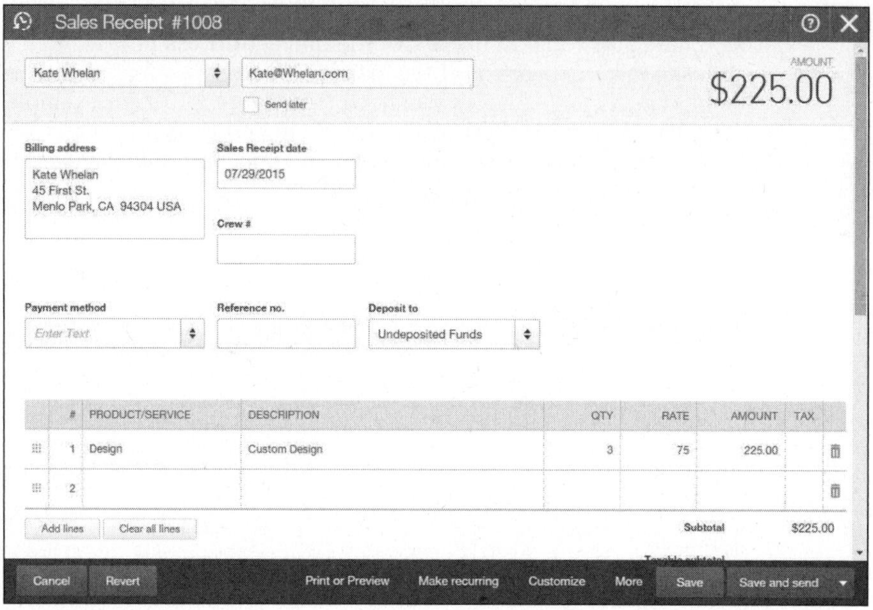

Figure 6-16:
A sales
receipt.

The sales receipt form closely resembles other sales forms you've seen in this chapter: You select a customer — QBO fills in customer billing address information and assigns today's date to the transaction — enter a payment method and optional reference number, and select the account into which QBO should place the funds. See the sidebar in this chapter, "Using the Undeposited Funds account," for information on selecting an account from the Deposit To list.

You fill out the rest of the Sales Receipt transaction the same way you fill out an invoice transaction; if you scroll down in the window, you'll find the same fields at the bottom of the Sales Receipt window as the ones that appear at the bottom of the Invoice window.

Giving Money Back to a Customer

It happens. It's a bummer, but, it happens. Occasionally, you need to return money you have received from a customer.

If a customer returns merchandise to you, issue a credit memo. Alternatively, if you need to refund money to a customer — perhaps because goods arrived damaged and the customer doesn't want to reorder them — issue a refund receipt.

Recording a credit memo

If a customer returns goods previously purchased or if you and your customer agree that the customer's outstanding or future balance should be reduced, record a credit memo in QBO.

By default, QBO automatically applies credit memos to outstanding or future invoices. If you want to change that behavior, open Company Settings (choose Gear menu ⇨ Company Settings) and click Advanced on the left. Scroll down to the Automation section on the right, and click the Automatically Apply Credits option.

You enter a Credit Memo transaction pretty much the same way you enter an invoice; to display the Credit Memo window shown in Figure 6-17, you can click the Create menu button and choose Credit Memo or, from the Sales Transactions page, you can click the New Transaction button and choose Credit Memo.

Select the customer, fill in the products or services for which you are issuing a credit memo, fill in the bottom of the Credit Memo window with appropriate information, and save the transaction. This transaction window is very similar to the Invoice transaction window: see the section "Preparing an Invoice" for details.

Figure 6-17: Entering a credit memo.

You can enter a credit memo for a customer even if that customer currently has no outstanding invoices; when you enter the customer's next invoice, QBO will apply the credit memo to the invoice.

When you enter a credit memo for a customer who has outstanding invoices, QBO applies the credit memo to an outstanding invoice; if you view the Sales Transactions list for that particular invoice, you'll notice that its Status is Partial, meaning that the invoice is partially paid (see Figure 6-18).

	DATE ▾	TYPE	NO.	CUSTOME	DUE DATE	BALANCE	TOTAL	STATUS	ACTION
☐	09/18/2015	Estimate	1001	Sonne...	09/18/...	$0.00	$337.50	Pending	Start invoice ▾
☐	09/18/2015	Payment		Freem...	09/18/...	$0.00	$0.00	Closed	
☐	09/18/2015	Credit ...	1038	Freem...	09/18/...	$0.00	$-10.00	Closed	Print ▾
☐	08/23/2015	Payment		Freem...	08/23/...	$0.00	$-387.00	Closed	
☐	08/23/2015	Payment		Cool ...	08/23/...	$0.00	$-1,67...	Closed	
☐	08/23/2015	Invoice	1035	Mark ...	09/22/...	$314.28	$314.28	Open	Receive payment ▾
☐	08/23/2015	Invoice	1037	Sonne...	09/22/...	$362.07	$362.07	Open	Receive payment ▾
☐	08/23/2015	Invoice	1036	Freem...	09/22/...	$467.50	$477.50	Partial	Receive payment ▾
☐	08/22/2015	Payment		Travis ...	08/22/...	$0.00	$-81.00	Closed	

Figure 6-18:
An invoice to which QBO has applied a credit memo.

Invoice with a credit memo applied

If you double-click the invoice to view it, you'll see the credit amount on the Amount Received line at the bottom of the invoice (see Figure 6-19).

Issuing a refund to a customer

Use QBO's Refund Receipt transaction if you need to refund money to a customer instead of reducing an outstanding or future balance. In this example, I'm going to issue a refund check to a customer, which will deduct the amount of the refund from a Bank account and reduce an Income account. The customer didn't return any items.

To account for refunds you issue when a customer doesn't return an item, first set up an account called something like Returns and Allowances and assign this account to the Category Type of Income. Then set up a service on the Products and Services list and call it something like Customer Refunds or even Returns & Allowances. Do *not* select Is Taxable for the service. Assign the service to the Returns and Allowances account and don't assign a default Price/Rate.

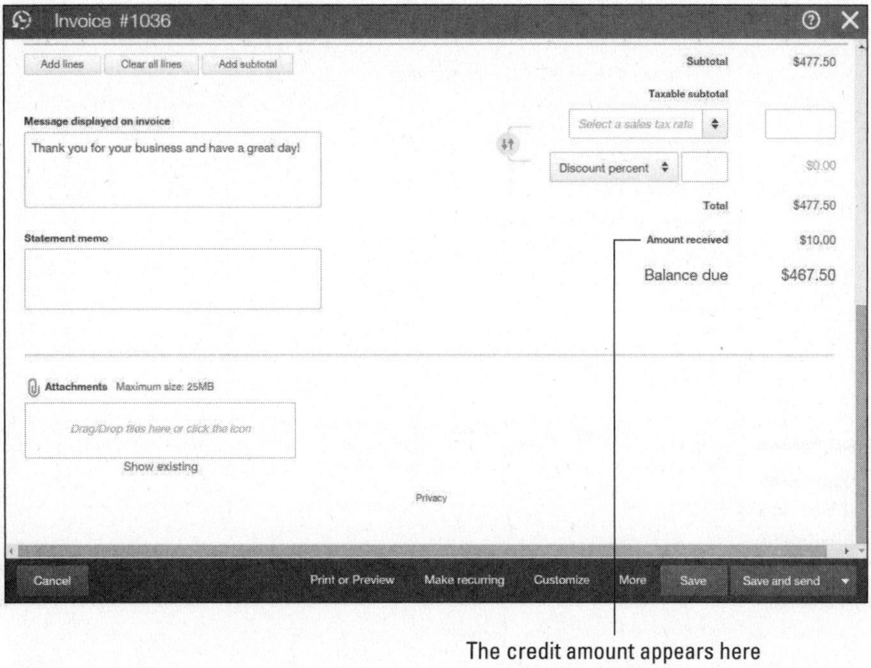

Figure 6-19:
By default,
QBO applies
credit
memos to
an existing
outstanding
invoice.

The credit amount appears here

Filling in the Refund Receipt window is very similar to filling in the Invoice window, so, if you need more details than I supply here, see the section "Preparing an Invoice." To display the Refund Receipt window shown in Figure 6-20, click the Create button — the plus (+) sign — and choose Refund Receipt in the Customers column. Select a customer, and QBO fills in related customer information.

Select a payment method and an account; if you select a Bank account like I did, QBO lists the Bank account's current balance and the next check number associated with the account. If you want, click the Print Later check box.

In my example, the customer isn't returning any items, so I selected the Refunds & Allowances service. If your customer is returning items, select the item in the Product/Service column that the customer is returning in exchange for the refund and don't select the Refunds and Allowances service shown in Figure 6-20.

You can scroll down to the bottom of the Refund Receipt transaction window and fill in all the same information available at the bottom of an invoice.

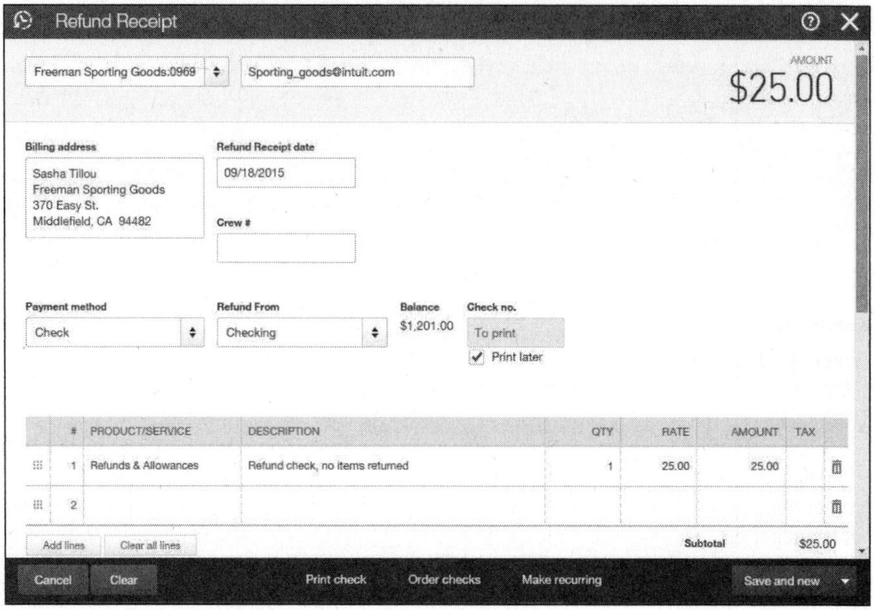

Figure 6-20: Issuing a refund check.

Creating Billable Time Entries

Your employees might work directly for you on activities needed to run your company (such as preparing customer invoices or entering accounting information into QBO), and they might also perform work directly related to your customers. In the latter case, you might want to track the time employees spend on client-related projects and then bill your customers for your employees' time.

To track time, you use either the Time Activity window or the Weekly Timesheet window; regardless of the window you use, QBO tracks the time entered and, when you prepare an invoice for a client for whom time was recorded, QBO prompts you to add the time to the invoice.

In this section, you learn to enter time using both the Time Activity window and the Weekly Timesheet window, and you see how QBO prompts you to include the billable time on a customer's invoice. Note that a time entry that you can bill back to a customer is called *billable time*.

Entering a single time activity

You open the Time Activity window using the Create plus (+) sign menu at the top of QBO. Follow these steps:

1. **Click the Create plus (+) sign button to open the Create menu.**

2. **In the Employees column, click Single Time Activity.**

   QBO displays the Time Activity window shown in Figure 6-21.

Figure 6-21:
The Time
Activity
window.

3. **From the Name list, select the employee or vendor who performed the work.**

4. **Enter the date the work was performed.**

5. **From the Customer list, select the customer for whom the work was performed.**

6. **From the Service list, select the service that was performed.**

7. **Place a check in the Billable box, which changes to the Bill At box, and supply an hourly rate.**

8. **If the work performed is subject to tax, place a check in the Taxable box.**

9. **In the Time box, enter the amount of time spent on this activity.**

   You can enter start and end times, including any break time, by checking the Enter Start and End Times box; QBO calculates the time spent and displays it below the Description box.

10. **Enter a description of the work that will appear, by default, on an invoice.**

    You can change the description after adding the time entry to the invoice.

11. **Click Save to save the entry or Save and New to enter another time activity.**

    If you click the arrow beside Save and New, you can choose Save and Close.

Using a timesheet to record time

If you prefer to enter time in a grid format that shows the days and dates for a week, then the Weekly Timesheet, shown in Figure 6-22, is for you. To enter time using this window, follow these steps:

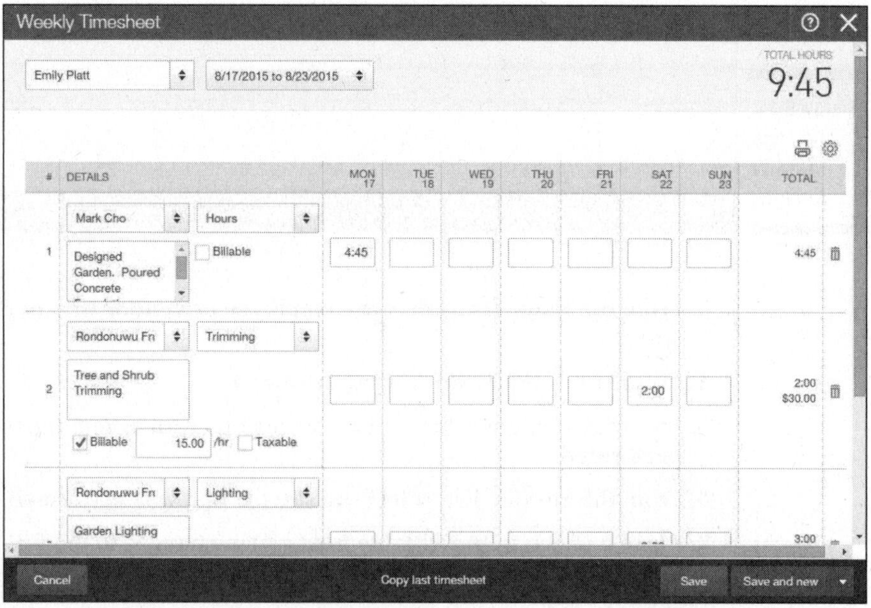

Figure 6-22:
The Weekly Timesheet.

1. **Click the Create button — the plus (+) sign — to open the Create menu.**

2. **In the Employees column, click Weekly Timesheet.**

3. **Select the name of the person whose time you're recording.**

4. **Select the week for which you want to record time.**

5. In the Details section, select a customer name, a service item, and, if appropriate, supply a description.

6. To bill the time back to a customer, select the Billable check box and provide a rate at which to charge the time.

7. Fill in the time worked on the appropriate day.

8. Click Save, Save and New, or click the arrow beside Save and New and select Save and Close.

Adding a billable expense to an invoice

You can add billable time entries to an invoice in a couple of ways. For example, if you view any customer's page, QBO displays a list of outstanding transactions, as shown in Figure 6-23. In the Action column of any billable time entry, QBO displays a Start Invoice button that you can click to start an invoice to the customer and include the billable expense on the invoice. To view a customer's page, click Customer in the Navigation bar and then click a customer's name.

Click here to display your customer list and select a different customer

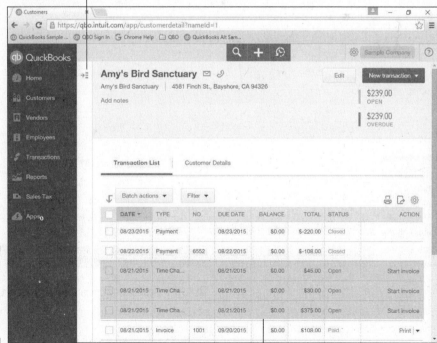

Figure 6-23: Viewing a customer's page in QBO.

These lines contain billable expenses

But you don't need to go looking for billable time entries. QBO prompts you to add them to any invoice you create for a customer for whom billable time entries exist. Start an invoice (from the Create menu — the plus sign — click Invoice) and select a customer. If the customer has billable time entries, they appear in the pane on the right side of the screen (see Figure 6-24).

Click the Add button in each billable time entry that you want to add to the invoice. Or, to add all the entries, click the Add All button at the top of the pane on the right. QBO enters each billable time entry's information on a line on the invoice, filling in the service, description, quantity, rate, and total amount. You can edit any information on the line as needed. Fill in the rest of the invoice as described in the section "Preparing an Invoice," adding other lines that might not pertain to time entries.

Don't forget that you can add a subtotal for time entries, if you choose. See the first section in this chapter, "Customizing Forms to Handle Subtotals," for details.

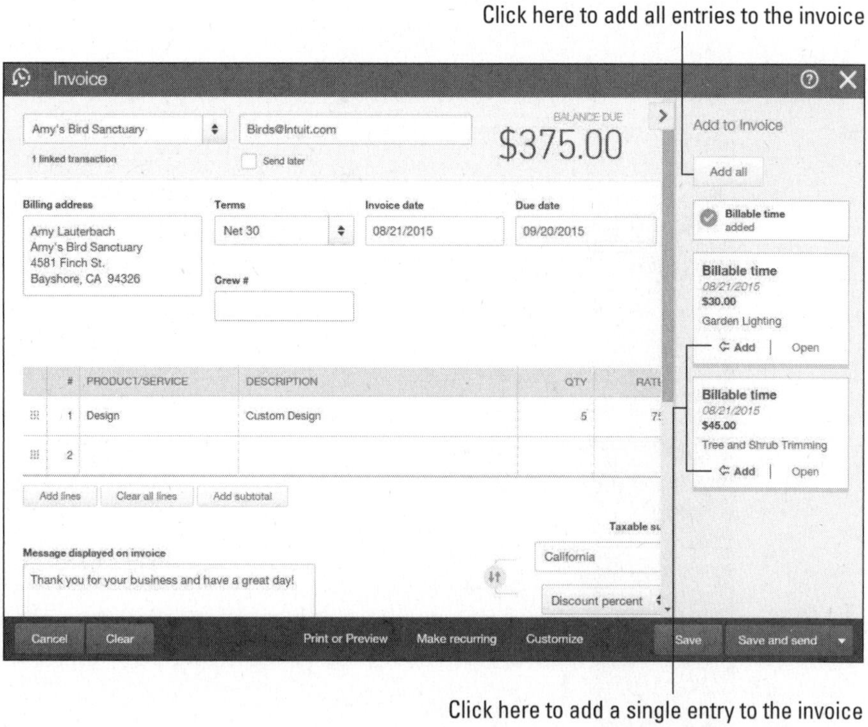

Click here to add all entries to the invoice

Figure 6-24: Creating an invoice for a customer with billable time entries.

Click here to add a single entry to the invoice

Chapter 7

Working in Registers

In This Chapter
▶ Examining registers
▶ Working with registers and transactions

Chapters 5 and 6 show you how to enter transactions such as checks, sales receipts, invoices, and customer payments using various QBO transaction windows. You also see ways to find and filter for certain transactions.

But transaction windows and lists aren't the only way to work with transactions in QBO. You can use registers. Some people are more comfortable entering transactions, particularly checks, into a register.

And many people find it easy to use a register to quickly view the transactions that affect a particular account and find particular transactions, as described at the end of this chapter.

Understanding Registers

Registers in QBO look very much like the registers that banks give you along with handwritten checks. In Figure 7-1, you see a Bank account register in QBO.

To help you focus on the register, I've collapsed the Navigation bar in this chapter.

The register page displays the name of the account and its ending balance at the top of the register, along with column headings that identify the contents of each column for every transaction. Unfortunately, as you scroll down to the bottom of the register, the column headings disappear from view. On the good news side, you shouldn't need to scroll down to the bottom of the register often; your latest transactions appear at the top of the register, and you can add transactions to a check register without looking for a blank line, as you read later in this chapter in the section "Entering transactions."

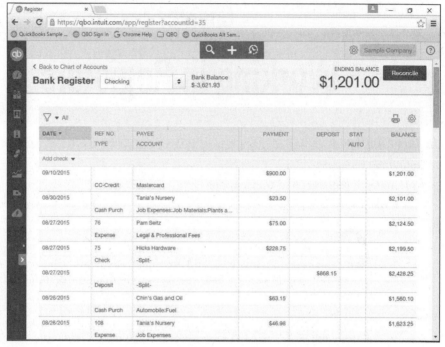

Figure 7-1:
A typical
Bank
account
register.

You can customize the appearance of the register to help you find a particular transaction; see "Other Things You Can Do in a Register" later in this chapter for details.

All the transactions in Figure 7-1 affect a Bank account — along with some other account, as dictated by the rules of accounting (*double-entry bookkeeping*, a founding principle of accounting, means that every transaction affects at least two accounts). The amount shown in the Balance column is a running balance for the account as long as the register is sorted by date.

If you sort by any column other than the Date column, the Balance column won't display any information because the information wouldn't make any sense.

Because this bank account is electronically connected to its counterpart at a banking institution, you also see the balance in the account as that financial institution reports it — and in this case, the balance at the bank is negative.

One rule you need to remember about registers: They are *not* available for all accounts. You'll find that registers are available for all *balance sheet* accounts except Retained Earnings. Balance sheet accounts fall into the following QBO account category types:

- ✔ Bank
- ✔ Accounts Receivable
- ✔ Other Current Assets
- ✔ Fixed Assets
- ✔ Other Assets
- ✔ Accounts Payable
- ✔ Credit Card
- ✔ Other Current Liabilities
- ✔ Long Term Liabilities
- ✔ Equity

You see these account category types when you add a new account to the Chart of Accounts. In addition, the Chart of Accounts page shows each account and its associated account category type.

If you use account numbers, then, generally, all asset accounts begin with 10000, all liability accounts begin with 20000, and all equity accounts begin with 30000. This numbering scheme is *not* carved in stone, but most accountants recommend that you follow these guidelines when you assign numbers to the accounts in your Chart of Accounts.

Entering and Editing Transactions

Many people are comfortable using a Bank account register to enter a check or a bill payment; some people are also comfortable entering a bill in the Accounts Payable register or an invoice in the Accounts Receivable register. But, even if you're not comfortable entering transactions in a register, many people find viewing a transaction in a register very easy and helpful.

You open a register from the Chart of Accounts page. To open the Chart of Accounts page, click the Gear icon beside your company's name and, from the menu that appears, click Chart of Accounts in the Settings column (see Figure 7-2).

From the Chart of Accounts page (shown in Figure 7-3), you can click the View Register link in the Action column beside any account that displays the link; all accounts displaying the link are balance sheet accounts.

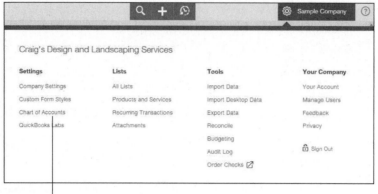

Figure 7-2:
Use the
Gear icon to
open your
company's
Chart of
Accounts
page.

Click here to display the Chart of Accounts page

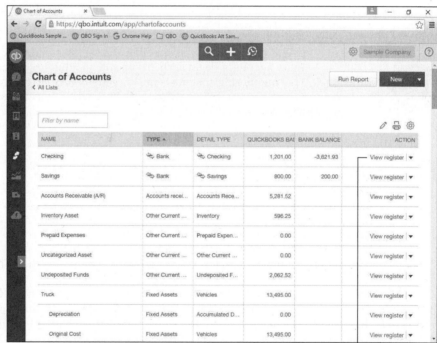

Figure 7-3:
The Chart of
Accounts
page.

Click here to open an account register

Entering a transaction

Because checks are the transaction most often entered using a register, I focus the discussion in this section on Bank account registers. After you click the Register button of a Bank or Credit Card account, you can enter a transaction into the register; follow these steps:

1. **Click the down arrow beside the Add button.**

   The Add button, which appears just below the Date column heading, is named Add Check in Bank accounts and Add CC Expense in Credit Card accounts.

   After you open the list box, QBO displays the list of available transaction types (see Figure 7-4).

   QBO displays only those types of transactions available in the account register you opened. For example, you can record a customer payment in a Bank account register, but you cannot enter a customer invoice. Similarly, you can record a check or a bill payment in a Bank account register, but you cannot enter a vendor bill.

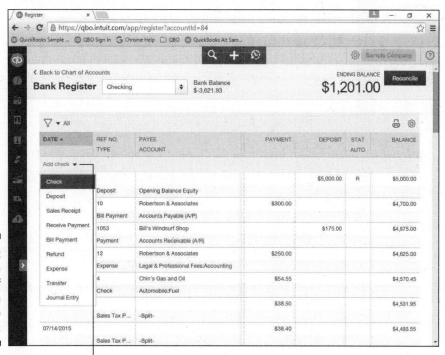

Figure 7-4: Select the type of transaction you want to enter.

Click here to display the available transaction types

2. From the list that appears, select the type of transaction you want to enter.

QBO fills in today's date and displays lines so that you can complete the transaction (see Figure 7-5).

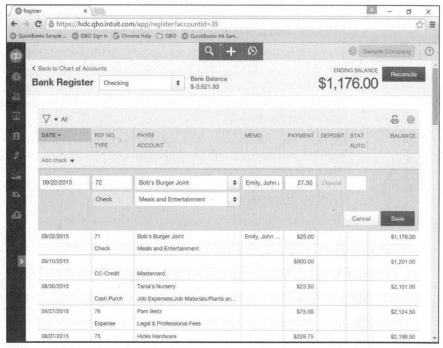

Figure 7-5:
Entering a
check in a
Bank
account
register.

3. If necessary, change the transaction date.

4. Press Tab and, if appropriate, change the check number for the transaction.

5. Press Tab and supply a Payee name.

For example, if you're recording a payment you received from a customer, select the customer's name. If you're writing a check, select the check recipient's name.

6. Press Tab and, in the Memo column, supply any memo information you want to record for the transaction.

7. Press Tab and, in the appropriate column, provide the amount of the transaction.

In a Bank account register, record a payment you're making in the Payment amount box and an amount you're depositing in the Deposit amount box.

8. **Press Tab.**

   QBO places the mouse pointer in the Stat Auto column, also known as the Reconcile and Banking Status column. This column displays a character representing the status of the transaction: C for Cleared or R for Reconciled. When the column is blank, the transaction is neither cleared nor reconciled. Typically this column is updated when you download or reconcile transactions.

9. **Press Tab.**

   QBO's placement of the insertion pointer depends on the type of transaction you're entering. For example, if you're entering a Sales Receipt, a Received Payment, a Bill Payment, or a Refund transaction, QBO places the insertion point in the area where you can save the transaction.

   If, however, you're entering a Check, a Deposit, an Expense, a Transfer, or a Journal Entry transaction, QBO places the insertion point in the Account column. Select the other account affected by the transaction (in addition to the account whose register you have opened). For example, if you're entering a check, select an Expense account. If you enter an account and press Tab, you can enter a memo for the transaction.

10. **Click the Save button that appears in the transaction.**

    QBO saves the transaction and starts another of the same type. You can click Cancel to stop entering transactions.

Editing a transaction

You can edit the transaction in the register by clicking the transaction and then making changes. Or, if you prefer to use the transaction window for the type of transaction you selected, click the Edit button. For example, if you opt to edit an Expense transaction in an account register, QBO displays the transaction in the Expense window. If you opt to enter a Check transaction, QBO displays the transaction in the Check window. See Chapter 5 for examples of transaction windows.

Other Things You Can Do in a Register

Registers wouldn't be all that useful if you could only add and edit transactions. You need to be able to find transactions easily. And, to make registers more helpful, you need to be able to control their appearance.

Sorting transactions

After a while, the number of transactions in a register can make the Register page very long, especially in a Bank account register. Looking for a transaction by skimming through the register — or *eyeballing* — can be a nonproductive way of finding a transaction. Instead, sort to help you find a particular transaction.

You can sort by any column in the register simply by clicking that column heading. In Figure 7-6, the transactions are sorted by date, in descending order from latest to earliest; note the downward-pointing arrow in the Date column.

Click a column heading to sort by that column

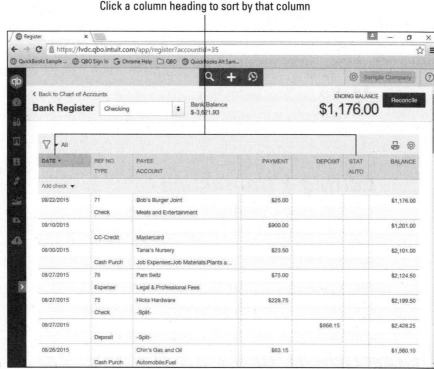

Figure 7-6:
Sorting transactions by date, from latest to earliest, is the default order QBO uses to display transactions.

To sort the transactions by date from earliest to latest, click the Date column; the arrow changes direction and becomes points upward. Or suppose you want to search for transactions for a particular payee. You can click the Payee column heading to sort transactions in alphabetical order by payee, and you can click the column heading a second time to sort in reverse alphabetical order.

You can sort by any column heading *except* Account and Balance. And, if you sort by any column other than Date, the Balance column won't display any information because the information wouldn't make any sense.

Filtering transactions

When sorting seems like the long way to find a transaction, try working with filters. Click the Filter button that appears just above the Date column, and QBO displays a variety of ways you can filter register transactions (see Figure 7-7).

Click here to view filter options

The currently selected filter

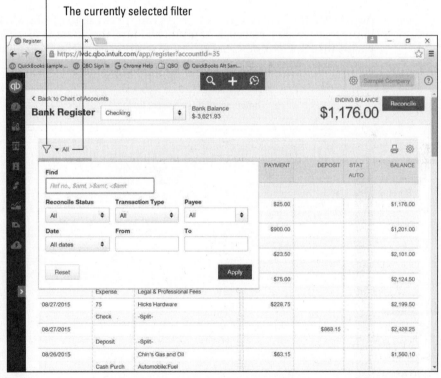

Figure 7-7: Displaying available filters.

The current filter appears just beside the Filter button. When you haven't selected any filters, you see All beside the Filter button.

If you're looking for a transaction of a certain dollar amount, enter the amount, making sure that you don't forget the currency symbol. When you filter by amounts, use these examples as a guideline:

- ✔ 1234 will find all checks or reference numbers with 1234.

- ✔ $500 will find all transactions that equal $500.

- ✔ >$25 will find all transactions with amounts over $25.

To go to a specific transaction date, enter the date in the first box and click Apply. Or supply both From and To dates to view transactions only within that time frame.

You can also filter by a transaction's reconciliation status, transaction type, or payee.

Any transactions that meet the criteria you specify in the Filter window appear in the register after you click Apply. In addition, the selected filter appears beside the Filter button (see Figure 7-8). You can click the Clear Filter/View All link to clear the filter and redisplay all transactions in the register.

The current filter appears here

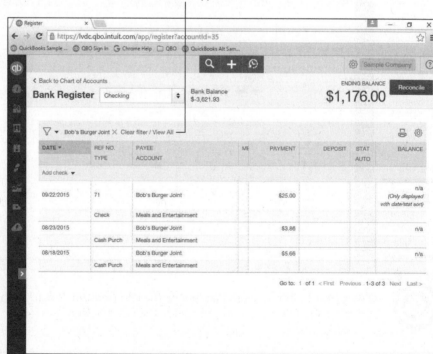

Figure 7-8: A list of transactions QBO found based on criteria specified in the Filter window.

Changing the appearance of a register

In addition to sorting and filtering transactions in a register, you can control the appearance of the register. In particular, you can

- ✔ Change the size of columns
- ✔ Control the number of rows on a page in your QBO company
- ✔ Reduce each register entry to a single line

To change the size of any column, slide the mouse pointer into the column heading area on the right boundary of the column. In Figure 7-9, I'm resizing the Ref No. Type column. When the mouse pointer changes to a pair of arrows pointing left and right connected to a pair of vertical bars, drag the pointer to the left to make the column narrower or to the right to make the column wider. As you drag, a solid vertical line helps you determine the size of the column. Release the mouse button when the column reaches the size you want.

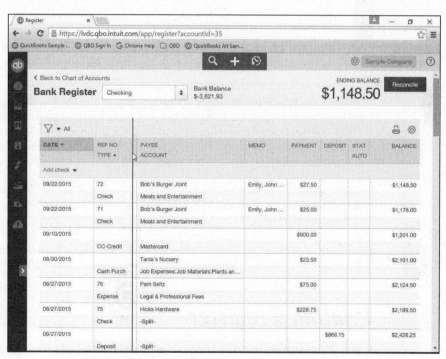

Figure 7-9: Resizing a column.

You can save space horizontally and vertically onscreen. Click the Gear icon above the Balance column (see Figure 7-10).

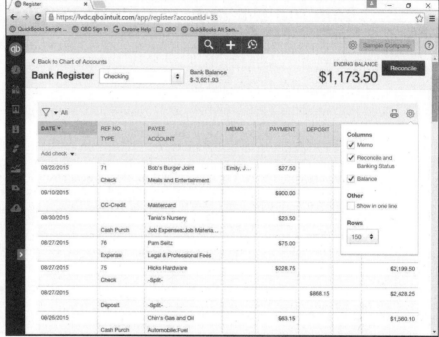

Figure 7-10:
Options you
can use to
control the
appearance
of the
register.

You can save space horizontally by hiding any of the Memo, Reconcile and
Banking Status (which are actually two columns merged into one when you
display transactions on two lines), and Balance columns. Click a column to
remove the check mark that appears beside it, and QBO hides the column in
the register.

To save space vertically, place a check mark in the Show in One Line box and
change the number of rows that appear on a page. You can display 50 rows,
150 rows, or 300 rows.

By default, if you opt to show transactions on a single line in the register,
QBO hides the Memo, Reconcile Status, and Banking Status columns.

Printing a register

When doing research, many people find it easiest to print the information
that appears in the register. To do so, click the Print button beside the register's Gear button (at the right edge of the register, just above the Balance
column; you can see the Print button easily in Figure 7-10). QBO displays the
Print tab, with your register formatted for printing (see Figure 7-11).

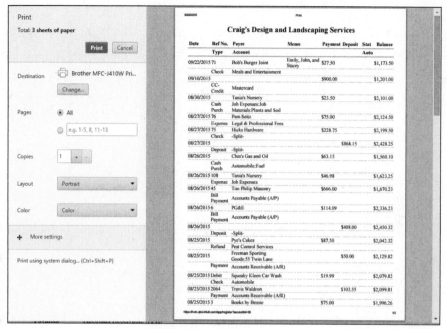

Figure 7-11:
Printing a
register.

Select the printer you want to use and make any other necessary selections, such as the pages to print, the number of copies, and the layout orientation. When you finish selecting settings, click Print. When the report finishes printing, you can close the Print tab to redisplay your register in your QBO company.

Chapter 8

Handling Bank and Credit Card Transactions

In This Chapter

▶ Managing the order and appearance of Bank accounts

▶ Connecting QBO Bank and Credit Card accounts to accounts at financial institutions

▶ Making bank deposits

▶ Reconciling a Bank account

*T*he real title of this chapter should have been "Handling Bank and Credit Card Transactions and Other Banking Tasks," but my editors said that title, although accurately descriptive, was too long.

So, in a nutshell, this chapter covers the ways you can connect Bank and Credit Card accounts in QBO to their counterparts at financial institutions. You also find out how to make bank deposits and reconcile your bank statement.

Controlling the Appearance of Bank Accounts

Before diving in to using Bank accounts, let's take a look at a few things you can do to make your life easier while working with Bank accounts.

Bank accounts appear on the QBO Home page and also on the Bank and Credit Cards page. You can control the order in which your accounts appear on these pages. For example, perhaps you'd like your accounts to appear in alphabetical order. Or maybe you'd like them to appear in most used order. Whatever works for you.

On the QBO Home page, click the pencil that appears to the right of Bank Accounts (see Figure 8-1). The pencil changes to the Save button. Then simply drag the accounts so that they appear in the order you want and click the Save button. Changes you make will appear on both the Home page and on the Bank and Credit Cards page.

Click here to change the order in which bank accounts appear

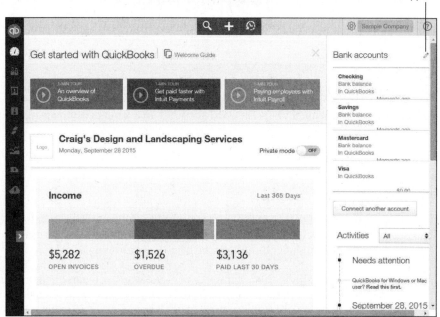

Figure 8-1:
Drag accounts to place them in the order you want.

In addition to changing the order of accounts, you can, to some extent, control the information that appears in the table on the Bank and Credit Cards page. For example, you can opt to

- ✔ Display check numbers
- ✔ Display Payee names
- ✔ Make the date field editable so that you can change it if necessary
- ✔ Display more detailed information about a transaction by displaying information provided by the bank
- ✔ Copy bank detail information into the Memo field

You can display the Memo field in an individual bank register; see Chapter 7 for details.

To display the Bank and Credit Cards page, choose Transactions ➪ Banking. To make changes to the page's appearance, click the Gear icon that appears just above the Action column (see Figure 8-2).

Click here

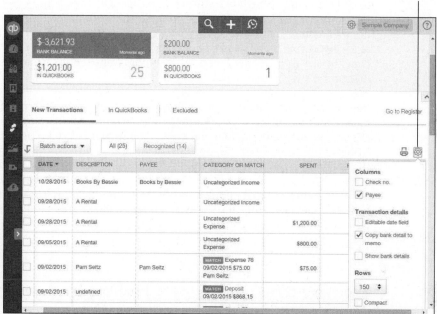

Figure 8-2:
Use the Gear icon to make changes to the Bank and Credit Card page table.

Connecting QBO Accounts to Financial Institutions

QBO offers three ways to connect QBO Bank and Credit Card accounts to corresponding accounts at financial institutions:

- ✔ Connect directly if your bank supports a direct connection.
- ✔ Use QuickBooks Web Connect.
- ✔ Import transactions stored in an Excel file.

You have a fourth option: You don't have to connect at all. If you choose this fourth option, skip to the end of this chapter, where I discuss making bank deposits and reconciling bank statements. If you aren't sure whether to connect, read through this section until you make up your mind.

Connecting . . . or not connecting

I don't think Shakespeare would mind if I paraphrased Hamlet: "To connect or not to connect, that is the question."

In QBO, you might be able to directly connect QBO Bank and Credit Card accounts to their counterparts at financial institutions. I say "might" because not all financial institutions support directly connecting to QBO. If you bank at an institution that doesn't support a direct connection, you can use the QuickBooks Web Connect method to export transactions from the financial institution's website into QBO.

Before I dive into connecting, it's important to understand that you *don't have to connect.* You can work along quite happily in QBO without ever connecting an account at a financial institution to one in QBO. You simply enter transactions that affect the appropriate account and, monthly, you reconcile the accounts.

So, why connect? Most people connect to accounts at financial institutions so that they can electronically verify (by matching) the transactions recorded in QBO with the ones recorded at the financial institution. Connecting is, therefore, primarily a matter of convenience.

Connecting Bank or Credit Card accounts

When you add a new Bank or Credit Card account, you can opt to connect it to a financial institution — or you can choose not to connect to a financial institution, as you read in the preceding section. The method you choose to add a new account depends on whether you want to connect it to a financial institution.

Connecting as a form of data entry . . . not!

Don't be tempted to use connecting as a method for entering information into QBO. You might think you'll save time because you won't have to fill out transaction windows in QBO, but, in reality, you won't save time. As you see later in this chapter, you need to review every downloaded transaction and confirm that it is properly assigned in QBO. And, even if you review transactions daily, you won't have an up-to-date version of your accounting information, because you will know about transactions that have not yet cleared your financial institution. That means that the account balances in QBO won't really be up-to-date unless you enter transactions in QBO and use connecting as a method of confirming that your QBO balances match financial institution balances. Long story short: It's safer to enter transactions and use connected account information to confirm QBO balances.

Just a reminder: See Chapters 5 and 6 for details on entering transactions that affect a Bank account. You typically use an Expense transaction to record credit card purchases and sales receipts to record refunds to a credit card.

Adding but not connecting

In Chapter 3, I show you how to create a new Bank account in QBO. The technique I use in Chapter 3 assumes that you do not want to connect the QBO Bank account to its corresponding account at a financial institution. If you want to set up and not connect a Credit Card account, you use the same technique. For example, follow these steps to set up a Credit Card account that you don't intend to connect to a financial institution:

1. **Click the Gear icon beside your company's name and, from the left side of the menu that appears, choose Chart of Accounts.**

   QBO displays the Chart of Accounts page.

2. **Click the New button on the Chart of Accounts page to open the Account dialog box (see Figure 8-3).**

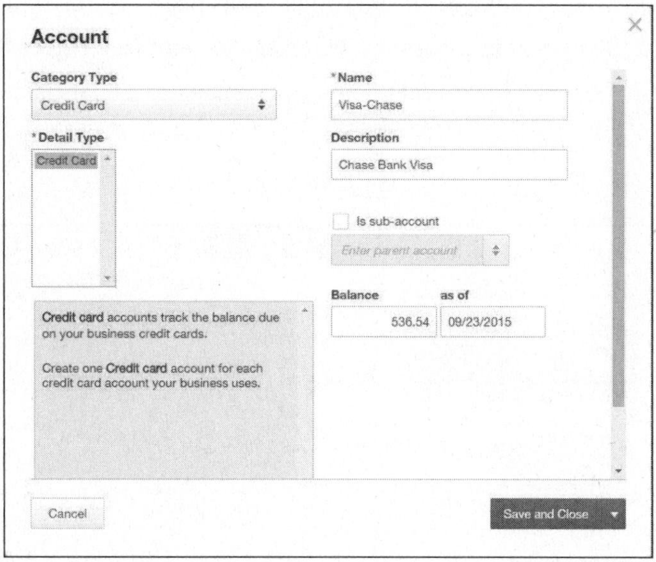

Account ✕

Category Type
Credit Card

*Detail Type
Credit Card

*Name
Visa-Chase

Description
Chase Bank Visa

☐ Is sub-account

Enter parent account

Credit card accounts track the balance due on your business credit cards.

Create one **Credit card** account for each credit card account your business uses.

Balance | as of
536.54 | 09/23/2015

Cancel | Save and Close ▼

Figure 8-3: The dialog box you use to create an account.

---

3. **Open the Category Type list and choose Credit Card.**

4. **If you're using account numbers, supply a number for the new account.**

5. **Optionally, you can enter your account's balance as it appears on the last statement.**

If you enter a balance, QuickBooks updates both the account balance and the Opening Balance Equity account, and your accountant probably won't be happy with you. I suggest that you not enter a balance.

6. **Click Save and Close.**

QBO redisplays the Chart of Accounts page and your new account appears in the list.

You'll need to enter expense transactions that have occurred since you received the last statement for this credit card account.

Adding and directly connecting

If, on the other hand, you want to create an account that is connected to a financial institution, you can do so if your financial institution offers the option to connect directly to QBO accounts. Gather up the user ID and password you use to log in to the financial institution online and follow these steps:

1. **In the Navigation bar, choose Transactions➪Banking.**

QBO displays the Bank and Credit Cards page.

2. **In the upper-right corner, click Add Account (see Figure 8-4).**

QBO starts a wizard that helps you connect to a financial institution.

Click here

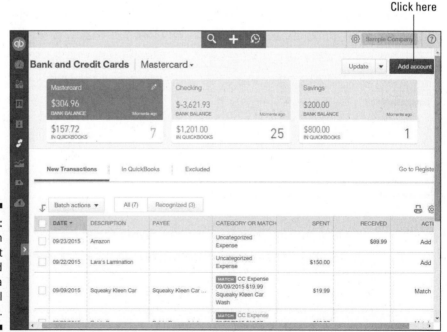

Figure 8-4: Adding an account connected to a financial institution.

3. **On the first wizard page, shown in Figure 8-5, you either provide your financial institution's website address, or you can click your financial institution's name if it appears on the page.**

   The screen that appears next depends on whether you typed a web address or clicked one of the popular banks onscreen. I clicked Chase.

Type a web address here

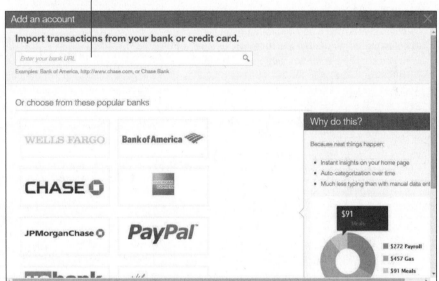

Figure 8-5:
Identify your financial institution.

4. **Supply your user ID and password and click the Log In button.**

   Follow any additional onscreen prompts you see to finish setting up the account.

Downloading activity

The method you use to download activity depends on the method you use to connect to your financial institution.

Downloading information for a directly connected account

This is kind of a silly heading for the book, but I needed a way to get your attention. You see, if you connected your account directly to a financial institution as described in the preceding section, transactions download automatically; you don't need to take any action. You can view downloaded transactions by choosing Transactions ⇨ Banking. I talk more about using the Bank and Credit Cards page that appears later in this chapter.

Directly connecting after the fact

Suppose that you originally decided that you didn't want to connect a Bank or Credit Card account to a financial institution, but now you've decided that you do want to connect, and your bank supports direct connection. You're not out of luck.

If you follow the steps outlined for setting up an account that is connected to a financial institution, you'll end up with two accounts on your QBO Chart of Accounts for the same account. And that's okay because you then merge the accounts so that the connected account ends up containing all the transactions from the unconnected account.

You cannot undo merging accounts, so be sure you want to take this action.

Follow these steps to merge the two accounts:

1. Click the Gear icon beside your company's name and choose Chart of Accounts from the drop-down menu.

2. Take note of the exact name of the account that is connected on the Chart of Accounts page.

3. Click the Edit button that appears above the Action column.

4. Change the name of the account that *isn't* connected to exactly match the name of the account that is connected.

5. Click the Save button, which appears above the Action column.

6. When the message appears that asks if you want to merge the accounts, click Yes.

Downloading information using QuickBooks Web Connect

If you can't connect your account directly to QBO, perhaps because your financial institution doesn't yet support QBO, you're not out of luck. Instead, you can use QuickBooks Web Connect, which has been around for years. If you were previously a QuickBooks desktop user, you might have used QuickBooks Web Connect. When you use QuickBooks Web Connect, you download transactions from your financial institution's website to your computer, and then you upload the downloaded transactions from your computer to QBO.

Because QuickBooks Web Connect files are not encrypted, you should not use a public computer to download information using QuickBooks Web Connect.

To use QuickBooks Web Connect, follow these steps:

1. **Log in to your financial institution's website and look for a link that enables you to download to QuickBooks.**

   Some banks have a "Download to QuickBooks" link. If you can't find the link, contact your financial institution and let it direct you to the link. After you find it, make note of where it appears on your financial institution's website for future use.

2. **Using the link you found in Step 1, select any of the following file formats:**

    - .qbo: QuickBooks

    - .qfx: Quicken

    - .ofx: Microsoft Money

    If you save your file to some other format, QBO won't be able to upload it.

3. **Select the dates for the transactions you want to download.**

    If you download transactions with dates that precede the opening balance you entered for the account in QBO, the account's opening balance will change.

4. **Save the file to a location on your computer where you'll be able to find it later.**

    Many people download to the Downloads folder or to their desktop.

    After you successfully import a QuickBooks Web Connect file, you should delete it because it is not encrypted and contains your account information.

5. **To upload the file to QBO, log in to QBO and, in the Navigation bar, choose Transactions ⇨ Banking.**

    QBO displays the Bank and Credit Cards page.

6. **At the right side of the page, click the arrow beside the Update button and choose File Upload (see Figure 8-6).**

    QBO starts the Upload Bank File wizard and displays the screen shown in Figure 8-7.

7. **Click the Browse button, navigate to the location where you saved the transactions you downloaded in Step 2, and select the downloaded file.**

8. **Click Next.**

    QBO displays a screen where you select the QBO account into which you want to upload the transactions.

9. **Select the QBO account where the transactions should appear and click Next.**

    QBO uploads the transactions to the selected QBO account (The process can take a few minutes.)

10. **When you see the confirmation screen, click Finish.**

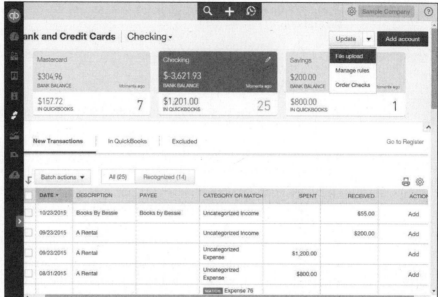

Figure 8-6:
Click the File
Upload
button or
click the
arrow
beside the
Update
button and
select File
Upload.

Figure 8-7:
Use this
screen to
navigate to
the transac-
tions you
downloaded
from your
financial
institution.

Importing transactions via Excel

If your bank supports downloading transactions to a CSV format (a *comma-separated values* format that can be read by Excel), you can download your banking activity to a CSV format and then import it into your QBO Bank account. First, log in to your bank's website and save your banking transactions. QBO can import CSV files formatted in either three or four columns, as shown in Tables 8-1 and 8-2.

Table 8-1	An Acceptable Three-Column Format	
Date	**Description**	**Amount**
1/1/2018	Example payment	-100.00
1/1/2018	Example deposit	200.00

Table 8-2	An Acceptable Four-Column Format		
Date	**Description**	**Credit**	**Debit**
1/1/2018	Example payment	100.00	
1/1/2018	Example deposit		200.00

Open your CSV file using Excel and make sure it matches one of these formats; if necessary, edit it. Then, follow these steps to import the transactions:

1. **Choose Transactions ⇨ Banking in the Navigation bar.**

2. **Click the File Upload button or the arrow beside the Update button and, from the menu that appears, click File Upload.**

   The Import Bank Transactions page appears.

3. **Click the Browse button, select the .CSV file you downloaded from your bank's website, and click Next.**

4. **Select the account into which you want to import transactions and click Next.**

5. **On the Map CSV Columns screen that appears, match the fields in QBO to the fields in your .CSV file and then click Next (see Figure 8-8).**

   The transactions you can import from your .CSV file appear, with a check box to the left of each transaction. To avoid importing a particular transaction, select its check box.

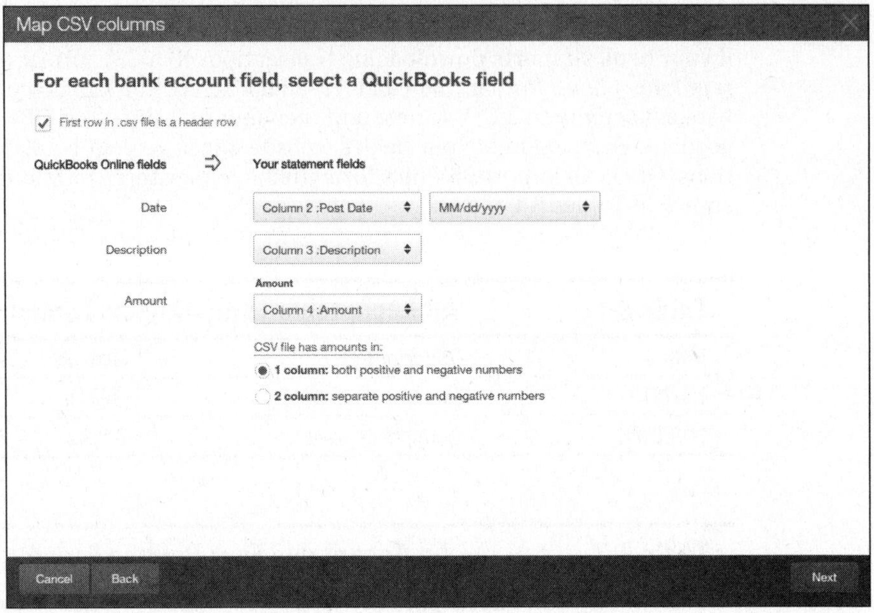

Figure 8-8:
Match QBO
fields to the
fields
in your
.CSV file.

6. **Click Next.**

   QBO displays the number of transactions that will be imported and asks if you want to import the transactions.

7. **Click Yes to import the transactions.**

   When QBO finishes importing the transactions, a confirmation screen appears.

8. **Click Finish.**

   The Bank and Credit Cards page appears, and the transactions you imported appear on the New Transactions tab.

Handling downloaded activity

After you download transactions using either download method, you need to evaluate each transaction and, as appropriate, use them to update QuickBooks. From the Bank and Credit Cards page, you match, exclude, or add transactions downloaded from a financial institution to your QBO company. Choose Transactions➪Banking to display the Bank and Credit Cards page (see Figure 8-9) and, if necessary, select an account.

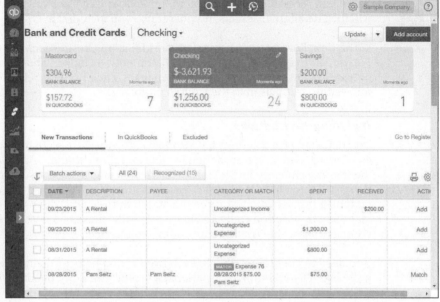

Figure 8-9:
Use this
page to
specify how
QBO should
handle each
downloaded
transaction.

Just above the list of transactions, three transaction status tabs appear:

- ✔ If you click New Transactions, transactions that you have downloaded but have not yet specified how you want to handle appear.
- ✔ If you click In QuickBooks, transactions you have downloaded and added to QBO appear.
- ✔ If you click Excluded, transactions you have downloaded and decided not to include in QBO appear.

To view the transactions you need to consider, click New Transactions. In the list of transactions, QBO attempts to suggest an account to which each transaction should be assigned. Further, QBO tries to identify downloaded transactions that potentially match transactions you entered in QBO.

Excluding transactions

As you evaluate new transactions, you need to decide first whether they belong in QBO. I suggest that you identify transactions to exclude and then exclude them before you deal with transactions you intend to include in QBO. That way, you eliminate transactions that need no further consideration. When might you exclude a transaction from QBO? Suppose that you accidentally used a business credit card to pay for groceries. This transaction is not a business expense and shouldn't be part of your QBO transactions. So, you can exclude the transaction from QBO.

When you reconcile your statement, remember that the statement balance will include all transactions, not just those you included in QBO.

In the New Transactions list, select the check box beside each transaction you intend to exclude, and click the Batch Actions button above the list of transactions. From the menu that appears, click Exclude Selected. QBO moves the transaction to the Excluded tab.

Including transactions

The remaining transactions fall into two categories: those that don't have an obvious matching transaction in QBO and those that do. And, you can identify the category into which a transaction falls using the Action column. If you see the Add button in the Action column, QBO couldn't find an obvious matching transaction; if you see the Match button, QBO did find a potentially matching transaction (refer to Figure 8-9). QBO makes its best guess for adding or matching transactions, but it isn't perfect.

You need to confirm or change each transaction before you include it in QBO. If the listed transaction information is correct, you don't need to individually add or match transactions as described in the rest of this section. Instead, you can select transactions using the check box in the left column, click the Batch Actions button, and click Accept Selected from the list that appears.

If you need to make the same change to a number of transactions, select those transactions and choose the Modify Selected option in the Batch Actions list.

When you click any transaction that you will add to QBO, QBO expands the transaction information so that you can change the details of the transaction. For example, you can use the option buttons above the transaction information to specify whether you want to add the transaction, search for a matching QBO transaction, or transfer the transaction information to another account. You also can change the account QBO suggests to one you deem more appropriate, as I'm doing in Figure 8-10, and you can click the Split button to distribute the transaction among multiple accounts. After you make your changes, you can click the Add button to add the transaction to QBO.

When you click a downloaded transaction that QBO suggests you match to an existing QBO transaction, QBO displays a different set of details (see Figure 8-11). You can select the correct matching transaction, search for other matching transactions, add the transaction (and supply account information for it), or transfer the transaction to a different account. After you make your choices in this window, you can click the Match button at the right edge of the window.

Repeat the process of adding and matching until you've handled all downloaded transactions.

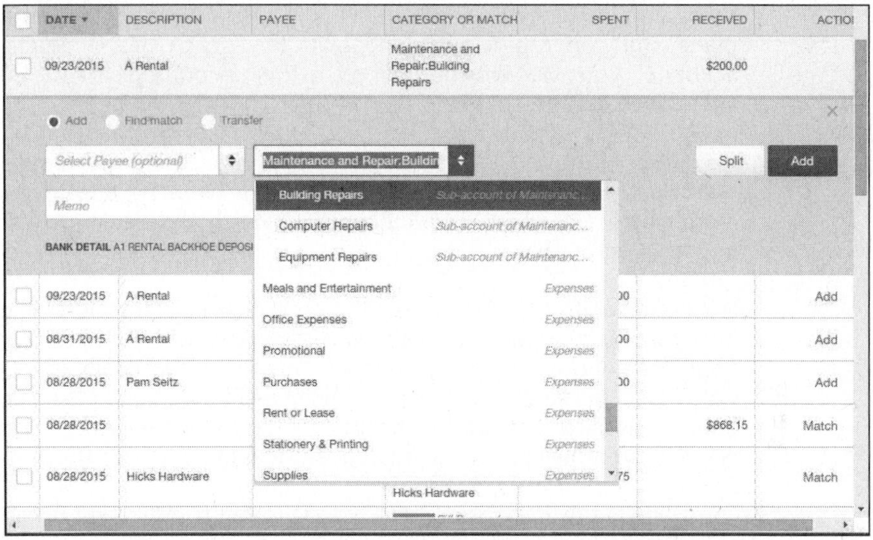

Figure 8-10:
When you click a transaction, QBO displays transaction details.

Figure 8-11:
The transaction details QBO displays when you click a transaction you plan to match to an existing QBO transaction.

Making a Bank Deposit

In Chapter 6, I show you how to record payments from customers, and I suggest that you use the Undeposited Funds account as you record a Receive Payment transaction. So, after receiving a customer payment and placing it in the Undeposited Funds account, your Bank account — where the money will eventually show up — hasn't yet been updated. That updating happens when you prepare a bank deposit.

You can think of the Undeposited Funds account as a temporary holding place until you prepare a bank deposit. "So, why use the Undeposited Funds account?" you ask. "Why not just place the customer payments into the Bank account where they belong?"

Excellent questions. And the answers revolve around making sure that the bank deposits in QBO match the ones at your bank, because if the deposits match, bank statement reconciliation — everybody's least favorite task — becomes quite easy.

For example, if you receive more than one customer payment on any given day, you'll take several checks to your bank that day. And you'll probably deposit all of them as a single deposit. Most banks typically don't record the individual checks that make up a deposit as individual deposits. Instead, the bank records the sum of the checks as your deposit — pretty much the same way you sum the checks on the deposit ticket you give to the bank teller.

"And why is this important?" you ask. This fact is important because, when you receive your statement from your bank, you need to match the bank's deposits and withdrawals with your own version of deposits and withdrawals. If you track each customer payment you receive as a deposit in the bank, then your QBO deposits *won't* match the bank's deposits. But if you record customer payments into the Undeposited Funds account, your deposits *will* match the bank's version of your deposits.

As I mentioned, the Undeposited Funds account in QBO acts as a holding tank for customer payments before you prepare a bank deposit slip. If you place customer payments in the Undeposited Funds account, you then use the Bank Deposit feature in QBO to sum up the payments you receive and intend to deposit simultaneously at your bank. And, if you don't go to your bank daily to make deposits, there's no problem. QBO records, as the deposit amount in your QBO Bank account, the amount calculated in the Bank Deposit window, which will match the amount you actually deposit at your bank. Then, your bank reconciliation process becomes quick and easy — okay, maybe not quick and easy, but certainly quicker and easier than if you were trying to figure out which customer payments make up various bank deposits.

To set up a bank deposit, follow these steps:

1. **Click the Create button — the plus (+) sign — and, from the Create menu, select Bank Deposit.**

   QBO displays the Deposit transaction window shown in Figure 8-12. Existing payment transactions appear in the Select Existing Payments section of the window. You can use the lines in the Add New Deposits section to add a new payment transaction that is not associated with an outstanding invoice.

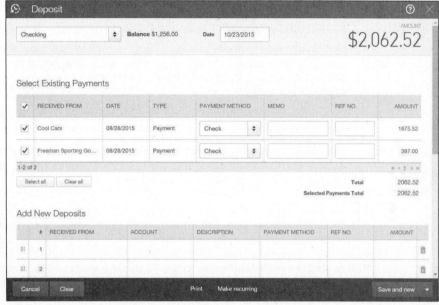

Figure 8-12:
Use the
Deposit
window to
select
payment
transactions
to deposit.

Don't try to record a payment from a customer for an outstanding invoice in the Add New Deposits section. QBO is unlikely to match the line on the Deposit transaction to the outstanding invoice. Instead, record the Receive Payment transaction; the transaction will then appear in the Select Existing Payments section of the Deposit transaction window.

2. **At the top of the window, select the account in which you plan to deposit the payments.**

3. **In the Select Existing Payments section, click the check box beside each transaction you want to include on the deposit.**

4. **For each transaction you intend to deposit, select the Payment method.**

Credit card companies often deposit credit card transaction receipts into your Bank account, and most of them make a daily deposit. To keep bank statement reconciliation as simple as possible, I suggest that you record separate QBO deposits for each credit card you accept. You can group the checks and cash payment methods on the same deposit.

5. **Optionally, you can supply a memo and a reference number.**

The total of the selected payments — and the amount you intend to deposit unless you add entries in the Add New Deposits section — appears below the Select Existing Payments list.

6. **Scroll down the Deposit transaction window.**

Optionally, supply a memo for the deposit.

Optionally, supply a cash back amount — money from the deposit total that you don't intend to deposit — along with an account in which to place the cash back amount and a memo to describe the purpose of the cash back amount.

Optionally, you can attach an electronic document to the deposit, such as a scanned copy of the deposit ticket you take to the bank.

To attach an electronic document to the deposit, click in the Attachments box and navigate to the document or drag and drop the electronic copy into the Attachments box.

7. **Click Save and Close.**

QBO moves the deposited amount from the Undeposited Funds account to the account you selected in Step 2.

All that's left to do is take a trip to the bank. Or if you're mobile-savvy, you might be able to remotely deposit checks via your cellphone; talk to your banker.

Reconciling a Bank Account

Most people's least favorite task is reconciling the bank statement. But, if you're diligent about entering transactions in QBO and recording bank deposits as described in the preceding section, reconciling your bank statement should be a fairly easy process.

To reconcile an account, follow these steps:

1. **Click the Gear icon beside your company name and, from the menu that appears, select Reconcile.**

2. **From the Reconcile page that appears, select the account you want to reconcile and click the Reconcile Now button.**

QBO displays the Start Reconciling dialog box shown in Figure 8-13.

3. **Enter the ending date and balance found on your bank statement, and then click OK.**

QBO displays the Reconcile page shown in Figure 8-14.

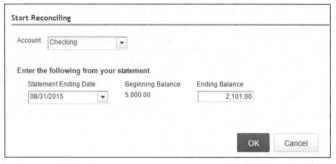

Figure 8-13:
Enter
information
found on
your bank
statement.

Figure 8-14:
Match
transactions
found on
your bank
statement
with those
shown on
the Recon-
cile page in
QBO.

4. **Select each transaction that appears on your bank statement and in the Reconcile page.**

    By selecting a transaction, you're marking it as having cleared the bank. Your goal is to have the Difference amount at the bottom of the Reconcile window equal $0.

    If you have lots of transactions, make sure that a check appears in the Hide Transactions After the Statement's End Date check box (upper-right corner of the window). Hiding those transactions can help you find transactions to clear. If the Difference amount isn't $0, then deselect the box to look for additional transactions to mark as cleared.

5. When the Difference amount equals $0, click the Finish Now button.

QBO redisplays the Reconcile page that appeared in Step 2 but wasn't shown. The reconciliation you just performed now appears in the Reconciliation History part of the screen (see Figure 8-15).

Figure 8-15:
A history of reconcilia-
tions for the
selected
account
appears on
the Recon-
cile page.

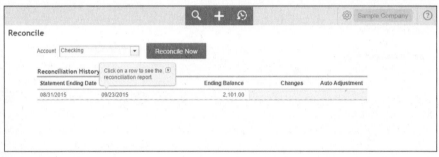

You can click any reconciliation on this page to see its Reconciliation report, which resembles the one shown in Figure 8-16.

You can drill down to view any transaction in the window where you created it; just click the transaction. And to produce a paper copy, click the Print button in the upper-left corner of the window.

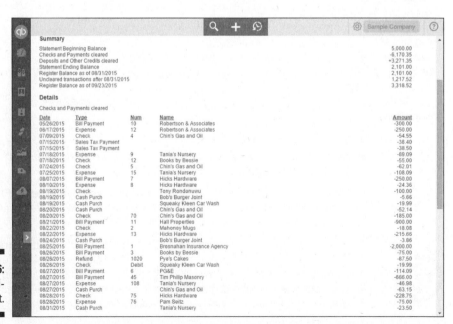

Figure 8-16:
A Reconcili-
ation report.

Chapter 9

Paying Employees

In This Chapter

▶ Turning on payroll and setting payroll preferences

▶ Preparing paychecks

▶ Handling payroll tax payments and returns

*I*t's important to understand that QBO users can prepare payroll in one of two ways: using QuickBooks Online Payroll (QBOP) or using Intuit Online Payroll. This chapter explores using QBOP.

A third alternative is to let Intuit prepare payroll, manage all payroll tax payments, and prepare and file all payroll tax returns (including W-2s at the end of each year) for you — for a fee, of course — using its Full Service Payroll option, found at `http://payroll.intuit.com/payroll-services/fullservice-payroll/`.

Understanding the payroll process

Just so you understand the job you're undertaking, be aware that running payroll is more than just issuing paychecks to your employees (although your employees will tell you that's the most important part of payroll). Yes, you first need to prepare accurate paychecks that account for withheld payroll taxes, deductions for benefits such as health insurance, and company contributions to, for example, retirement plans. But then, after you've prepared paychecks, you also need to electronically deposit withheld payroll taxes, remit amounts withheld for deductions and benefits to the appropriate parties, and file payroll tax returns with the appropriate taxing authorities. And all this work needs to be done according to a timetable that the IRS has established based on the size of your business's payroll tax liability.

If you or your accountant opt to use Intuit Online Payroll, you prepare payroll outside of QBO; the data you enter using Intuit Online Payroll can be imported into QBO. Generally speaking, Intuit Online Payroll is a pretty straightforward online payroll processing tool; you can take a tour at `http://payroll.intuit.com/online-payroll/`, and you can watch videos that show you the basics of using it. You also can sign up for a 30-day free trial.

Getting Started with QBO Payroll

When you prepare payroll, the process involves setup work so that you can accurately calculate payroll checks. You must also account for payroll taxes withheld from each employee's paycheck. You will remit federal and state payroll taxes to the appropriate tax authorities. You will also remit any required deductions and contributions that affect each employee's paycheck to appropriate agencies.

This section examines the payroll setup process in QBOP.

Turning on QBOP

QBOP uses a wizard to walk you through the setup process. You start by first turning on payroll in QBO. Then, the wizard walks you through setting up your company so that you can pay your employees.

Click the Employees link in the Navigation bar, and then click the Get Started with Payroll button (see Figure 9-1).

The Get Ready for Payroll wizard starts. On the first page, QBO fills in information you provided when you initially set up your company. Double-check the information and click the Continue button in the lower-right corner of the screen.

On the next screen of the wizard, you indicate whether you've been paying employees during the current year or whether you are about to start paying employees for the first time.

If you indicate that you have previously done payroll and are now switching to QBOP, the wizard displays two additional questions for you to answer, as shown in Figure 9-2. Answer the questions and click the Continue button in the lower-right corner of the screen. If you indicate that you've not previously paid employees, no additional questions appear, so you can just click Continue.

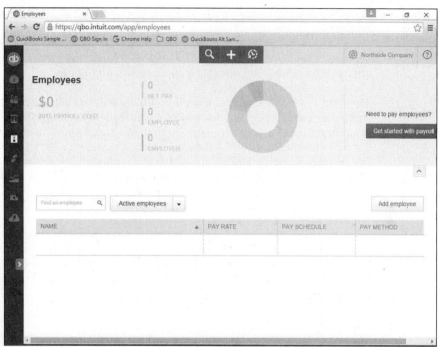

Figure 9-1:
Turning on
QBOP.

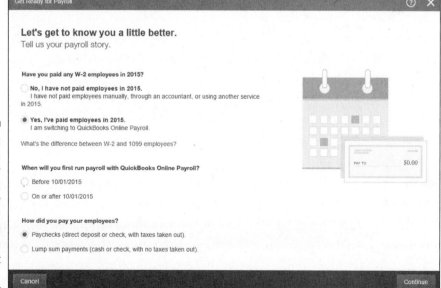

Figure 9-2:
Indicate
whether
you've
previously
paid
employees
during the
current
year.

For this example, I'm going to assume that you've not previously paid any employees. If you have, I suggest that you use the payrolls you have completed as your learning tools and enter them into QBOP as described in the section, "Preparing Payroll." That way, you'll learn how to prepare payroll and simultaneously get your payroll accounts up to date.

The next page of the wizard asks if you have collected completed W-4 forms from your employees. W-4 forms are the Internal Revenue Service's form that employees complete to specify their withholding allowance. If you need to complete Form W-4 for any employee, you can click the Need W-4 Forms link in the Payroll Setup wizard to display and print or save a PDF version after printing the form; the form QBO displays is not an editable form. For an editable form that you can complete using your computer, visit www.irs.gov and click the W-4 link in the Forms & Pubs section to display editable PDF forms.

After you indicate that you have received completed W-4 forms from your employees, click Continue. QBO displays the Enter Employee Pay Details page, shown in Figure 9-3. Click the Add Employee link and the wizard begins to walk you through setting up employees.

Figure 9-3:
Add an
employee.

Enter employee pay details

TOTAL PAY
$0.00

Bank account
Select bank account

Pay period
Select pay period

Pay date
09/25/2015

NAME	HOURS		TOTAL PAY

Add employee — Ready to add your employees? We'll help you set them up.

Back

Preview payroll

The wizard prompts you for the information shown in Figure 9-4:

✔ Name.

✔ Form W-4 information.

This information includes the employee's address, social security number, marital status, withholding amount, and state payroll tax — which varies from state to state, but QBOP prompts you to supply information for the state in which your business operates. The prompts for all this information appear when you click the Enter W-4 Form button.

To identify your state's payroll tax requirements, visit your state's website and search for *payroll taxes*.

✔ The frequency with which you pay the employee and the next expected pay date. When you supply pay frequency information, QBO creates a pay schedule that you can apply to subsequent employees you create.

✔ The amount you pay the employee.

✔ Whether the employee has any deductions.

✔ The method you want to use to pay the employee (such as paper check or direct deposit).

After you answer questions 2–5, if you need to make changes, click the pencil icon beside the answer. As you supply information, QBOP updates the preview of the sample check on the right side of the window.

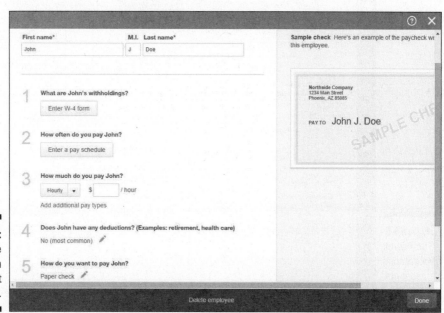

Figure 9-4:
Provide information for the first employee.

When you finish supplying the employee's information, click Done, and QBO redisplays the Employees page; the employee you set up appears in the list, and you can click the employee to edit the information, or you can click the Add Employee button to add additional employees. You can display the Employees page at any time and click the Add Employee button to set up additional employees.

Setting payroll preferences

In addition to adding employees, you should review payroll preferences and set up payroll taxes.

To review payroll preferences, click the Gear icon beside your company's name and, from the menu that appears, click Payroll Settings to display the Preferences page shown in Figure 9-5. The page contains a series of links that you can click to review or establish various settings related to payroll. Understanding this page might make you feel less overwhelmed by what you see.

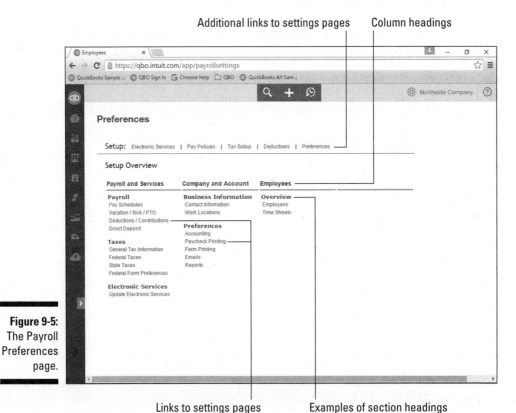

Figure 9-5:
The Payroll
Preferences
page.

The Setup Overview page is divided into three columns: Payroll and Services, Company and Account, and Employees. Within each column, you find additional headings — I refer to these additional headings as *section headings* — that summarize the types of settings you find as you click each link in that section. For example, under the Company and Account column, you find section headings for Business Information and Preferences. In the following bullets, I describe the kind of information you find as you click the links under each section heading on the Setup Overview page.

In addition, links appear above the Setup Overview heading; good news here — these aren't additional settings that you need to review. Instead, these links lead to the same pages as some of the links listed in the columns and section headings on the Setup Overview page. For example, the Electronic Services link at the top of the page displays the same page as the Update Electronic Services link in the Electronic Services section under the Payroll and Services column heading. And clicking the Pay Policies link displays the same page as clicking the Pay Schedules and Vacation/Sick/PTO links in the Payroll section under the Payroll and Services column heading.

In the bullets that follow, you find a description of the pages that appear as you click the links beneath each section heading:

✔ In the Payroll section (under Payroll and Services), you can set up additional pay schedules; establish vacation, sick, and paid time off policies; define deductions and contributions used by your company during payroll; and set up direct deposit.

✔ In the Taxes section, you establish general company tax information (such as your company's legal organization); set up your federal tax ID number and your filing and tax deposit schedule requirements; set up your state's payroll requirements, which vary from state to state; and designate whether you have a third-party or paid form preparer. To identify your state's payroll tax requirements, visit your state's website and search for *payroll taxes.*

✔ Use the Electronic Services section to enroll in electronic services for filing and paying payroll taxes.

✔ Use the Business Information section to ensure that your contact information is accurate.

✔ Use the Preferences section to establish the following:

- Wage and tax accounts for payroll

- Paycheck and W-2 form printing settings

- Payroll-related email preferences such as receiving reminders about preparing payroll, making tax payments, and filing tax forms

- Report settings to identify reports you want available after you prepare payroll

✔ In the Overview section, the Employees link takes you to the Employees page; clicking Employees on the Preferences page has the same effect as clicking Employees in the Navigation bar.

✔ Use the Time Sheets link in the Overview section to establish the way you want to enter employee hours.

Setting up payroll taxes

Before you start using payroll, you should use the wizard QBOP provides to set up payroll tax form and filing information. The wizard asks you for federal and state tax details such as your federal Employer ID number (EIN) and your corresponding state account number, how often you're required to remit payroll taxes, and whether you want to file and pay taxes electronically or manually using paper coupons. Choose Taxes ➪ Payroll Tax in the Navigation bar to display the Payroll Tax Center before you set things up (see Figure 9-6).

Click Continue, and the wizard displays the Employee Details page, which lists each of your employees. Fill in a birth date and hire date (in mm/dd/yyyy format) and click the W-4 Info link to confirm that the employee's W-4 details are correct.

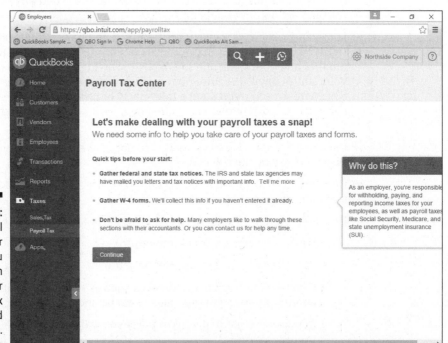

Figure 9-6: The Payroll Tax Center before you establish settings for payroll tax forms and payments.

After you check each employee, click Continue. On the next screen, the wizard displays the Business Details page shown in Figure 9-7. Confirm or change information the wizard supplies about your business, including the address you use when filing tax forms, the first time you'll be running payroll using QBOP, the time frame during which you hired your first employee, and your workers' compensation insurance status.

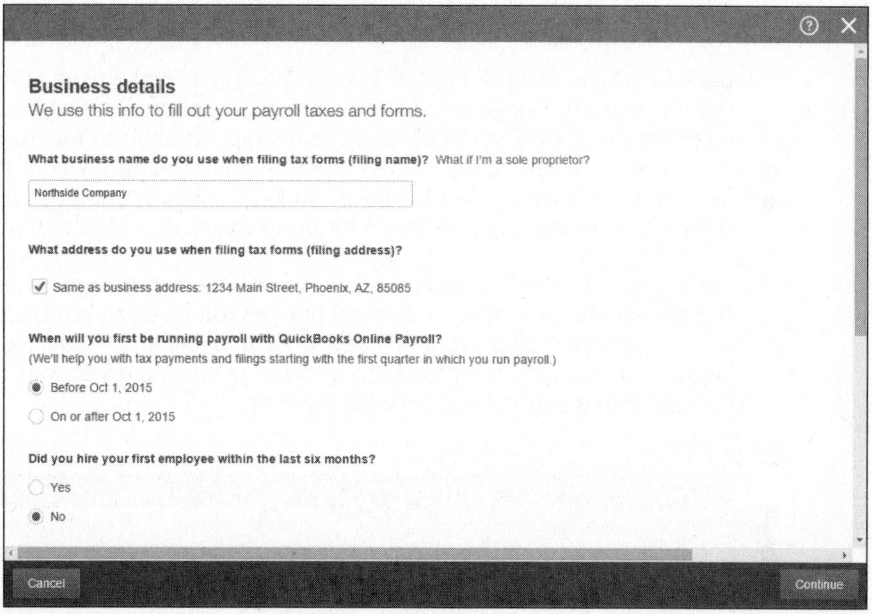

Business details
We use this info to fill out your payroll taxes and forms.

What business name do you use when filing tax forms (filing name)?   What if I'm a sole proprietor?

Northside Company

What address do you use when filing tax forms (filing address)?

☑ Same as business address: 1234 Main Street, Phoenix, AZ, 85085

When will you first be running payroll with QuickBooks Online Payroll?
(We'll help you with tax payments and filings starting with the first quarter in which you run payroll.)

● Before Oct 1, 2015

○ On or after Oct 1, 2015

Did you hire your first employee within the last six months?

○ Yes

● No

Cancel   Continue

Figure 9-7:
The
Business
Details
page.

Getting up and running

The date you start using QBOP determines the "as of" date of historical information you need to collect. Try to start using QBOP on January 1 of any year — that way, you don't need to enter any historical information. If you can't start using QBOP on January 1, try to start using it on the first day of an accounting period — either on the first day of your company's fiscal year or on the first day of a month.

If you are starting on a date other than January 1 and have issued payroll checks during the current year and prior to using QBOP, I suggest that you use these prior payrolls as a learning tool. You can enter the paychecks and then record the tax payments and prepare the tax forms without e-filing anything you've already filed; that way, this year's payroll history will be recorded in QBOP.

Chapter 3 includes the sidebar, "Proper account balances." If you opted to set an opening balance on the bank account from which paychecks are paid, you can't use prior payrolls as your learning tool because you'll mess up your bank account balance. Instead, I suggest that you contact Intuit QuickBooks Support for help entering historical payroll information.

See the "Getting up and running" sidebar for information about the date you intend to run your first QBOP payroll. Then, click Continue.

The Payroll Tax setup wizard next displays the Federal Tax Details page shown in Figure 9-8. Supply your federal Employer Identification Number (EIN), and confirm the payroll tax form you use and how often you must remit payroll taxes. You should also specify whether your company is a federally recognized non-profit organization that is not required to pay federal unemployment taxes (FUTA).

Click Continue, and the Payroll Tax setup wizard displays the State Tax Details page. This page is the state counterpart of the Federal Tax Details page. On the State Tax Details page, you supply details about your state payroll account, including the number, the State Unemployment Insurance (SUI) rate assigned to your business, and your state payroll tax deposit schedule. You also supply details for other taxes, if any, in your state.

Click Save, and QBO displays the E-pay and E-file Setup page, where you specify whether you want to file and pay payroll taxes electronically or manually, using paper coupons. If you opt to file and pay electronically, you then supply information about the bank account from which you want to pay, including your routing and account number.

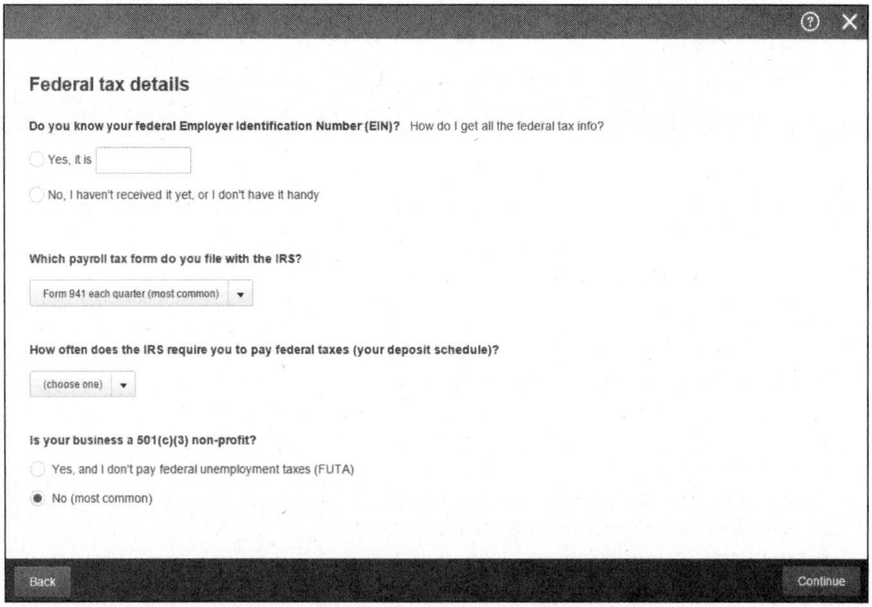

Federal tax details

Do you know your federal Employer Identification Number (EIN)?   How do I get all the federal tax info?

○ Yes, it is [   ]

○ No, I haven't received it yet, or I don't have it handy

Which payroll tax form do you file with the IRS?

[Form 941 each quarter (most common) ▼]

How often does the IRS require you to pay federal taxes (your deposit schedule)?

[(choose one) ▼]

Is your business a 501(c)(3) non-profit?

○ Yes, and I don't pay federal unemployment taxes (FUTA)

● No (most common)

Back   Continue

Figure 9-8:
The Federal
Tax Details
page.

When you finish supplying information about how you want to file and pay your taxes, click Next. QBO confirms that you've finished setting up your payroll taxes. Click Done, and QBO redisplays the Payroll Tax Center screen (see Figure 9-9).

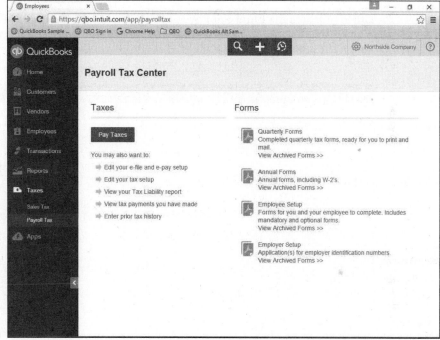

Figure 9-9: The appearance of the Payroll Tax Center screen now that you've finished setting things up.

You can use the links on the Payroll Tax Center screen to make changes to any of the settings you provided as you worked through the wizard.

Preparing Payroll

Once you get past the setup work, you're ready to process payroll — essentially a three-step process:

- ✔ Record paycheck information
- ✔ Review paycheck information
- ✔ Generate paychecks

Recording payroll information

To start preparing paychecks, click the Employees link in the Navigation bar. On the Employees page, click the Run Payroll button on the top-right side of the page.

QBOP presents the Enter Employee Pay Details window shown in Figure 9-10, which lists all your employees (I have only two employees in this company, so my list is short).

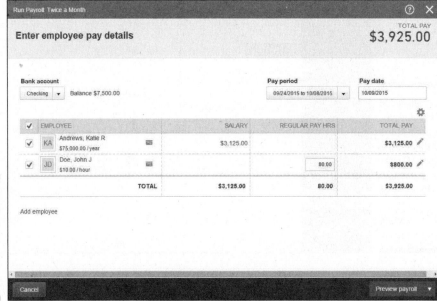

Figure 9-10: Use this screen to enter payroll information for your employees.

Select the bank account from which you'll pay employees and double-check pay period and pay date information. Then, for each employee paid on an hourly basis, supply the hours worked during the pay period.

You can view hours entered on timesheets by time tracking employees. Before you start payroll, click the Create (+) button at the top of QBO, select Weekly Timesheet, and then select the employee. If you prefer, you can print information: Run a Time Activity by Employee report (click the Reports link in the Navigation bar and then search for *Time Activities by Employee Detail*. Then, customize the report to display the payroll time frame. For information on reports, see Chapter 10.

Letting employees use timesheets

If you use QBO Plus, you can set up *time tracking users* who can log in with limited privileges that enable them to complete timesheets (and do nothing else).

To add a time tracking user, follow these steps:

1. **Click the Gear icon beside your company name and, from the menu that appears, click Manager Users.**

2. **Click the New button and, from the window that appears, click Time Tracking Only.**

3. **Click Next and select the employee (or vendor) you want to fill out timesheets.**

4. **Supply the employee's (or the vendor's) email address.**

5. **Click Next and then click Finish.**

QBO sends to the user an email containing a link that he clicks to complete the Time Tracking Only setup process. If the user already has a QBO sign-in name and password, he can use it. Otherwise, he needs to create a sign-in name and password.

Once the user has signed in, the Single Activity Time Sheet screen appears; if the employee prefers to use the Weekly Timesheet screen, she can click the tab at the top of the screen. Because most employers don't pay their employees based on hours reported on timesheets — employers instead use timesheets to bill clients for time spent on client projects — see Chapter 6 for details on entering time.

Reviewing and generating payroll checks

Once you finish entering employee pay details, click the Preview Payroll button in the lower-right corner of the Enter Employee Pay Details window (shown previously in Figure 9-8). QBOP displays the Review and Submit page, similar to the one shown in Figure 9-11.

When you're satisfied with the information on this page, click the Submit Payroll button in the lower-right corner of the screen.

Printing payroll reports

Once you complete payroll, you might want to print payroll-related reports. Click the Reports link in the Navigation bar to display the Reports page (see Figure 9-12).

Then, click the All Reports link on the page and QBO displays the All Reports page. Scroll down the page to find the Manage Payroll link and click it.

Figure 9-11:
Reviewing
paychecks
before
generating
them.

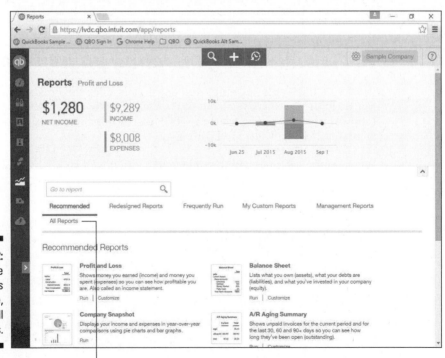

Figure 9-12:
From the
Reports
page,
display all
reports.

Click here

You can click any payroll report to print it to the screen and, subsequently, to your printer. To preview the information on a report, slide the mouse pointer over the icon beside the report, and QBO displays a sample of the information on the report (see Figure 9-13). To customize reports, see Chapter 10.

Figure 9-13:
Preview the
content of
any report.

Mouse pointer

Managing Payroll Taxes

As I mention at the beginning of this chapter, the payroll process doesn't end with preparing and producing paychecks. On a schedule determined by the IRS, you need to remit payroll taxes and file payroll tax returns.

Paying payroll taxes

Using rules established by the IRS, you pay payroll taxes weekly, monthly, or quarterly, depending on the amount you owe (called your *payroll tax liability*).

Payroll-related due dates

Payroll and unemployment tax payments are due on a different schedule than the corresponding tax forms. To summarize, payroll tax payments are due weekly, monthly, or quarterly, depending on the size of your payroll tax liability. The payroll tax form (Federal Form 941) is due quarterly.

Federal unemployment tax payments are typically due quarterly, but the federal unemployment tax return (Federal Form 940) is typically due annually.

If you do business in a state that imposes a personal income tax, then you also have state payroll tax obligations. In addition, most states impose an unemployment tax.

Last, but not least, localities within any given state might also impose payroll tax obligations.

The due dates for these state and local payments and their corresponding returns vary from state to state; to determine the due dates for your state and locality, check at the state's website.

You must make Federal tax deposits by electronic funds transfer. Most people make Federal tax deposits using the Electronic Federal Tax Payment System (EFTPS), a free service provided by the United States Department of Treasury, and QBOP makes use of the EFTPS.

To pay your payroll taxes, choose Taxes ⇨ Payroll Tax to display the Payroll Tax Center (refer to Figure 9-6). Once you've paid employees, the Payroll Tax Center displays taxes that are due, along with their due dates and e-payment cutoff dates. You can preview how much you owe by printing the Payroll Tax Liability report; click the View Your Tax Liability Report link on the Payroll Tax Center page.

When you click the Pay Taxes button, QBO displays the Pay Taxes page (see Figure 9-14), which shows payroll tax amounts that you owe to various taxing authorities.

If you "look ahead," that is, opt to view payroll tax liabilities before their due date, the amounts you see are estimates of your liabilities.

When you click the Create Payment link beside a line, QBO shows you the amount you owe, allocated by tax item (see Figure 9-15). At the top of the screen, you can opt to pay the liability electronically using EFTPS or make the payment yourself. If you're entering historical payrolls to set up accurate payroll information for the current year, choose to make the payment yourself (because you've probably already made the payment and you simply want to record it in QBOP).

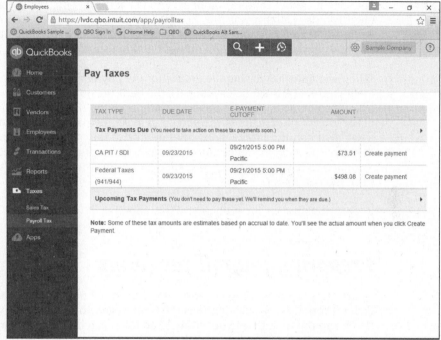

Figure 9-14:
Your payroll
tax liabilities,
separated
by payroll
tax authority.

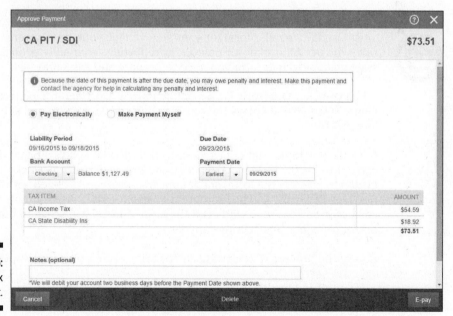

Figure 9-15:
A payroll tax
payment.

I'm working in the sample company, and I'm showing you this potential payment two days after it was due. So, QBO displays a note at the top of the screen indicating that late payments might be subject to interest and penalties and providing information on what action I should take.

When you finish reviewing the details for the payment, including the payment method (electronic or manual), the bank account from which you'll make the payment, and the payment date, click the Approve or E-pay button in the lower-right corner of the screen to make the payment. QBO displays a payment confirmation window that describes the payment method, type, liability, due date, payment date, and payment amount. If you opted to use a coupon to pay the taxes, QBO displays a button you can click to view and print the coupon.

Repeat this process for each payroll tax liability.

Preparing payroll tax forms

Quarterly, you must complete and submit a federal payroll tax return using Federal Form 941, which identifies the total wages you paid, when you paid them, and the total taxes you withheld and deposited with appropriate taxing authorities throughout the quarter. The IRS permits you to file the form electronically or to mail the form.

If you live in a state that imposes a personal income tax, then you typically must also file a similar form for your state; check your state's website for the rules you need to follow for payroll tax reporting. Your state probably has a state unemployment form you need to prepare and submit as well.

When you click Quarterly Forms on the Payroll Tax Center page (refer to Figure 9-9), QBOP displays the reports you need to prepare and submit (see Figure 9-16).

Click the link to the right of each form, and QBOP displays a page where you can opt to file the form electronically and preview the form. Click the View button to preview the form, and it appears onscreen, prefilled with information (see Figure 9-17). The form preview also includes a set of tools that you can use to review, save, and print the form. And, as you scroll to the bottom of the form, filing instructions appear.

Repeat the process of reviewing and printing each form as appropriate.

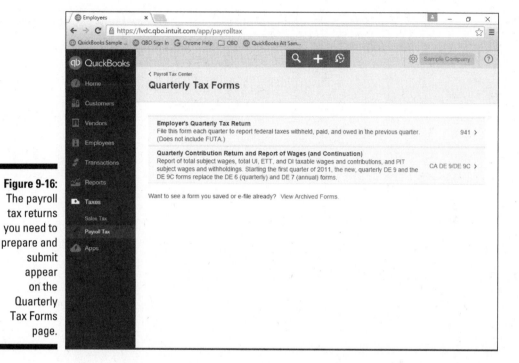

Figure 9-16:
The payroll tax returns you need to prepare and submit appear on the Quarterly Tax Forms page.

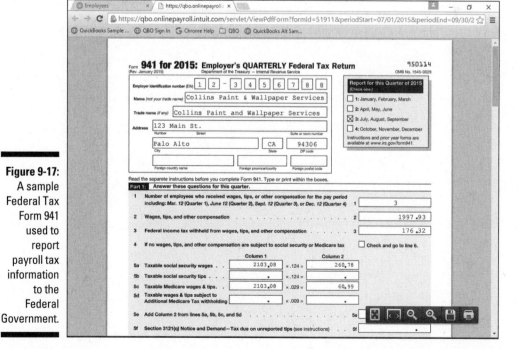

Figure 9-17:
A sample Federal Tax Form 941 used to report payroll tax information to the Federal Government.

Chapter 10

How's the Business Doing?

*N*o big surprise here: To help you measure and evaluate your business's health, you use reports. The reports reflect the information in QBO, so, keeping QBO up to date with your daily activities helps ensure that correct information appears on the reports you run.

Quickly Review Income and Expenses

When you click Reports on the Navigation bar, you see a page like the one shown in Figure 10-1.

The graphic at the top of the page shows profit and loss information and is interactive; for example, if you click anywhere in the graphic — on the Net Income number, on either the Income or the Expenses number, or on any of the bars in the chart — QBO displays the Profit and Loss report shown in Figure 10-2. This version of the Profit and Loss report breaks down income and expenses by week for the period of the graphic.

You can click Reports in the Navigation bar to redisplay the Reports page shown in Figure 10-1, or you can click your browser's Back button.

Don't want the income and expense numbers displayed onscreen? Click the upward-pointing carat at the bottom-right edge of the graphic on the Reports page, and QBO hides the graphic.

Click here to hide the graphic

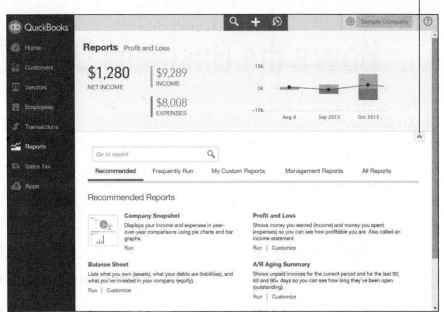

Figure 10-1:
The Reports
page.

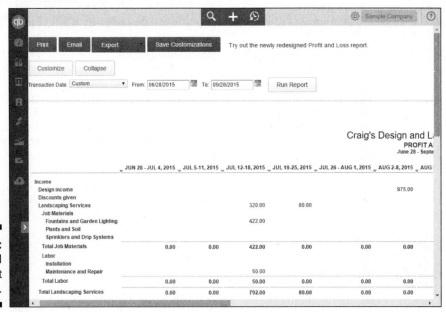

Figure 10-2:
A Profit and
Loss report
by week.

Finding the Report You Want

Reports in QBO are organized into five categories:

- ✔ Recommended Reports
- ✔ Frequently Run Reports
- ✔ My Custom Reports
- ✔ Management Reports
- ✔ All Reports

These categories appear on the Reports page below the graphic and function as tabs; that is, you click a tab to see the reports in that category.

Examining recommended reports

QBO lists reports on the Recommended Reports tab of the Reports page based on features you use in QBO, preferences, and add-ons.

In Figure 10-3, I've hidden the graphic at the top of the Reports page to give the reports on the Recommended Reports tab a bit more screen real estate. Remember, the reports I display in the figure might differ from the ones you see when you review recommended reports.

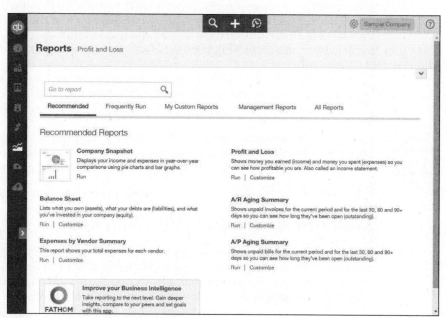

Figure 10-3:
Typical re-
commended
reports.

Each listed report also displays a graphic to the left of the report title. If you have not turned on Redesigned Reports and you pass your mouse pointer over one of these graphics, QBO displays a sample of the report's appearance (see Figure 10-4).

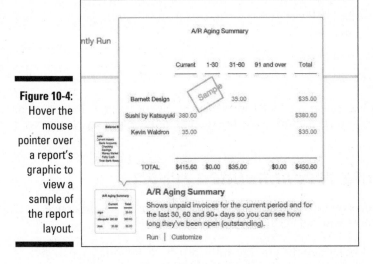

Figure 10-4:
Hover the mouse pointer over a report's graphic to view a sample of the report layout.

What are redesigned reports?

Intuit is in the process of redesigning reports to make them more professional looking and easier to customize. At the time I wrote this, Redesigned Reports was a QuickBooks Labs feature you need to turn on. (See Chapter 3 for details on enabling a QuickBooks Labs feature.)

To get a feel for the difference in appearance between the original version of a report and a redesigned version, Figure 10-5 shows the original version of the Profit and Loss report and Figure 10-6 shows the redesigned version.

If you click the Advanced button in the upper-right corner of the redesigned report, you see additional customization options that let you control the column and row data on the report, set period comparisons, and more.

Looking at frequently run reports

No surprise here: On the Frequently Run tab, QBO lists the reports you run most often. When you first start using QBO and haven't run reports yet, the Frequently Run tab doesn't contain any reports. Instead, it contains a message that describes what you'll see after you start running reports.

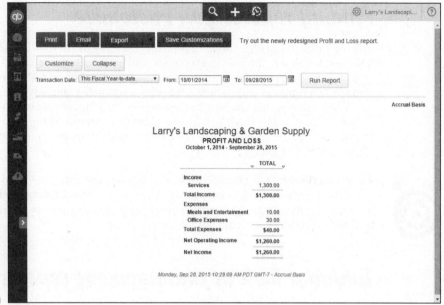

Figure 10-5: The original version of the Profit and Loss report.

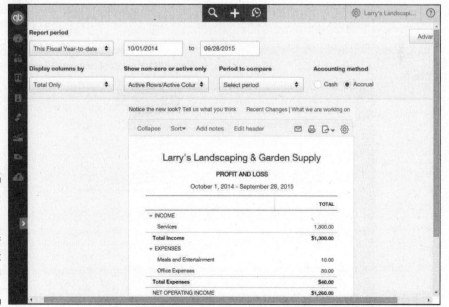

Figure 10-6: The redesigned version of the Profit and Loss report.

Finding reports you customize

The My Custom Reports tab lists reports you have printed — whether to your display or a printer — customized, and saved, either as single reports or in a report group. Like its cousin, Frequently Run reports, the My Custom Reports tab remains empty until you print, customize, and save a report as described later in this chapter in the section, "Saving a customized report." In that section, I also show you how to place a customized report into a group, and you get a look at the My Custom Reports page after it contains a report saved to a group.

If you're a former QuickBooks desktop user, be aware that saving a report in QBO is the equivalent of memorizing a report in QuickBooks desktop, and saving a report to a group in QBO is conceptually the same as creating a memorized report group in QuickBooks desktop.

Taking a look at management reports

The Management Reports tab, shown in Figure 10-7, lists three predefined management report packages you can prepare and print by clicking the View link in the Action column. Each package contains a professional looking cover page, a table of contents, and several reports that relate to the report package's name:

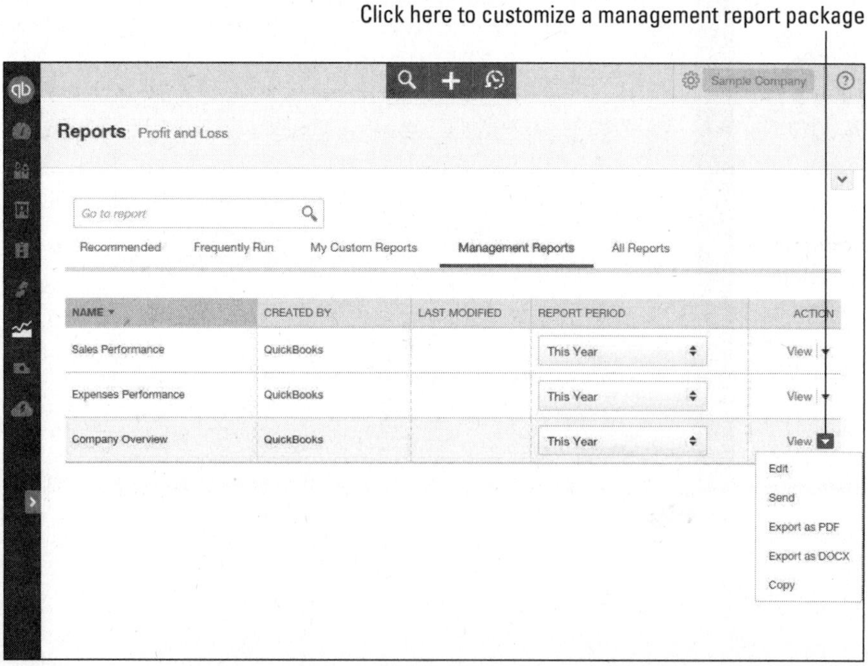

Click here to customize a management report package

NAME ▼	CREATED BY	LAST MODIFIED	REPORT PERIOD	ACTION
Sales Performance	QuickBooks		This Year	View ▾
Expenses Performance	QuickBooks		This Year	View ▾
Company Overview	QuickBooks		This Year	View ▾

Edit
Send
Export as PDF
Export as DOCX
Copy

Figure 10-7: The Management Reports page.

✔ The Sales Performance management report contains the Profit and Loss report, the A/R Aging Detail report, and the Sales by Customer Summary report.

✔ The Expenses Performance management report contains the Profit and Loss report, the A/P Aging Detail report, and the Expenses by Vendor Summary report.

✔ The Company Overview management report contains the Profit and Loss report and the Balance Sheet report.

The management report appears in its own window, where you can scroll through and print it. You can also customize these reports; click the downward-pointing arrow beside a report to see your choices.

If you opt to edit a report package, you can add more reports to the package and you can include an executive summary and end notes to the package.

Exploring all QBO reports

The All Reports tab gives you a way to find any QBO report. The page lists a series of categories for reports, such as Business Overview and Manage Accounts Receivable. When you click a particular category, you see a page similar to the one shown previously in Figure 10-3, which lists all the reports for the selected category. If you haven't turned on the redesigned reports feature, a graphic appears beside each report, and you can hover your mouse pointer over the graphic to identify the report's layout and content.

Once you select a category, you can redisplay the All Reports page by clicking the All Reports link that appears above the report category name.

Searching for a report

You don't need to use the tabs to find a report. Instead, you can click in the Go To Report box; when you do, QBO displays all reports, listed alphabetically, in a drop-down list (see Figure 10-8).

If you see the report you want, you can click it, and QBO displays it onscreen. If you don't see the report you want, you can type some keywords into the Go To Report box, and QBO narrows the reports displayed in the drop-down list to those whose names contain the keywords you typed.

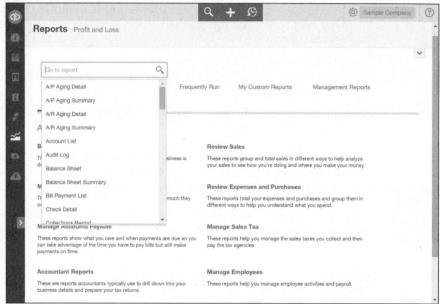

Figure 10-8:
Searching
for a report.

Printing a Report

To produce any report, simply click the report's title. QBO automatically displays the report with a standard set of settings. To redisplay reports, click Reports in the Navigation bar.

On most reports, you can *drill down* to view the details behind the report's numbers. For example, from the Profit and Loss report, you can click any Income or Expense account value, and QBO displays the transactions that make up the number on the Profit and Loss report. I clicked the dollar amount for Design income, and QBO displayed the Transaction report shown in Figure 10-9.

To redisplay the original report, you can click the Back to Summary Report link on the left side of the report page.

 If you want to keep the original summary version of the report open and also view the details from drilling down, duplicate the tab containing the summary version of the report before you drill down to view details. When you finish working with the details, you can close the tab containing the details. To duplicate a tab in Chrome, right-click the tab and select Duplicate. To duplicate a tab in Firefox, press and hold down the Ctrl key as you click the browser refresh button, which appears at the right edge of the address bar.

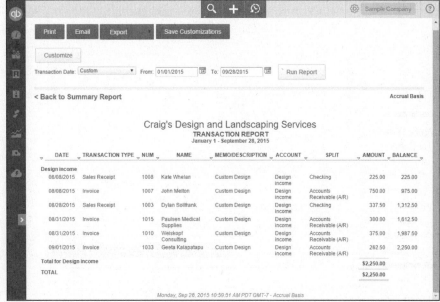

Customizing a report

You can customize most reports in a variety of ways. For all reports, you can change the date range covered by the report by opening the Transaction Date list box and making a selection or by setting specific dates in the From and To boxes. After you make your selection, click the Run Report button to refresh the report and display information only in the date range you selected.

To set more detailed custom settings, click the Customize button at the top of the report. QBO displays the Customize dialog box shown in Figure 10-10; from this dialog box, you can make changes that affect the information QBO displays on the report.

First, although you see tabs down the side of the dialog box, the Customize dialog box contains one long list of settings you can control. The tabs help you scroll down quickly to a particular type of setting.

Second, it's important to understand that the settings (and the tabs) that appear in the Customize dialog box vary, depending on the report you are customizing. Figure 10-10 shows the settings in the General section of the Customize Profit and Loss dialog box. From this section, you can, for example, opt to display the report using the accrual basis of accounting rather than the cash basis of accounting.

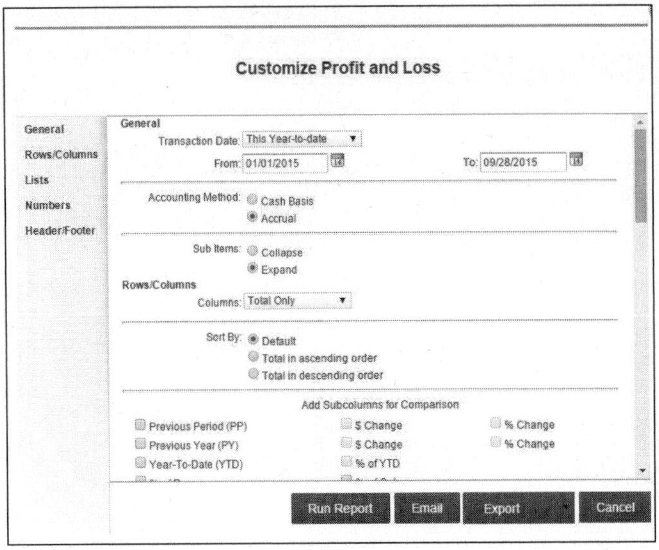

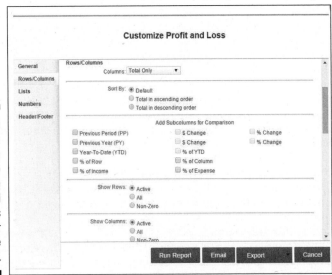

Figure 10-10:
The General
tab of the
dialog box
you use to
customize a
report in
greater
detail.

From the Rows/Columns section of the Customize Profit and Loss dialog box
(see Figure 10-11), you can control the columns and rows that appear on the
report as well as the order in which they appear. You also can add a variety
of comparison columns.

Figure 10-11:
Use this tab
of the dialog
box to
control the
rows and
columns
that appear
on the
report.

From the Lists section, shown in Figure 10-12, you can control the entries from the Customer, Vendor, Employee, and Product/Service list that QBO includes on the Profit and Loss report.

Figure 10-12 also shows the settings you can control for numbers on the report and the beginning of the report header and footer settings. If you click Header/Footer on the left side of the dialog box (or you scroll down in the dialog box), you see the rest of the report header and footer settings you can control, along with a preview of the header and footer settings you select.

Figure 10-12: The Lists and Numbers settings you can control on the Profit and Loss report.

When you're finished customizing the report, click Run Report, and QBO displays the report onscreen using your customized settings. With the report onscreen, you can click the Print button to print the report to paper or to a PDF file. Or, you can click the Email button to email the report or the Excel button to export the report to Excel.

You can email the report or export it to Excel from the Customize dialog box, but I suggest that you use the Run Report button to display the report on-screen first and make sure that what you see is what you want to send.

When you use Chrome to export a report to Excel, a button with the title "report1.xls" appears in the bottom-left corner of the screen; click that button to open the report in Excel. Be aware, too, that QBO automatically saves a copy of the report to the local hard drive; mine appeared in the Downloads folder. If you don't delete the reports, QBO increments the report name for subsequent reports you export to Excel.

To find the folder where QBO stores the report, click the down arrow on the right side of the report's button in the lower-left corner of the QBO screen and choose Show in Folder.

Saving a customized report

Once the report looks the way you want, you might want to save it so that you don't need to apply the same customizations each time you run the report. Click the Save Customizations button at the top of the report page to display the Save Report Customizations dialog box shown in Figure 10-13.

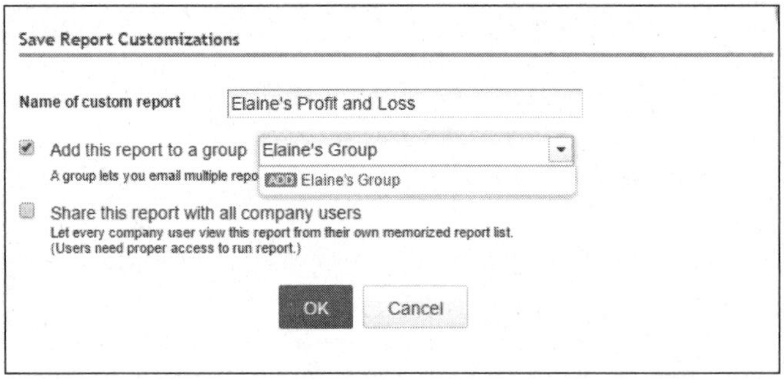

Figure 10-13:
Use this
dialog box
to save a
customized
report.

> **Save Report Customizations**
>
> **Name of custom report**   Elaine's Profit and Loss
>
> ☑ Add this report to a group   Elaine's Group ▼
> A group lets you email multiple repo [ADD] Elaine's Group
>
> ☐ Share this report with all company users
> Let every company user view this report from their own memorized report list.
> (Users need proper access to run report.)
>
> [OK]   [Cancel]

Supply a name for the customized report; you can use the QBO name for the report, but you'd be better off including some information in the name that helps you remember the customizations — unlike the one I used in the figure, which really doesn't tell you much other than the report isn't the standard Profit and Loss report.

You can add the report to a group you create; creating a group is useful if you want to email several reports simultaneously.

Once you click OK in the Save Customizations dialog box, the saved report appears on the My Custom Reports tab of the Reports page. And, if you created a group, the report appears in that group (see Figure 10-14). In Figure 10-14, my customized version of the Profit and Loss report appears in a group called Elaine's Group.

To print the report, I click its title, and the report appears onscreen. I also can take any of the following actions if I click the down arrow in the Action column beside the report:

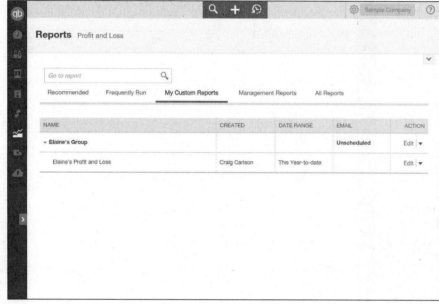

Figure 10-14:
The My
Custom
Reports
page after
creating a
custom
report.

- ✔ Create a PDF version of the report by clicking Export as PDF.
- ✔ Move the report to a different group by clicking Group.
- ✔ Export the report to Excel by clicking Export as Excel.
- ✔ Delete the customized report by clicking Delete.

To change a report's name or group, click the Edit link beside the report.

If you select the Edit link in the Action column beside a report group, you can set an email schedule for the report group; QBO displays the Report Group Settings page shown in Figure 10-15. Select the Set the Email Schedule for This Group check box to display and edit scheduling information.

If you select the Attach the Reports as Excel Files option, QBO sends the reports in Excel format; if you don't select this option, QBO sends the reports in HTML format.

Fill in the Email information; QBO will use the same subject each time it emails the report group. By default, QBO chooses monthly as the email interval, but if you click the Edit Schedule button, QBO lets you customize the email schedule (see Figure 10-16).

If you click Delete at the bottom of the Report Group Settings page, you delete the report group and all custom reports the group contains.

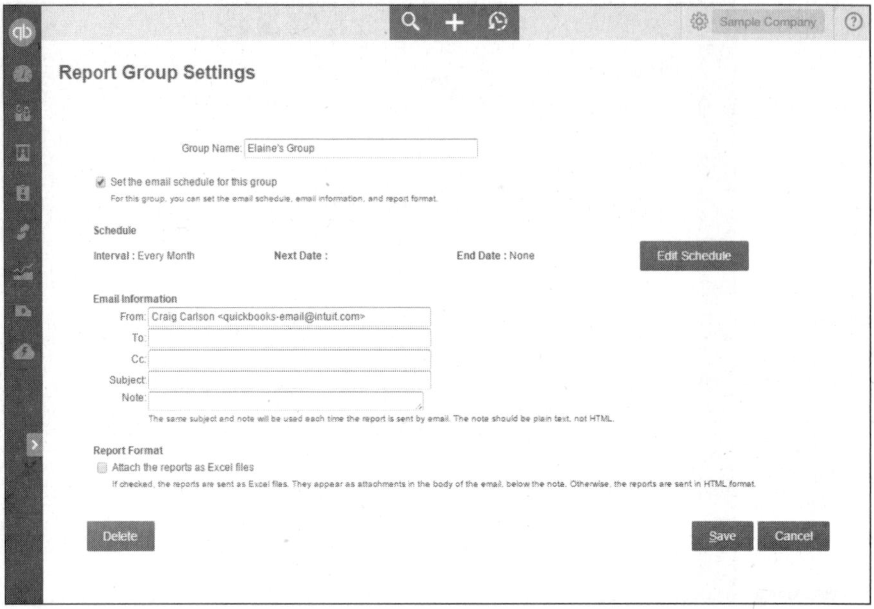

Figure 10-15:
Set an email schedule for a report group.

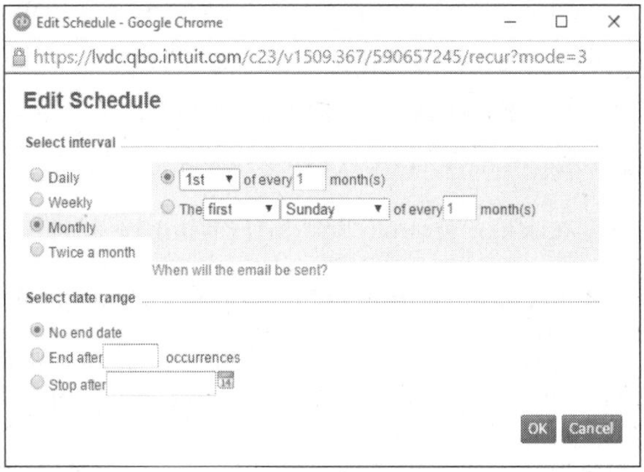

Figure 10-16:
Set up a recurring schedule to email the reports in a report group.

Part III
Managing the Books for the Accountant

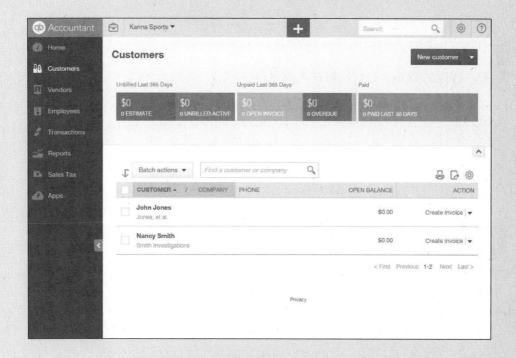

Check out the free articles at www.dummies.com/extras/quickbooksonline to read details about data conversion and its limitations if you plan to convert a desktop QuickBooks company to a QBO company.

In this part . . .

- ✔ Examine the QBOA interface, set up QBOA users, and work with the QBOA Client List, free company, and sample company.

- ✔ Learn how to add clients to the Client List, including importing desktop QuickBooks companies.

- ✔ Become familiar with working with a client QBO company from QBOA.

- ✔ Learn how to use notes and tasks to keep track of information and how to communicate with clients from within their QBO companies.

- ✔ Use tools available to accountants to manage client QBO companies.

Chapter 11

Setting Up Shop in QBOA

· ·

In This Chapter

▶ Signing up for QBOA

▶ Signing into and out of QBOA

▶ Understanding the QBOA front-end interface

▶ Setting up multiple users in a QBOA account

▶ Using the Client List page

▶ Working with the free QBOA company and the sample company

· ·

*P*art I covers the details of QBO, and QBO is the product you use to enter transactions into a company.

Because accountants need to work in multiple QBO companies, they use QuickBooks Online for Accountants (QBOA). QBOA provides a front-end interface that acts as a portal you use to open client QBO companies. When you open any particular client's company, you have available to you the features for the client's subscription level: Simple Start, Essentials, or Plus.

As you see in this chapter, the interface for a client QBO company opened in QBOA varies slightly from the interface your client sees when opening the company.

Signing Up for and into QBOA

Setting up a QBOA subscription account is free, and your QBOA subscription remains free for the first 180 days starting from the day you enroll. You can sign up for the Intuit Wholesale Pricing program and receive discounted rates for each client subscription you manage; contact Intuit for details.

When you sign up for a QBOA subscription account, you get, as one of the perks, a free QBO company that you can use for your own QuickBooks company.

To create a QBOA account, open your browser and navigate to `http://quickbooks.intuit.com/accountants/quickbooks-accountant`. On the web page that appears, click the Overview link in the QuickBooks Online Accountant bar (see Figure 11-1).

Figure 11-1: Navigating to the QBOA sign-in page.

Click here   QuickBooks Online Accountant bar

Once you click Overview, a Sign Up Free link appears at the right edge of the QuickBooks Online Accountant bar; click it to display the web page shown in Figure 11-2. Provide your email address and the rest of the requested information, including your company name, and then click the Sign Up button.

QUICKBOOKS ONLINE ACCOUNTANT
Sign up now, it's free!

◉ I'm a new Intuit user   ○ I have an Intuit user ID

Product region

| Please select region ▾ |

Name

| First | | Last |

Accounting firm name

Firm phone number

optional

Email

User ID

Password

By clicking Sign Up below, you acknowledge you have read and agree to the Terms of Service.

[Sign Up] 🔒 Secure Server

No credit card needed

Quick and easy setup

Live expert help
9am - 5pm, PT

Be sure to use one of these browsers for the all-new QuickBooks Online Accountant

[–]
Feedback

Figure 11-2:
Provide a limited amount of information to create a QBOA account.

Just as you'd expect, by clicking the Sign Up button, you're agreeing to Intuit's Terms of Service, the End-User License Agreement, and the Privacy Policy for QBOA.

QBOA uses the company name to create the free company you can use to manage the books for your own business. You can read more about this company later in this chapter, in the section "Understanding and Using the Free QBOA Company."

Your new company is created and the Home page in QBOA appears. In addition, the "Take a Tour" video, lasting less than two minutes, provides some tips to get you started. When the video finishes, you'll see that your Client List page is empty except for links to two other "getting started" videos and to a PDF version of the 16-page QuickBooks Accountant Welcome Guide, which you can use to help you work in QBOA.

Once you've created a QBOA account, you use the same page to log in to your QBOA account that your client uses to log in to QBO. Navigate to https://qbo.intuit.com to view the web page shown in Figure 11-3 and supply your login credentials.

Examining the QBOA Interface

The QBOA interface focuses on giving accountants access to tools they need to manage multiple clients. Although the view in the QBOA interface changes, depending on where you're working, two common elements appear in the QBOA interface:

- ✔ The Navigation bar (navy blue) runs down the left side of the page.
- ✔ The QBOA toolbar (green) runs across the top of the page.

You use the Navigation bar to display the various pages in QBOA. The Navigation bar contains two choices that display different views and affect the choices in the QBOA toolbar: the Your Practice and Your Books views. The following two sections explore the Navigation bar and the QBOA toolbar in each of these views.

Working with the Your Practice view

By default, the QBOA Home page displays, in the Navigation bar, the links for the Your Practice view and the Clients page, as you see in Figure 11-4.

QBOA toolbar

Figure 11-4:
The Your Practice view of the Navigation bar in QBOA.

Navigation bar

On the Client List page, you can search for a client, see overview material about each client, and open a client's QBO company. You can also control the appearance of the Client List page. See the section "Controlling the Appearance of the Client List" later in this chapter for details on working with the Client List page.

When you click Team in the Navigation bar, you can set up the users in your firm who will have access to various client companies. For more information, see the section "Setting Up Your Team."

When you click ProAdvisor, you see information about the Intuit ProAdvisor program.

Across the top of the interface, you find a toolbar with the following buttons, from left to right:

- ✔ **The Accountant button:** This button contains the QuickBooks logo and offers you another way to display the Client List shown in Figure 11-4.

- ✔ **The Go to Client's QuickBooks button:** You can use this list box to display a list of your clients; clicking a client name opens the client's company.

- ✔ **The plus sign (+) icon:** This button displays the Create menu, which you use to create a client, a user, or a request (typically for information).

- ✔ **The Search box:** When you click in this box, a list of recent transactions or reports appears; you can type in the box to search for the transaction or report of your choice or you can click an item in the list.

- ✔ **The Gear button:** Click this button to display the Gear menu (see Figure 11-5). The Gear menu shows the settings you can establish for your own company, your client's company, and your QBOA account.

You also can open the QBO sample company from the Gear menu; read more about opening and working in the sample company later in this chapter, in the section "Working with the Sample Company."

- ✔ **The Help button:** Click this button to open the Help menu so that you can search for help on any topic. Help in QBOA is context sensitive and available from all screens. When you open the Help menu from a transaction screen, the suggested choices that appear are based on the type of transaction you were viewing when you clicked Help.

Gear button

Figure 11-5: The choices available from the Gear menu.

Long For Success LLC

Settings	Lists	Tools	Your Company
Company Settings	All Lists	Import Data	Your Account
Custom Form Styles	Products and Services	Import Desktop Data	Your Team
Chart of Accounts	Recurring Transactions	Export Data	Videos and Welcome Guide
Payroll Settings	Attachments	Reconcile	Sample Company
QuickBooks Labs		Budgeting	Feedback
Company Templates		Audit Log	Refer a Friend
		Order Checks	Privacy
		Resolve Duplicate Clients	Switch Company
			🔒 Sign Out

Working with the Your Books view

When you click Your Books in the Navigation bar, you open your own QBO company, and, with the exception of the Your Practice link and the Your Books link in the Navigation bar, you and your client see the same links (see Figure 11-6).

QBOA toolbar

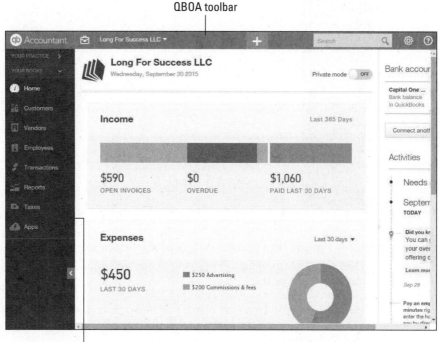

Figure 11-6:
The view of
a QBO
company
from QBOA.

Navigation bar

The view when you open your own company's books in QBOA matches the view you see when you open any client's QBO company; the only difference onscreen is the name of the company that appears on the QBOA toolbar.

The Home screen of a company displays overview income, expense, and profit and loss information in interactive filters; you can click part of any graphic on this page to display the details that make up that part of the graphic.

The QBOA toolbar in a QBO company changes somewhat when you display the Your Books view. In particular, beside the Accountant button, you see a suitcase button that I call the Accountant Tools button; you can click this button to display, well, tools accountants need frequently when working in a client's company (see Figure 11-7). See Chapter 15 for details on these tools.

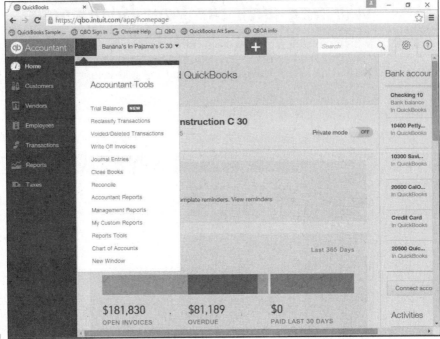

The List Box button beside the Accountant Tools button displays the name of the currently open QBO company; when you click Your Books, your company's name appears.

The Create button (the plus sign), the Search box, the Gear icon, and the Help button all work the same way in the Your Books view as they do in the Your Practice view.

While any company is open, you can open the list box displaying the company's name to switch to a different client company. Also, you can redisplay the Client List page at any time by clicking the Accountant button on the QBOA toolbar.

Setting Up Your Team

If your accounting firm has more than one person who need access to client QBO companies, the person who creates the QBOA account — called, in QBOA parlance, the *master administrator* — can set up the other users. The other users get their own login credentials and access to those clients that the master administrator specifies; for those clients, the user can access the Accountant tools described in Chapter 15. The master administrator also specifies the user's level of access to the firm's information; a user can have basic, full, or custom access.

Using separate QBOA login information helps maintain security in QBOA, because a lot of financial information (product subscriptions and billing information, for example) is tied to login information.

So, what's the difference, status-wise, between basic, full, and custom access?

- ✔ Those users with full access can open and work in the firm's books as well as in client QBO companies and can access the Team page and make changes to any user's privileges.

- ✔ Those users with basic access can access only client QBO companies.

- ✔ Those users with custom access have nothing more than basic or full access with at least one privilege set differently from QBOA's defaults for basic or full access.

To set up multiple users in a QBOA account, the master administrator or any firm member with full access privileges to QBOA sets up other members of the firm; during the process, QBOA sends an email to the other firm members whom, for this discussion, I call *invitees*. Once an invitee accepts the invitation, QBOA prompts the invitee to set up his own QBOA login credentials. Follow these steps to set up a new user in a QBOA account:

1. **Log in to QBOA.**

2. **Click Team in the Navigation bar.**

   The Team page appears (see Figure 11-8).

3. **Click the Add User button.**

   The Add User wizard begins.

4. **On the first page of the Add User wizard, fill in the name, email address, and title of the team member you want to add.**

   The team member's title is optional.

5. **Click Next.**

   The second page of the Add User wizard appears (see Figure 11-9). On this page, you identify the privileges related to your firm that you want to provide to the team member.

Figure 11-8:
View, edit, and add members to your QBOA team.

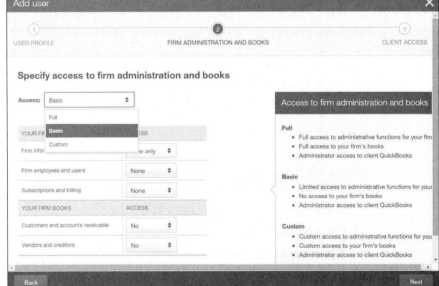

Figure 11-9:
Specify the new user's access level to your firm's administration and books.

6. Select the type of access you want to give to the team member.

You can assign Basic, Full, or Custom access; a description of each type of access appears on the right side of the page. Assign Full access to those team members who should have access to your own company's books. Assign Basic access to give a team member access to QBO client companies only.

You can make changes to individual settings; if you do, QBOA sets the team member's access to Custom by default.

7. Click Next.

The last screen of the Add User wizard appears (see Figure 11-10). On this page, you identify the clients for whom the team member should be able to perform work.

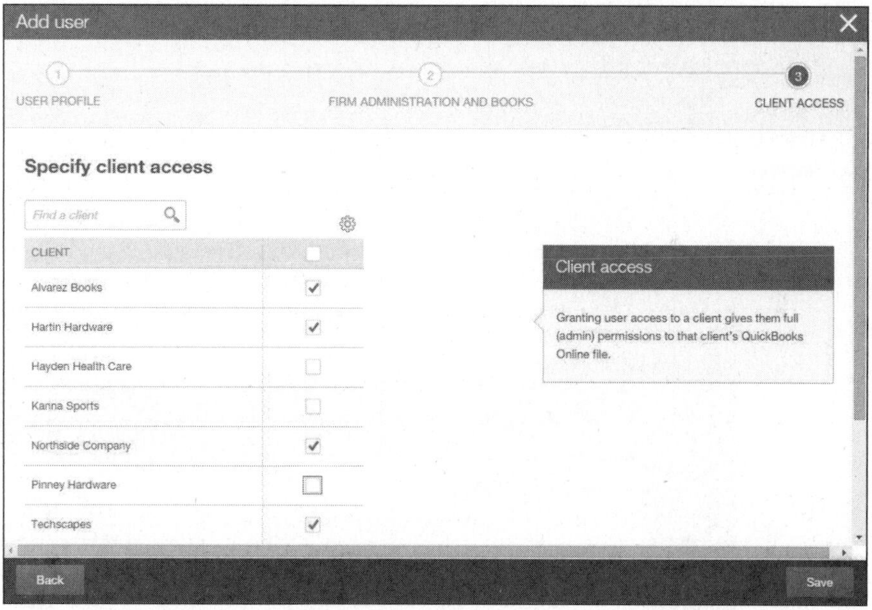

Figure 11-10:
You can provide a team member access to your firm's clients on a selective basis.

Add user ✕

① ② ③
USER PROFILE · · · · · · · · · · · · · · · FIRM ADMINISTRATION AND BOOKS · · · · · · · · · · · · · · · CLIENT ACCESS

Specify client access

Find a client 🔍	⚙

CLIENT	☐
Alvarez Books	☑
Hartin Hardware	☑
Hayden Health Care	☐
Kanna Sports	☐
Northside Company	☑
Pinney Hardware	☐
Techscapes	☑

Client access

Granting user access to a client gives them full (admin) permissions to that client's QuickBooks Online file.

Back   Save

8. Deselect clients as needed.

9. Click Save.

QBOA adds the new user to your team and assigns a status of Invited to the user. In addition, the Status column on the Team screen indicates that QBOA sent an email invitation to the user, inviting the user to join your team. After the user responds to the QBOA invitation, the user's status changes to Active on the Team page in QBOA.

The email invitation that QBOA sends looks like the one shown in Figure 11-11.

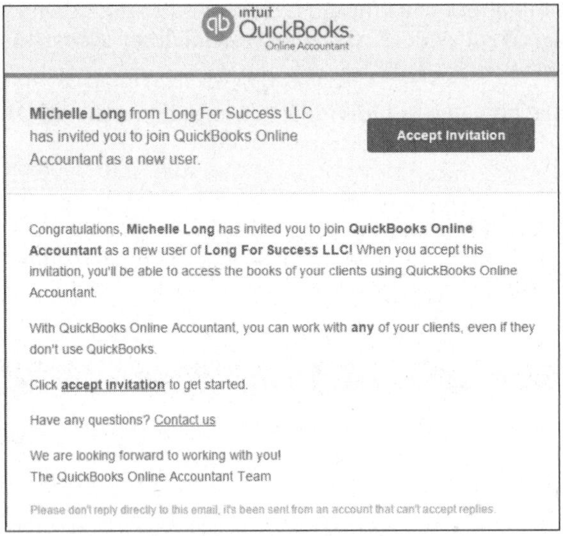

Figure 11-11:
An email
invitation to
use a QBOA
account.

The recipient clicks the Accept Invitation button, and, assuming the invitee doesn't already have login information for QBOA, the page shown in Figure 11-12 appears. On this page, the invitee sets up QBOA login

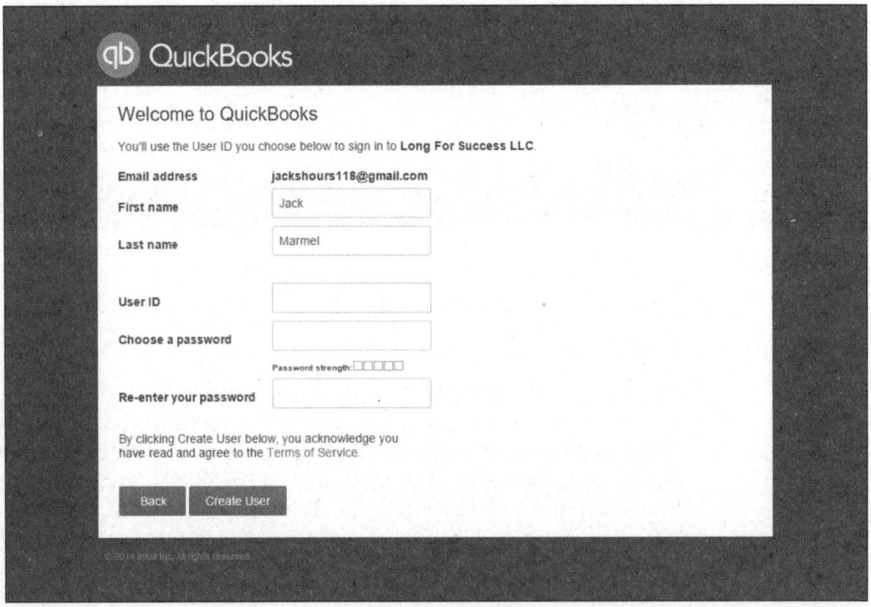

Figure 11-12:
An invited
team
member
sets up her
own login
information.

information by providing a user ID (which does not need to be an email address) and a password. Once the invitee clicks Create User, QBOA confirms that the user ID is available, sets up the login information, and displays a page on which a Sign In button appears. Clicking the Sign In button signs the user into QBOA with the user's assigned privileges.

To log into QBOA in the future, the team member navigates to https://qbo.intuit.com and supplies her login credentials.

Controlling the Appearance of the Client List

You can use the Client List page to open any client's QBO company, and you can control the appearance of the Client List page, shown in Figure 11-13.

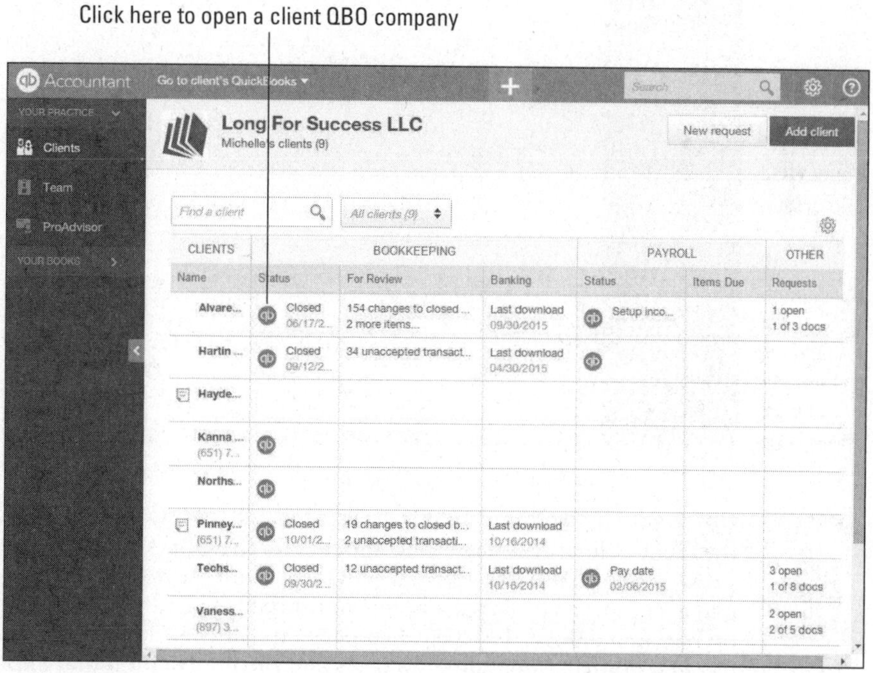

Click here to open a client QBO company

Figure 11-13:
Click a QuickBooks logo or use the Go to Client's QuickBooks list to open a client QBO company.

To open any client's QBO company, click the QuickBooks logo in the Status column of the Client List page. Or, if you prefer, open the Go to Client's QuickBooks list box on the QBOA toolbar to select the QBO company you want to open.

If you click a client's name — rather than the QuickBooks logo — you don't open the client's company. Instead, you see overview details about the client. And the QuickBooks logo that appears in the Payroll Status column opens the client's company and displays payroll information for the client company.

You can control the appearance of the Client List page. For example, you can control the number of clients listed on the page by limiting the number of rows that appear. You also can specify the columns of information that appear on the Client List page. Click the Gear icon that appears just above the list of clients and make choices from the list that appears (see Figure 11-14).

Click here

Figure 11-14:
Control the number of rows and the information appearing on the Client List page.

QBOA actually contains multiple Gear menus, and two of them appear on the QBOA Client List page. One appears on the QBOA toolbar; you use it to provide information about your QBOA account, establish settings, view lists, and access tools to, for example, import data. The other Gear menu appears on the right side of the Client List page, just above the list of clients, and you use it to control the number of rows and the information that appears on the page. The Gear menu on the QBOA toolbar appears at all times, even when you open a client QBO company.

Understanding and Using the Free QBOA Company

As I mention at the beginning of this chapter, QBOA users get one free company to use for their own company. To open the company reserved for you, click the Your Books link in the Navigation bar, and QBOA opens your company. The interface you see when you open your company looks just like the interface you see when you open any client's QBO company; remember, this interface varies slightly from what a client using QBO sees.

You can use the free QBOA company to enter your own company's information using transactions, or if you've been tracking your business in desktop QuickBooks, you can, with some limitations, import information from your desktop QuickBooks company. To enter information using transactions, you can read the chapters in Part I of this book, because you as a QBOA user and your clients as QBO users enter transactions in the same way.

You can import desktop QuickBooks information, and you can import only list information. For details on importing lists, see Chapter 4. If you want to try importing a desktop QuickBooks company, see Chapter 12 for details as well as the Part III articles at www.dummies.com/extras/quickbooksonline, which describe the limitations associated with importing information.

The Your Books company is not intended to house a client's data. The Your Books company ties into QBOA and updates as clients are added to QBOA. So, if you use it to store a client's data, that data will be messed up as you add other clients.

Working with the Sample Company

If you've been a desktop QuickBooks user, you know that desktop QuickBooks comes with a variety of sample companies that you can use to test company behavior. Like its desktop cousin, QBOA also comes with a sample company.

To open the sample company, follow these steps:

1. **Click the Gear icon on the QBOA toolbar.**

   QBOA opens the Gear menu.

2. **In the Your Company section, click Sample Company.**

   QBOA displays a warning message that you will be logged out of QBOA if you continue.

3. Click Continue.

QBOA signs you out of your company and opens the sample company. The interface looks like the QBOA interface you see when you open a client's company. For example, you see the Accountant button in the upper-left corner and the QBOA toolbar to the right of the Accountant button. The QBOA toolbar contains the same tools you see when you open a client QBO company. Note, though, that the sample company name appears on the Client Home page (click Home on the Navigation bar) as Craig's Design and Landscaping Services, but the name of the company beside the Gear icon on the QBOA toolbar is Sample Company (see Figure 11-15).

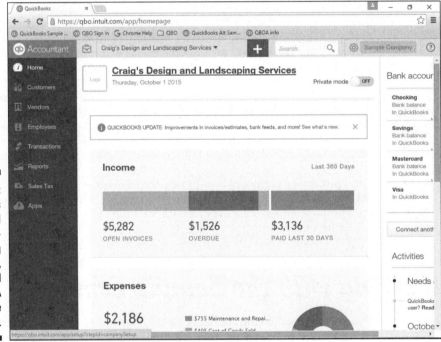

Figure 11-15: Craig's Design and Landscaping Services, the QBO and QBOA sample company.

End users (your clients) also have access to this sample company, but opening it isn't quite as easy as it is for you. Direct your clients to www. quickbooks.intuit.com/online and tell them to scroll down and click the Take a Test Drive button.

Closing Companies and QBOA

You don't close companies in QBOA the way you might using desktop QuickBooks. When you switch from one client QBO company to another, you automatically close the first client's company.

To work in two client QBO companies simultaneously, you can use two different browsers, two instances of a single browser, or Chrome's User feature (if you're using Chrome). (For details on using Chrome, see Chapter 17.)

To close QBOA, click the Gear icon on the QBOA toolbar and choose Sign Out (see Figure 11-16).

Figure 11-16:
Exit from
QBOA by
signing out.

Click here

Chapter 12

Adding Companies to the QBOA Client List

In This Chapter

▶ Adding client QBO companies to the QBOA Client List

▶ Importing company data from desktop QuickBooks to QBO

▶ Switching between client QBO company files in QBOA

*A*fter signing up for QBOA and logging in, the next step for the accountant is to populate the Client List with QBO clients, which can happen in a couple of ways. In addition, you might be helping a client set up a QBO company either by creating a new company or by importing information into the QBO company.

This chapter shows you how to add client companies to the Client List and how to import company information from the desktop QuickBooks product.

Adding a Client's Company to the Client List

You can add a client company to the Client List in two ways:

✔ By letting your client create the company and then inviting you to access the company

✔ By creating a client's company for the client

If you create a client's company for the client and you participate in the Intuit Wholesale Pricing program, you can opt to manage the client's subscription for him. In this case, Intuit bills you for the client's subscription and you then bill your client. Alternatively, the client can opt to manage his QBO subscription. At the time this book was written, Intuit was running specials on QBO through its main website. In addition, Intuit was offering discounts for QBO companies created by accountants using QBOA regardless of whether the accountant or the client ultimately managed the client's QBO subscription.

The method you choose for creating a client company doesn't permanently affect the method chosen to manage the subscription; if you belong to the Intuit Wholesale Pricing program, you can always change subscription management later.

If you plan to manage your client's subscription as part of the Intuit Wholesale Pricing program, consider creating your client's company for her. For details on signing up for the Intuit Wholesale Pricing program, contact Intuit.

Adding a company created by a client

If a client creates his own company, he retains billing responsibility for the company. Even so, your client can invite you to access the company using the Invite Accountant process in QBO. Your client should follow these steps:

1. **Have the client open her company in QBO and click the Gear icon beside the company name.**

   QBO displays the client's Gear menu in QBO (see Figure 12-1).

2. **In the Your Company column, have your client click Manage Users.**

   The Manage Users page appears. This page identifies the company's Master Administrator, enables the client to add users to the QBO subscription (assuming it is not a Simple Start subscription), and also displays accounting firms the client has invited to access the QBO file (see Figure 12-2).

3. **Have your client click the Invite Accountant button.**

   If your client hasn't allowed pop-ups in the browser, he might see a message indicating that a pop-up was blocked. Have your client enable pop-ups for qbo.intuit.com.

   The window shown in Figure 12-3 appears.

4. **Have your client provide your email address and click Next.**

   The Finish Inviting Account page appears, explaining that, when the client clicks Finish, an email will be sent to the accountant that invites the accountant to sign in to the client's company.

5. **Click Finish.**

   The email message is sent and the Manage Users page is updated to indicate that the accountant has been sent an invitation.

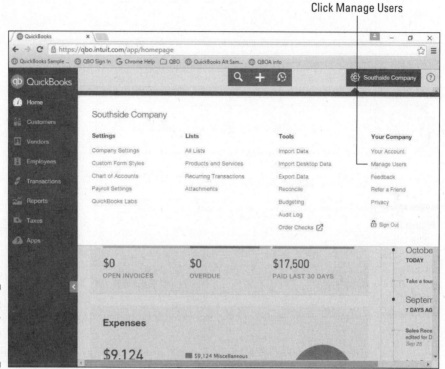

Click Manage Users

Figure 12-1:
The Gear
menu in
QBO.

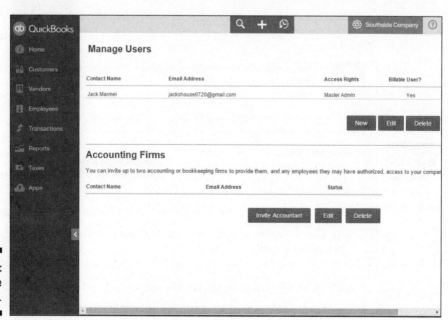

Figure 12-2:
The Manage
Users page.

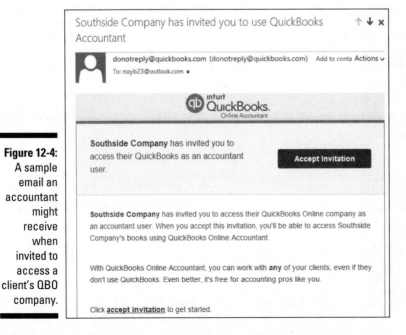

Figure 12-3:
The client
fills in the
accountant's
email
information.

When you receive your client's email, it will look something like the one
shown in Figure 12-4.

Figure 12-4:
A sample
email an
accountant
might
receive
when
invited to
access a
client's QBO
company.

Before you accept an invitation, you should make sure that you have disabled any browser ad blockers or configured them to allow *.intuit.com; otherwise, you'll have trouble accepting the invitation.

Click the Accept Invitation button, and your default browser opens to the QBOA login page. Fill in your QBOA email or user ID and password, and QBOA opens; the new client appears in your list on the Client List page.

Creating a QBO company for a client

You, the accountant, can create a new QBO company for a client instead of having the client create the company. If you have signed up for the Intuit Wholesale Pricing program, billing responsibility for the QBO company you create becomes a matter of choice:

- ✔ You can pay for the client's subscription and then bill the client back for the cost of the subscription.
- ✔ You can transfer billing responsibility to the client.

When an accountant creates a client's company

If you create a company for a client through QBOA, it's important to understand that the QBO company *does not* get a 30-day trial period. However, ProAdvisor discounts can be applied to companies created through a trial period offer.

Further, it's important to understand that you, the accountant, become both the Master Administrator and the Accountant user for any QBO company you create and add to your billing subscription. Therefore, you must retain the Master Administrator role to receive wholesale pricing for the life of the client's subscription. If your client is going to assume billing responsibility, then, as you create the company, you can assign Master Admin privileges to your client. If you retain the Master Administrator role, but, at some later time, you want to stop managing a client's subscription — for example, you stop working for the client — you can transfer Master Admin privileges back to the client. See the section "Transferring Master Administrator rights back to your client."

To create a company for your client, follow these steps:

1. **Open QBOA.**

2. **Click Clients in the Navigation bar to make sure you're displaying the Client List page.**

3. **From the Client List page, click the Add Client button in the upper-right corner above the list.**

   The Add Client wizard begins, and you see the Client Contact Info page (see Figure 12-5).

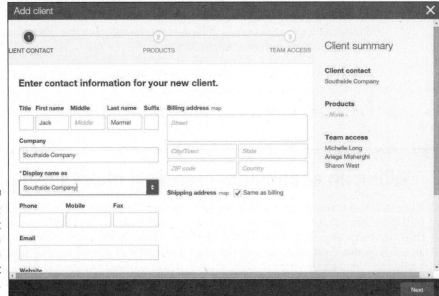

Figure 12-5: The Client Contact Info page of the Add Client wizard.

4. **Provide a name for the new company.**

5. **Optionally, supply other information on this screen.**

6. **Click Next.**

   QBOA displays the QuickBooks Products page of the Add Client wizard, shown in Figure 12-6.

7. **Click the QuickBooks Products list box to open the list and display the available QBO products.**

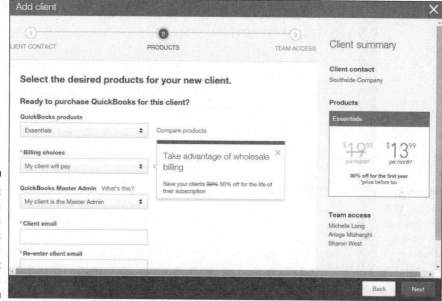

Figure 12-6:
The
QuickBooks
Products
page of the
Add Client
screen.

8. **Select a QBO product for the client.**

   You can choose Essentials, Essentials with Payroll, Essentials with Full Service Payroll, Plus, Plus with Payroll, or Plus with Full Service Payroll.

   After you select a product, the Billing Choices list box appears.

9. **Click the Billing Choices list box and make a selection.**

   If you select My Client Will Pay, you can opt to be the Master Admin instead of your client; if you make your client the Master Admin, you then need to supply the client's email address.

   If you select My Firm Will Pay (Wholesale), you don't need to supply any additional information; QBOA assigns you as the Master Admin and displays the email address you assigned to the QBOA Master Admin.

10. **Click Next.**

    QBOA displays the last screen of the wizard, where you select the members of your team who should have full administrative permissions when accessing the books of the client you're adding.

    You can change access privileges later.

11. **Click Save.**

    QBOA does some work and creates the company, which appears in the list of companies on the Client List page (see Figure 12-7).

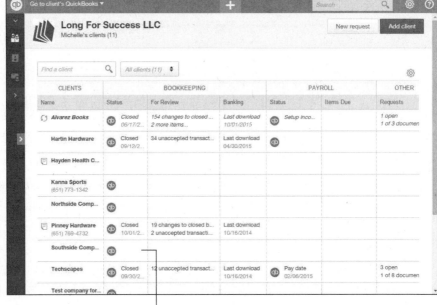

New company added

Transferring Master Administrator rights back to your client

As you see in the preceding section, when you create a company for a client, you can assign yourself as the Master Administrator; in this case, QBOA also assigns you as the Accountant user for the company. But you can transfer the Master Administrator role back to your client; this process won't affect your status as the Accountant user.

If you manage the subscription billing for your client — that is, you pay for the QBO subscription and then bill your client for it through the Intuit Wholesale Pricing program — you won't be able to transfer Master Administrator rights to your client.

The process of transferring the Master Administrator role to a client involves first inviting the client to become a Company Administrator. After the client accepts the invitation to become a Company Administrator, you can transfer the Master Administrator role to the client — again, using an invitation process.

Inviting the client to become a company administrator

As the first part of the process, create a Company Administrator for the new company. Follow these steps:

1. **Open the client company using the Go to Client's QuickBooks list on the QBOA toolbar.**

   The first time you open a client QBO company, the Welcome to QuickBooks wizard walks you through some basic setup steps, where you fill in the client's contact information, industry, and legal organization as well as some additional basic information, and QBO creates a Chart of Accounts for you.

2. **Click the Gear icon on the QBOA toolbar and choose Manage Users.**

   QBO displays the Manage Users page, which also contains the list of accountant users in the Accounting Firms section. In Figure 12-8, note that the accountant user in the Accounting Firms section at the bottom of the page and the Master Administrator in the Manage Users section at the top of the page belong to the same QBOA user.

Click here to invite your client to become the
Company Administrator for his QBO account

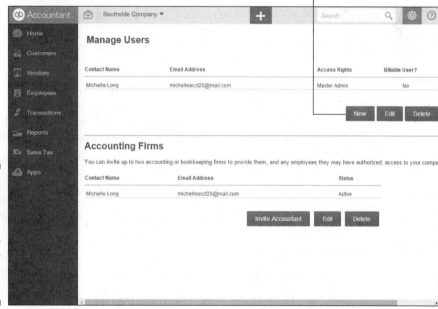

Figure 12-8:
The Manage Users page for a company created for a client by a QBOA user.

3. **Click New in the Manage Users section to add a new Company Administrator user.**

   A wizard starts.

4. **On the Choose User Type page, shown in Figure 12-9, select Company Administrator and click Next.**

Figure 12-9:
Select
Company
Adminis-
trator.

5. **On the Enter User's Email Address page, shown in Figure 12-10, provide the client's email address (and optionally, name) and click Next.**

   The Finish Adding User page appears and explains that QBO will send an email invitation to the user to sign in to the company. The email explains that he must create a QBO user ID unless he already has one. In most cases, if you set up a company for a client, the client doesn't yet have a QBO login.

6. **Click Finish.**

   The new user appears on the Manage Users page in Pending status (see Figure 12-11).

Figure 12-10:
Identify the user you want to set up as a Company Administrator.

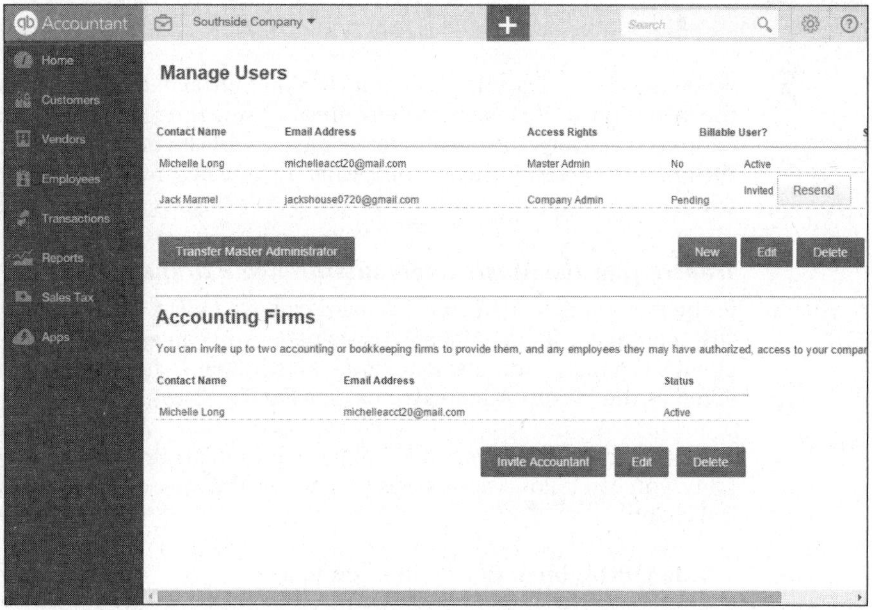

Figure 12-11:
The Manage Users page after successfully sending a message to a client to become a Company Administrator.

When the client receives the email invitation to become the Company Administrator, the invitation looks something like the one shown in Figure 12-12.

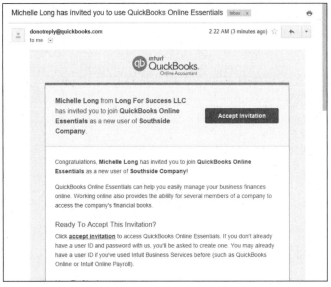

Figure 12-12:
The sample
email a
client
receives
when
invited to
become a
QBO
Company
Adminis-
trator.

When the client clicks the Accept Invitation button in the email to accept the invitation, a QBO login screen appears using the `qbo.intuit.com` web address. Typically, the client doesn't have a QBO login yet and so goes through the process of creating a new one; when he finishes, he's logged in to QBO and receives a message indicating that he successfully accepted the invitation.

Transferring the Master Administrator role to the client

In the meantime, you, the QBOA user, can use QBOA to open the client's QBO company. On the Manage Users page, you can see that the status of the client's Company Administrator role is no longer Pending, but you are still listed as the Master Administrator (see Figure 12-13).

Now that you've established a Company Administrator for the client company, you can follow these steps to transfer the Master Administrator role to the client:

1. **In QBOA, open the client's company.**

2. **Click the Gear icon on the QBOA toolbar and choose Manage Users.**

   The Manage Users page still lists you as the Master Administrator.

3. **Click Transfer Master Administrator.**

   The Transfer Master Administrator Role page appears (see Figure 12-14).

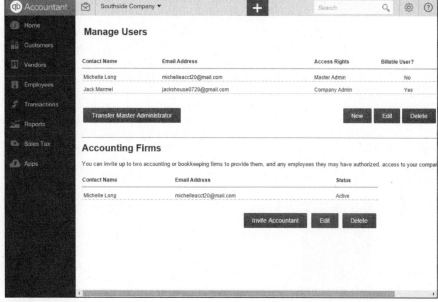

Figure 12-13:
The client's new role as Company Administrator is now active, but you're still the Master Administrator.

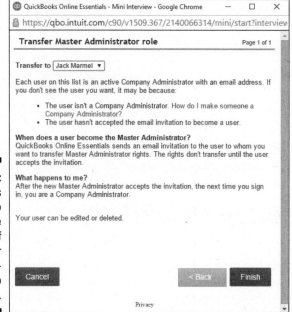

Figure 12-14:
Use this page to transfer the role of Master Administrator to your client.

4. **Select a user who should assume the Master Administrator role.**

5. **Click Finish.**

QBOA sends an email invitation to your client to become the Master Administrator; the email looks very much like the one shown earlier in Figure 12-12, and the client can accept or decline. Assuming the client accepts, he's prompted to log in to QBO. Once he does, he sees a page that explains that the Master Admin role has been successfully transferred to him and that an email explaining such will also be sent to the former Master Administrator — and that's you.

If you once again use QBOA to open the client's company and view the Manage Users page, you'll notice that you no longer appear in the Manage Users section and your client is the Master Administrator for the company (see Figure 12-15).

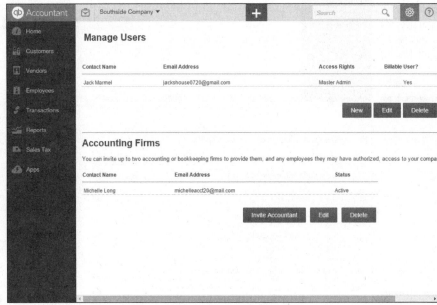

Figure 12-15: The client company's Manage Users page after transferring the Master Administrator role.

Importing Desktop QuickBooks Information

If you've been using QuickBooks for Windows Pro or Premier 2008 or later in the United States and Canada, and your QBO subscription is less than 60 days old, you can import your company's information into a QBO company. You also can help your clients import their desktop QuickBooks companies into QBO companies.

Users in countries other than the U.S. and Canada might be able to import desktop QuickBooks information into QBO with the help of an outside service; contact Intuit for more information. Users of QuickBooks for Windows 2007 and earlier, QuickBooks for the Mac, and QuickBooks Enterprise should contact Intuit for details on importing their data into QBO.

Assuming that you meet the criteria previously outlined, read on.

General conversion considerations

Before you dive into converting your data, stack the odds in your favor by doing some homework. First, examine your desktop QuickBooks data file to make sure that it will convert. In your desktop product, open your company and press F2 to display the Product Information dialog box shown in Figure 12-16. In particular, take note of the number of targets listed. If your data file's number of targets falls below 350,000, you can proceed.

Figure 12-16: Check the number of targets in your desktop QuickBooks company.

Total targets

If your data file's number of targets exceeds 350,000, consider importing lists only, as described in Chapter 4.

Next, using the U.S. version of the desktop QuickBooks product, verify your data file and then condense it so that it includes approximately one year's data. Condensing reduces the size of your data file and removes inactive list entries, and smaller data files tend to convert better. On the File menu, choose Utilities ⇨ Condense Data.

If you suspect the desktop company data isn't in good shape — for example, you get errors while verifying or condensing — you can try rebuilding the data and then rerunning the Condense Data function. If you still get errors, consider importing lists only as described in Chapter 4.

You should plan to keep your desktop data file around, if for no other reason than to refer to it for historical data as needed. Many people opt to run desktop QuickBooks and QBO simultaneously for a month or two to make sure QBO is performing as they expect.

Importing a desktop QuickBooks company

When you convert a QuickBooks desktop company to QBO, some data fully converts, some partially converts, and some doesn't convert at all. In addition, QBO contains comparable alternatives for some desktop QuickBooks features and doesn't contain alternatives for others.

In several web extra articles found at `www.dummies.con/extras/quickbooksonline`, you'll find information that describes the limitations you'll encounter if you import a desktop QuickBooks company. I suggest you review those articles so that you know what to expect. After you've reviewed the general considerations in the preceding section and the limitations for importing found at `www.dummies.con/extras/quickbooksonline`, you're ready to import your desktop QuickBooks company into QBO.

If the Multiple Currency preference in the desktop QuickBooks company has ever been enabled for the company you want to import, importing will not work.

Updating your edition of QuickBooks

The first step you should take in the process of importing data from a desktop QuickBooks company is to make sure that your edition of desktop QuickBooks is up to date. Follow these steps:

1. **Open the desktop edition of QuickBooks.**

2. **Choose Help ⇨ Update QuickBooks.**

   The Update QuickBooks window appears.

3. **Click the Update Now tab (see Figure 12-17) and select all updates.**

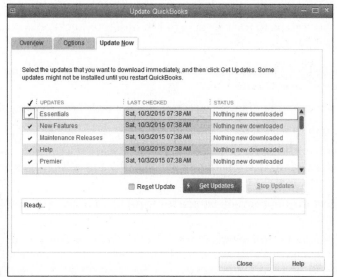

Figure 12-17:
Select all
update
areas.

4. **Click Get Updates.**

   QuickBooks goes through the process of downloading updates.

5. **Once the updating process finishes, click Close.**

Next, exit from QuickBooks and restart it; if QuickBooks downloaded updates, it will prompt you to allow the updates to be installed; make sure you install the updates.

Now, check the following in the desktop QuickBooks product to help you avoid errors during the export/import process:

- ✔ Make sure you're working in Single User mode: Click the File menu and make sure you see the Switch to Multi-user Mode command. Don't click it; just make sure you see it, because its availability lets you know you're working in Single User mode.

- ✔ To eliminate errors that might be introduced by working over a network, move the company file to your local drive.

Okay. You're ready to start the process of exporting a desktop QuickBooks company data and then importing it into a QBO company.

You can import a desktop QuickBooks company only during the first 60 days of a subscription with one exception: You can import your own data into the free company that comes with QBOA at any time.

Transferring data from a desktop company into QBO

During the transfer process, you're given the option to overwrite an existing QBO company or create a new one. In the steps that follow, I set up an empty QBO company before I started and allowed the process to overwrite it. Follow these steps to transfer data from a desktop QuickBooks company into a QBO company:

1. **In desktop QuickBooks, choose Company ⇨ Export Company File to QuickBooks Online.**

   A wizard starts to walk you through the process of exporting the data.

2. **Sign in to your QBO account.**

   If you don't have a QBO account yet, you can click Create a New Account and walk through the process of supplying a user ID — typically an email address — and a password.

3. **Select the appropriate choice for turning on inventory, and then click Continue.**

   If you opt to turn on inventory, select the date you want to use to calculate inventory value using the FIFO method. Intuit recommends that you use the first day following your company's last tax filing period.

4. **Select the appropriate choice for the location of your QuickBooks company data (see Figure 12-18).**

   I selected an empty company I created using the steps found earlier in this chapter in the section "Creating a QBO company for a client."

5. **Click Continue.**

   QBO makes a copy of your desktop QuickBooks company file and imports it into your QBO company. A message appears, letting you know that you'll receive an email when the process finishes (see Figure 12-19).

6. **Click OK, Got It.**

7. **You can close the desktop QuickBooks product.**

When the email arrives, the message will resemble the one shown in Figure 12-20. You can click the Continue to Account Setup button to log in to the QBO company, or you can use the QBO interface.

If you click the Continue to Account Setup button in the email, a new browser tab appears displaying the QBO sign-in page.

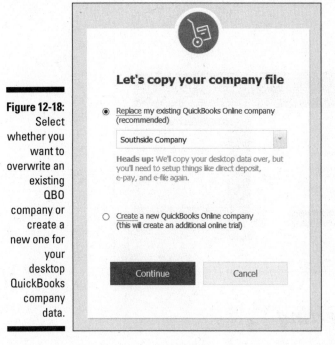

Figure 12-20:
A sample of the email message you receive after exporting a desktop QuickBooks company to QBO.

After converting . . .

After conversion finishes, you need to double-check things to make sure your data looks the way you expected. In both the desktop QuickBooks company and in the QBO company, I suggest you run and compare the Profit & Loss report, the Balance Sheet, Accounts Receivable, Accounts Payable, sales tax liability, and, if appropriate, payroll liability reports. Be sure you run these reports using the Accrual basis with the dates set to All.

Want to undo an import?

Suppose you're not happy with the results of importing and you decide that you simply want to enter data manually into your company. You can clear the data from the QBO company by purging it. Open the company and click Home so that you're viewing the QBO company home page.

In the browser address bar, change the address to `https://qbo.intuit.com/` `app/purgecompany` and press Enter or refresh the page. A page appears that describes what will be deleted and asks if you're sure. Type **yes** in the lower-right corner and click OK, and QBO purges the data from your company.

Warning: You cannot purge data from the Your Books company.

Need a do-over? During the first 60 days of a subscription, you get a do-over on importing data into a QBO company, which can be useful if things don't import as you expect. Just go through the process of importing again.

And, here's a checklist of things you probably need to do to make the imported QBO company ready for use:

- ✔ Set up company users.
- ✔ Set up sales tax items.
- ✔ Set up payroll, either through Intuit Online Payroll or QBOP.
- ✔ Reconcile accounts as needed.
- ✔ Set up recurring transactions to replace desktop QuickBooks memorized transactions.
- ✔ Review inventory.
- ✔ Customize and, if appropriate, memorize reports.
- ✔ Set up a closing date password.

Switching between Client QBO Companies

As you've worked through Chapters 11 and 12, you might have noticed that client QBO companies don't, by default, open in a separate tab in your browser. So, what do you do when you want to stop working in one client's books and start working in another's?

Well, you can click the Accountant button on the QBOA toolbar at any time to redisplay the QBOA interface and your list of clients. And, you can click the QuickBooks logo beside any client's name to open that client QBO company.

But you really don't need to take two steps to switch between client QBO companies; instead, take advantage of the Go to Client's QuickBooks list box on the QBOA toolbar.

When you're working in a client QBO company, the name of that company appears in the Go to Client's QuickBooks list box; if you click the company name, a list of all your client QBO companies appears. Just click the name of the company you want to open. No need to worry about saving work; QBO automatically saves as you work.

Chapter 13

Exploring a Client's Company from QBOA

In This Chapter

▶ Opening a client QBO company from QBOA

▶ Reviewing client QBO company settings

A client's QBO company looks a little different when viewed using QBOA. This chapter explores the interface you see when you open a client QBO company from QBOA. It also covers some facets of a client QBO company you might want to review for your client to make sure things flow smoothly for both of you.

Opening a Client's Company

You can open a client's company in QBOA from the Client List page; on the client's line in the list, click the QuickBooks logo (the circle with the letters *q* and *b* in it). Alternatively, you can use the Go to Client's QuickBooks list on the QBOA toolbar, which remains visible at all times, making it easy for you to switch from one client QBO company to another. Simply open the list and select the name of the company you want to open (see Figure 13-1).

You don't need to take any special action to close a client QBO company; you can simply open another client QBO company, or you can sign out of QBOA from the Gear menu on the QBOA toolbar.

To access two different companies simultaneously, you can't just open another browser tab and sign in to QBOA. Instead, you need to use separate browsers. Or, if you're using Chrome, you can sign into Chrome as a different user. See Chapter 17 for details on Chrome users.

Click here

Figure 13-1:
You can
click the
QuickBooks
logo or use
the list on
the QBOA
toolbar
to open a
client's QBO
company.

Click here

Reviewing a Client QBO Company

You'll probably want to review the company setup information for client QBO companies to make sure that things are set up properly for your client. In particular, you'll want to review the settings, the Chart of Accounts, and the lists of client QBO companies.

The first time you open a client QBO company that you have created, a wizard walks you through establishing basic setup information. But you can review and change that information at any time.

Examining company setup information

You review company setup information to make sure that the client QBO company uses the correct accounting method, employer EIN, and legal business organization. To review company settings, follow these steps:

1. **Open the client QBO company you want to review.**

   You can click the QuickBooks logo on the Client List page of QBOA, or you can use the list of clients in the QBOA toolbar.

2. **Click the Gear icon on the right side of the QBOA toolbar to display the Gear menu (see Figure 13-2).**

Gear icon

Figure 13-2:
The Gear
menu.

3. **From the Settings group on the left side of the Gear menu, click Company Settings.**

   The Company tab (selected on the left side of the Settings dialog box) appears (see Figure 13-3).

4. **Review the settings.**

   In particular, set or correct the following:

   - The accounting method
   - The Employer ID (EIN)
   - The tax form

   To make changes, click any setting. QBO makes the setting options available; make your changes and click Save.

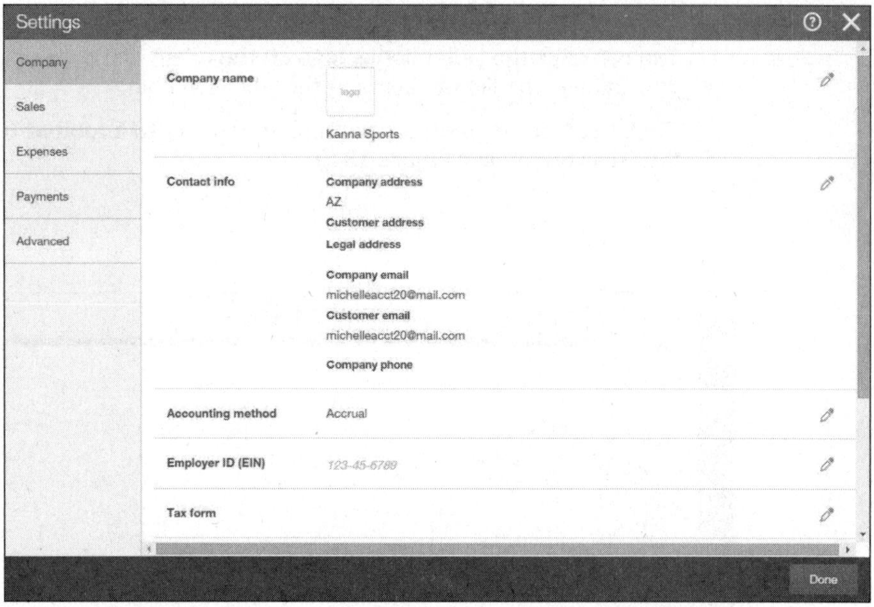

Figure 13-3:
The Settings
dialog
box for a
client QBO
company.

5. Click Advanced on the left side of the Settings dialog box.

The settings on the Advanced page of the Settings dialog box appear (see Figure 13-4).

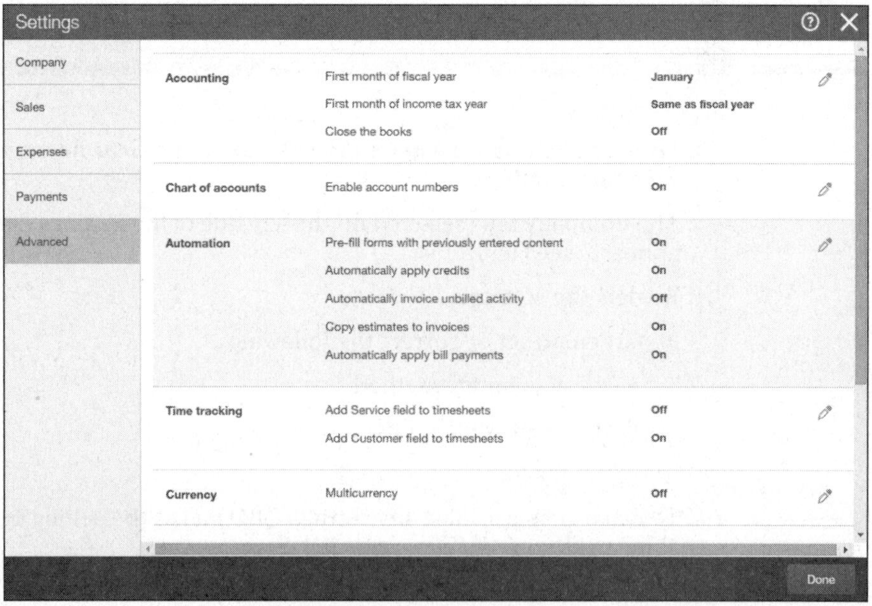

Figure 13-4:
Review
and, if
necessary,
make
changes
to settings
on the
Advanced
tab of the
Settings
dialog box.

6. **Review the settings.**

   In particular, set or correct the following:

   - The settings in the Accounting section

   - The settings in the Chart of Accounts section

   - The settings in the Other Preferences section, which isn't shown in Figure 13-4 but includes displaying warnings when duplicate check numbers and bill numbers are used

7. **Click Done to save your changes.**

   QBO displays a message at the top of the screen indicating that your changes were saved.

Taking a look at the Chart of Accounts

In addition to checking company settings, you should review your client's Chart of Accounts to make sure it looks the way you want. In the client QBO company, click the Accountant Tools button and choose Chart of Accounts to display the Chart of Accounts page shown in Figure 13-5.

Batch Edit button

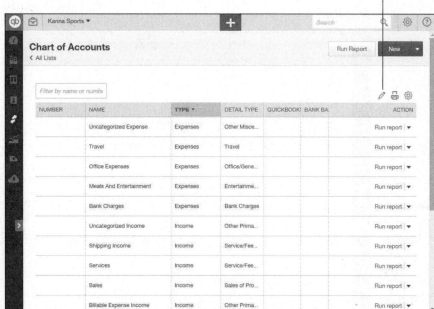

Figure 13-5: From the Chart of Accounts page, you can add and edit accounts.

You also can open the Chart of Accounts from the Navigation bar (under Transactions) and from Gear menu on the QBOA toolbar. All roads lead to Rome.

If you chose to enable the option to use account numbers while you were reviewing company settings (refer to Figure 13-4), the Chart of Accounts page displays a column for account numbers at the left edge of the Chart of Accounts page and the Batch Edit button in the upper-right corner. You'll use the Batch Edit button to add account numbers, as described later in this chapter, in the section "Adding account numbers."

Editing or adding accounts

You might need to edit an account to change an account's Category Type or its name, and you use the Account window to make the change.

If you decide to add account numbers to the Chart of Accounts, you can add an account number in the Account window; but, there's a much easier way, which I show you in the next section, "Adding account numbers."

To display the Account window, click the down arrow in the Action column at the right side of the account and, from the menu that appears, click Edit (see Figure 13-6).

Click here to create a new account

NUMBER	NAME	TYPE ▾	DETAIL TYPE	QUICKBOOKS BANK BA	ACTION
	Uncategorized Expense	Expenses	Other Misce...		Run report ▾
	Travel	Expenses	Travel		Run report ▾
	Office Expenses	Expenses	Office/Gene...		Edit / Delete
	Meals And Entertainment	Expenses	Entertainme...		Run report ▾
	Bank Charges	Expenses	Bank Charges		Run report ▾
	Uncategorized Income	Income	Other Prima...		Run report ▾
	Shipping Income	Income	Service/Fee...		Run report ▾
	Services	Income	Service/Fee...		Run report ▾
	Sales	Income	Sales of Pro...		Run report ▾
	Billable Expense Income	Income	Other Prima...		Run report ▾

Figure 13-6: To edit an account, use the down arrow in the Action column.

Click here to edit an account

Or, if you need to create a new account, click the New button above the list. The window you see when creating a new account looks just like the one you see when you edit an existing account.

If you double-click an Asset, Liability, or Equity account, QBO displays the account's register (except Retained Earnings, which displays a report). If you double-click an Income or Expense account, QBO displays a QuickReport for the account. You also can click the Register and Report links in the Action column to display a register or a report.

Adding account numbers

I promised I'd show you an easy way to add account numbers to a QBO company Chart of Accounts. First, make sure you enable the setting on the Advanced tab of the Settings dialog box (in the Chart of Accounts section), shown previously in Figure 13-4.

Then, on the Chart of Accounts page, click the Batch Edit button to display the page shown in Figure 13-7.

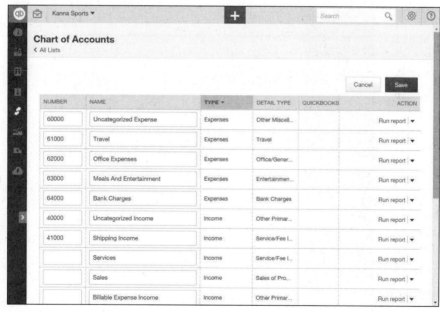

Figure 13-7: Use this page to set up account numbers for the Chart of Accounts.

Type account numbers in the Number column. Save buttons appear at the top- and bottom-right corners of the page; click either button after you finish entering the account numbers.

Because a QBOA session times out by default after 60 minutes of non-use, you might want to save periodically as you enter account numbers.

After you enter account numbers, you can sort the Chart of Accounts in account number order by clicking Number in the column headings on the Chart of Accounts page.

Reviewing list information

You also can review list information. Using the links in the Navigation bar, you can view overview information about customers, vendors, and employees. In Figure 13-8, you see the Customers page.

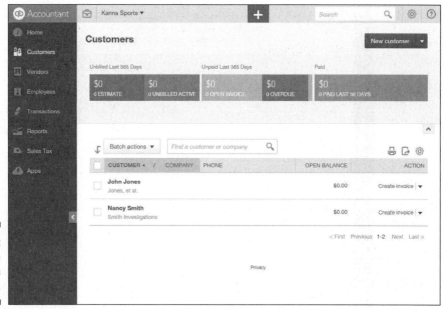

Figure 13-8: The Customers page.

On any of these pages, you can use the bar at the top of the page to filter the list to view a particular category. For example, you can filter the list of customers on the Customers page to view only overdue invoices. And you can use the Batch Actions button (just below the filter bar) to perform, well, batch actions, such as emailing a batch of customers. If your list is long, use the text box beside the Batch Actions button to search for a particular list entry. You also can sort the list by name or by open balance; just click the appropriate heading below the Batch Actions button.

TIP

You can import names into a people list. For more information, see Chapter 4.

To review other lists, click the Gear icon in the QBOA toolbar. In the Lists section of the Gear menu that appears, you can opt to view any of three common lists (the Products and Services list, the Recurring Transactions list, or the Attachments list). Or, you can click All Lists at the top of the Lists section to display the Lists page shown in Figure 13-9, which you can use to navigate to any list other than a people-oriented list.

For more extensive details on working with lists, see Chapter 4.

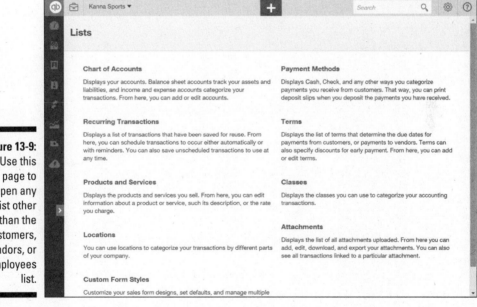

Figure 13-9: Use this page to open any list other than the Customers, Vendors, or Employees list.

Chapter 14

Working in a Client's Company

In This Chapter
▶ Navigating with shortcuts
▶ Working with transactions
▶ Communicating with clients

*Y*ou work in a client's QBO company in much the same way your client does; see Chapters 4 to 10 for detailed information. In this chapter, I focus on ways you can navigate easily, review and search for transactions, and communicate with clients.

Making Navigation Easy

Much of mouse navigation is obvious; click here and click there. But, you can use a few not-so-obvious tricks to navigate easily, including some keyboard shortcuts. Some common navigation techniques are specific to Chrome; see Chapters 16 and 17 for more information.

Using keyboard shortcuts

Hidden away in QBO companies are keyboard shortcuts that you might want to use. I show them here in Figure 14-1, and you also can find them on this book's cheat sheet, located at www.dummies.com/cheatsheet/quickbooksonline.

To view these shortcuts (and the current client QBO Company ID), press and hold Ctrl+Alt and then press the forward slash (/) key. Mac users, substitute Option for Alt here and in the next paragraph. If you press Ctrl+Alt+/ without opening a client QBO company, the Company ID you see is your own.

Your Company ID is 724935425 H90

Keyboard Shortcuts

To take advantage of shortcuts, simultaneously press
[ctrl] and [alt or option] and one [key from the list below]

REGULAR PAGES: HOMEPAGE, CUSTOMERS ETC.		TRANSACTION PAGES: INVOICE, EXPENSE ETC.	
SHORTCUT KEY	ACTION	SHORTCUT KEY	ACTION
i	Invoice	x	Exit transaction view
w	Check	c	Cancel out
e	Estimate	s	Save and New
x	Expense	d	Save and Close
r	Receive Payment	m	Save and Send
c	Customers	p	Print
v	Vendors		
a	Chart of Accounts		
l	Lists		
h	Help		
f	Search Transactions		
? or /	This dialog		

OK

Figure 14-1:
Keyboard
shortcuts
you can use
while
working in a
client QBO
company.

To use any of these shortcuts, press and hold Ctrl+Alt and then press the appropriate key to perform its associated action. For example, to open the Invoice window, press Ctrl+Alt+I.

Opening multiple windows

Many times, accountants want to work with multiple windows, and you can do that in QBO. Within the same QBO company, you can duplicate a browser tab using the New Window command on the Accountant Tools menu on the QBOA toolbar (see Figure 14-2). You can read more about the other commands on the Accountant Tools menu in Chapter 15.

If you're using Chrome to work in QBO, you also can duplicate a browser tab by right-clicking the tab and choosing Duplicate. In Firefox, you can duplicate a browser tab by clicking in the address bar and pressing Alt+Enter.

When you click the New Window command, QBO opens a new browser tab and displays the same information that appears in the original browser tab. But, from that point, you can display different information for the same company in each browser tab. And, if you're working in Chrome on multiple monitors, you can split the tabs onto different monitors. Drag the tab you want to place on a different monitor in a downward direction, and it splits away from the browser. You can immediately drag it to another monitor, or you can release the mouse button, in which case a second instance of Chrome appears. You can then drag either instance to a different monitor.

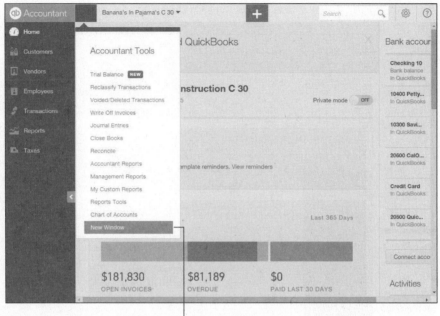

Figure 14-2:
Use the
New
Window
command
while
working
in a QBO
company to
duplicate
the window
you're
viewing.

Click here to duplicate the current browser tab

The same technique works in Firefox; drag a Firefox tab downward and release the mouse button. The tab splits away and appears in a second instance of Firefox. You can then drag either instance to a different monitor.

Working in two companies simultaneously

Suppose that you're done working with one client and want to open a different client. As described in Chapter 12, you can click the Go to Client's QuickBooks button on the QBOA toolbar and select a new client. Or, you can click the Accountant button in the upper- left corner of the QBOA interface to redisplay the Client List page and then click the QuickBooks icon for the client QBO company you now want to open. Either way, QBOA displays the information for the newly selected client.

That brings up the question, "How do I work in two different companies simultaneously?" Well, you can open a different browser, sign into QBOA, and open a second client QBO company. For example, if you're working in Chrome, you could open Firefox using the same QBOA login information. You can then open two different companies, as I did in Figure 14-3.

One company open in Chrome

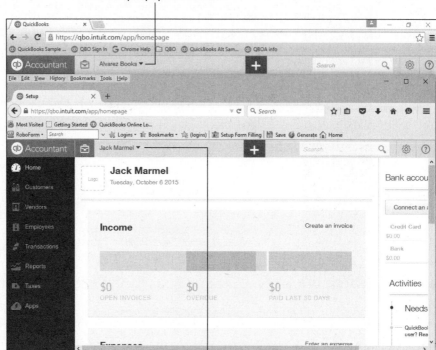

Figure 14-3:
To work
in two
companies
at the same
time, you
can use two
browsers.

Different company open in Firefox

If you're working in Chrome, you also can take advantage of Chrome users and open Chrome as a different user. You'd have, effectively, two instances of Chrome running simultaneously. See Chapter 17 for more information on Chrome users.

Examining Available Transaction Types

In Chapters 5 to 9, I cover transactions in some detail, so I'm not going to repeat that information here. But you can see the available transactions by opening a client QBO company and then clicking the Create menu (the plus sign) shown in Figure 14-4. Available transactions are organized on the menu by the type of people to which they pertain. And the Create menu contains an "Other" category for transactions that don't pertain to particular types of people — like bank deposits.

Before you open the Create menu, its button appears as a plus sign (+), but after you open it, as I did in Figure 14-4, the button changes to an X.

If you want to view only the more commonly used transactions, click the Show Less link in the lower-right corner of the Create menu. The link changes to the Show More link so that you can redisplay all types of transactions.

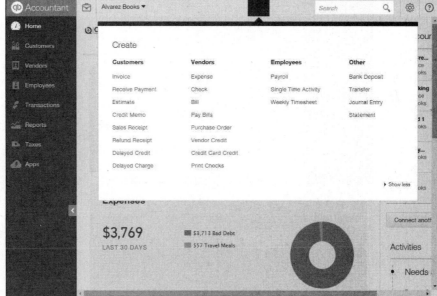

Figure 14-4: The transactions you can create while working in a QBO company.

Searching for Transactions

More often than not, you'll be searching for transactions in a client QBO company rather than creating them. You can search for transactions using the Search box on the QBOA toolbar at the top of the client QBO company window (see Figure 14-5). When you click in the Search box, QBO displays a list of recent transactions and reports.

If you see the result you want, you can click it to open it in the appropriate window. If you *don't* see the result you want, you have a couple of options.

First, you can type in the Search box, and QBO responds with sample results. If you still don't see the result you want, try your second option: Click Advanced Search in the lower-right corner of the menu, and QBO displays the Search page (see Figure 14-6).

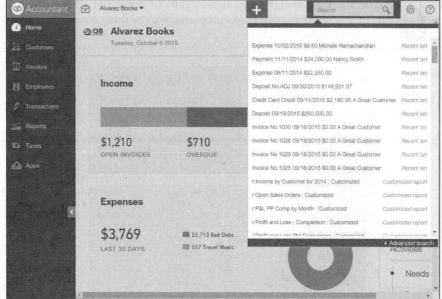

Figure 14-5:
Type any
phrase you
want to use
as a search
filter or click
Advanced
Search at
the bottom
of the
Search list.

Figure 14-6:
Set criteria
for a more
specifically
defined
search.

You can limit the search to a particular transaction type, choose to search for any of several types of data, and specify whether the search should contain, not contain, be equal to, or not be equal to the search criteria.

From any transaction window, you can view recent transactions of that type by clicking the button that appears in the transaction's title bar, immediately to the left of the name of the transaction type. The button image looks like a clock.

Communicating with a Client

Using QBO and QBOA tools, you can communicate with clients. You can

✔ Communicate via email concerning a particular transaction.

✔ Send an email request to a client for documents.

You also can send an email from QBOA without opening your email client. In the Client List, click the client's name. On the page that appears, click the client's email address. Your email program opens and displays the window where you type a new email message; the message is already addressed to your client.

Using the Client Collaborator tool

QBO and QBOA contain a tool called the Client Collaborator that you can use to communicate with your client about existing transactions. The Client Collaborator is a two-way tool; you or your client can send a message, and the message recipient can answer. Think of the Client Collaborator as a way to send a text message using QBOA or QBO.

You can communicate about certain types of transactions but not others. In general, you can communicate about posting transactions such as invoices, bills, payments to customers, checks to vendors, and credit card transactions. But you won't find the Conversation button referred to in this section in windows for cash and non-posting transactions such as sales receipts, expense transactions, billable expenses, delayed charges, credit memos, and paycheck and payroll-related windows.

Although either you or your client can initiate messaging, I'll start from the QBOA interface and post a message to a client. Follow these steps:

1. **Open the client company.**

2. **Open the transaction you question.**

   For this example, I opened a bill.

3. **In the upper-right corner of the transaction window, click the Conversation button (see Figure 14-7).**

   QBOA displays the bottom of the message, which contains an Activities section.

   The Activities section doesn't appear while you're creating a new transaction; it appears only on previously created transactions.

Figure 14-7:
Creating a
message to
a client.

4. **In the Activities section, click the drop-down list to select a message recipient.**

5. **Type your message.**

6. **Click Post.**

   QBOA sends an email message to the recipient, and the posted message appears at the bottom of the Activities section, along with the date and time the message was posted (see Figure 14-8).

Figure 14-8:
Posted
messages
appear
below the
Activities
section.

When the message recipient opens the email, a message like the one shown in Figure 14-9 appears, explaining that a message concerning a particular transaction has been posted in the recipient's QBO company.

Figure 14-9:
An email
message
generated
by the Client
Collaborator
tool.

To view the message and respond, the recipient can click the link in the message; the link initially displays the QBO sign-in page so that the client can sign in to his company. If your client initiates the conversation, the QBOA sign-in page appears.

Once the client signs in, the Conversation button appears in the upper-right corner of the QBO company Home page, beside the Gear icon (see Figure 14-10). The Conversation button contains the number 1, indicating that the client has one message, and the client can click the Conversation button to view the message.

Figure 14-10:
When messages exist, the Conversation button displays the number of waiting messages.

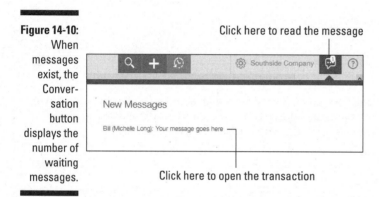

Click here to read the message

New Messages

Bill (Michelle Long): Your message goes here

Click here to open the transaction

If the client then clicks the message, the transaction from which the message originated opens. The client can then scroll to the bottom of the message, and, in the Activities area shown earlier in Figure 14-7, respond to the message by selecting a recipient, typing a message, and posting it. The Client Collaborator continues the process, sending an email notification of a message to the recipient, who clicks the link in the message to open the company and read and respond. The message conversation continues to appear at the bottom of the transaction.

Requesting documents from clients

You can, from within QBOA, request documents you need from your clients. When you do so, QBOA generates an email, sending it to the client for you; in addition, QBOA helps you track the status of the document request. To request a document from a client, follow these steps:

1. **Display your Client List page.**

   That is, make sure you have not opened a particular client.

2. On the QBOA toolbar, click the Create button and, from the Create menu that appears, click Request.

QBOA displays the Create New Request screen shown in Figure 14-11.

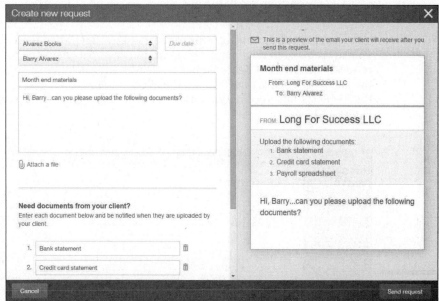

3. From the list box at the top left of the screen, select the client QBO company from which you need documents.

QBOA fills in the username associated with the client QBO company.

4. Optionally, type a due date for receiving the documents.

Including a due date can help you assign some urgency to your message and might help make your client react more quickly.

5. If prompted, type the client's email address.

6. Type a subject for the email message.

7. Type any message or questions in the box below the subject.

8. Attach any files you need to send to the client.

9. List any documents you need from your client.

The right side of the screen shows a preview of the email message the client will receive.

10. **Click Send Request.**

    The first time you send a request, QBOA prompts you to set up a Box account, and you see extra screens not shown here; on the first one, click Turn on Box, and on the second one, click Grant Access to Box.

    QBOA sends an email to your client, requesting the information you specified.

You can check the status of your request at any time; when your client sends you any requested document, QBOA notifies you. To check the status of a request, display the Client List page of QBOA and click the client's name in the list. QBOA displays details for the client, organized on four tabs. Click the Requests tab; information about your request appears onscreen (see Figure 14-12).

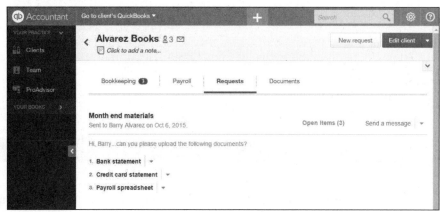

Figure 14-12: Track your document requests.

Any documents your client has sent appear with a green check beside them; you can click the Documents tab to see a list of all shared and private documents.

Chapter 15

Using Accountant Tools

Accountant tools are available to anybody who opens a client QBO company from QBOA.

You can become a user in a QBO company in one of two ways:

✔ As described in Chapter 12, your client can invite you to be the Accountant user on his account. But each QBO company can have only two Accountant users.

✔ As described in Chapter 11, the Master Administrator of the QBOA account can set up users. Any user established by the Master Administrator can log in to QBOA, open any client QBO company for which the user has privileges, and use the tools found on the Accountant Tools menu that I describe in this chapter.

In addition to the tools found on the Accountant Tools menu, this chapter covers reporting and paying sales tax — an activity that accountants often perform for their clients, so I start off with that information.

Reporting and Paying Sales Taxes

You or your client can manage and pay sales tax. Open any client QBO company and, in the Navigation bar on the left, click Sales Taxes to display the Sales Tax Center shown in Figure 15-1.

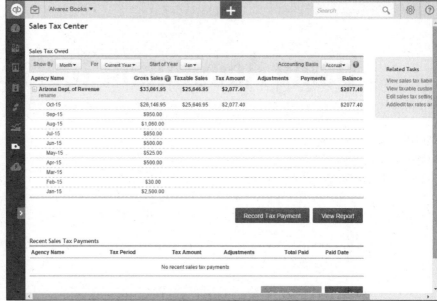

Figure 15-1:
Use the
Sales Tax
Center to
manage
and pay
sales tax.

If the client QBO company uses QBO payroll (QBOP), you might need to click Taxes before you can click Sales Tax in the Navigation bar.

You can click the View Report button to display the Sales Tax Liability Report, and on the right side of the Sales Tax Center page, you'll find a link to view a list of taxable customers.

Also on the right side of the page, you'll find links you can use to edit sales tax settings and add or edit tax rates and agencies.

You can click Record Tax Payment to pay sales tax; when you do, QBO displays the Record Sales Tax Payment dialog box shown in Figure 15-2.

QBO calculates the amount due to a sales tax agency, and you can confirm the amount or adjust it. Notice that the payment is made to the sales tax agency. Be aware that QBO doesn't treat the agency as a vendor. You won't see the sales tax agency on the Vendor List page, and you can't use the Check window or the Pay Bills window to pay a sales tax agency. In this way, QBO helps avoid applying sales tax payments incorrectly.

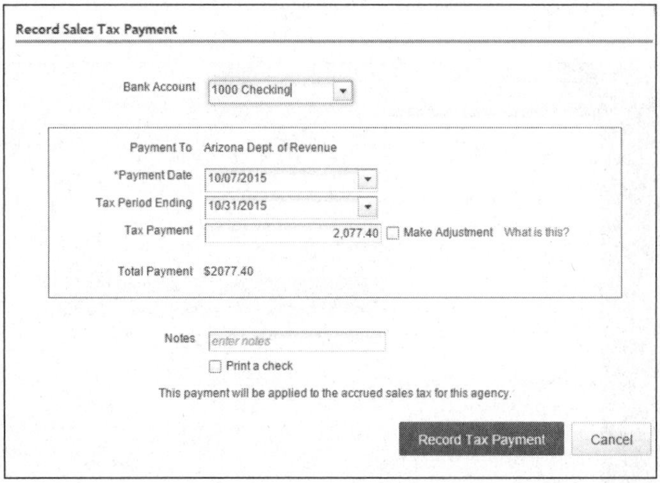

Record Sales Tax Payment

Bank Account	1000 Checking
Payment To	Arizona Dept. of Revenue
*Payment Date	10/07/2015
Tax Period Ending	10/31/2015
Tax Payment	2,077.40 ☐ Make Adjustment What is this?
Total Payment	$2077.40
Notes	enter notes
	☐ Print a check

This payment will be applied to the accrued sales tax for this agency.

[Record Tax Payment] [Cancel]

Figure 15-2:
Use this dialog box to record a sales tax payment.

Facilitating Accountant Activities

Accountants often need to reclassify transactions, examine voided and deleted transactions, write off invoices, and perform other activities. QBOA contains tools to make performing these activities easy.

To view and use the tools QBOA makes available to accountants, open any client QBO company. Then, on the QBOA toolbar, click the Accountant Tools button (the one that contains the icon that looks like a suitcase). QBOA displays the Accountant Tools menu, shown in Figure 15-3.

Understanding the Trial Balance page

You use the Trial Balance tool to display the Trial Balance page. The page you see initially presents a working trial balance like the one shown in Figure 15-4.

If you prepare a client's tax return using Intuit Tax Online, Intuit's cloud-based tax preparation software, you'll want to make sure that your client's accounts are mapped properly to lines on tax forms. The Trial Balance feature automatically maps account balances to lines on tax forms you'll file for corporations using IRS Form 1120 (for corporations) or 1120s, partnerships that use IRS Form 1065, and sole proprietorships using IRS Form 1040. For other business organization types, you can manually assign accounts to tax form lines. You also can manually assign lines on tax forms for accounts the tool doesn't recognize, and you can change tax line assignments as needed.

Click here

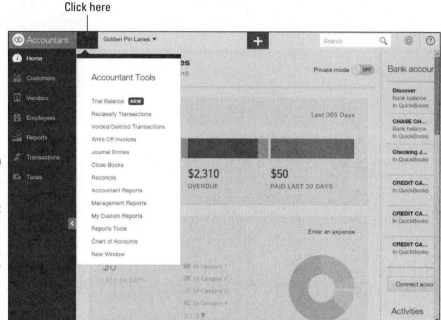

Figure 15-3:
The
Accountant
Tools menu
contains
commands
specifically
designed to
aid the
accountant.

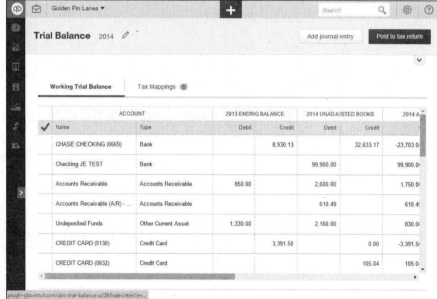

Figure 15-4:
The
Working
Trial
Balance tab
of the Trial
Balance
page.

Click the Tax Mappings tab on the Trial Balance page to see the page you use to map last year's client QBO company information directly to tax forms (see Figure 15-5).

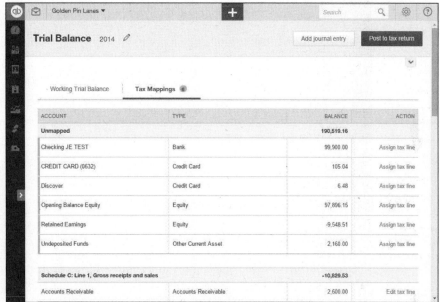

Figure 15-5:
The Tax
Mappings
tab of the
Trial
Balance
page.

To assign an account to a tax form line or edit the line to which an account is assigned, click the appropriate link in the Action column. QBOA displays a list box from which you select the appropriate tax form line. Then click Save.

Once you map your client's accounts, you can use the Working Trial Balance page (refer to Figure 15-4) to make adjusting journal entries that affect both the tax return and the client's books. When you're ready, you can click Post to Tax Return to transfer the information to Intuit Tax Online and generate a tax return. You don't pay anything to use the Trial Balance feature; you pay only when you print or e-file a return from Intuit Tax Online.

Reclassifying transactions

When you choose Reclassify Transactions from the Accountant Tools menu, the Reclassify Transactions page appears (see Figure 15-6). You can use this page to reclassify transactions without worrying about the company's closing date.

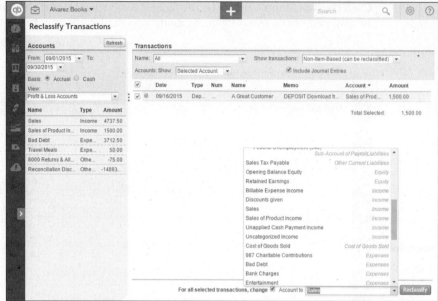

Figure 15-6:
Use this
page to
reclassify
transac-
tions.

You use the information in the gray areas of the Accounts section on the left
side of the page and the Transactions section on the right side of the page to
filter for the date range and type of accounts you want to consider. You then
select an account on the left side of the page, and QBOA displays transactions that meet the criteria on the right side of the page. You can reclassify,
individually or as a group, transactions that display a green circle.

Follow these steps to reclassify transactions:

1. **On the left side of the page, set the date range you want to consider,
   along with the accounting basis.**

2. **From the View list box, select the type of accounts you want to
   consider — Profit and Loss accounts or Balance Sheet accounts.**

3. **Click an account in the list below the View list box to examine that
   account's transactions.**

   The transactions in the account appear on the right side of the page.

4. **Above the list of transactions on the right side of the page, set
   filters to display the types of transactions that you might consider
   reclassifying.**

   You can make changes to transactions that display green circles.

   You can click a transaction to open it in its transaction window and then
   make changes to it.

5. To change several transactions simultaneously, select them by clicking the check box beside them.

6. At the bottom of the page, select the For Select Transactions, Change check box.

7. From the Account to list, specify a different account.

8. Click the Reclassify button.

Examining voided and deleted transactions

You can click Voided/Deleted Transactions on the Accountant Tools menu to display the Audit Log. The default view of the Audit Log (see Figure 15-7), shows information about those transactions that have been voided or deleted. But, you can click the Filter button to set a variety of different filters to view other types of transactions and events.

Click here to display more than voided or deleted transactions

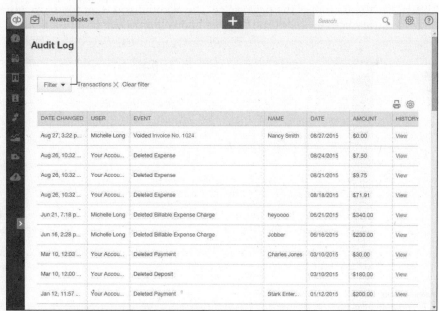

Figure 15-7:
Use the
Audit Log to
view all
kinds of
activity in
the QBO
company.

Writing off invoices

Choosing Write Off Invoices from the Accountant Tools menu displays the Write Off Invoices page, which enables you to view invoices you might want to write off, and then write them off to an account of your choice. At the top of the page, you set filters to display the invoices you want to review. Select the age of the invoices to view those

✔ Greater than 180 days

✔ Greater than 120 days

✔ In the current accounting period

✔ In a custom date range you set

You also can set a balance limit.

As you can see in Figure 15-8, QBOA displays the date, age, invoice number, customer name, original invoice amount, and the amount still due on the invoice. To write off any invoices, click the check box beside them. Then, at the bottom of the page, select the account you want to use to write off the invoices and click the Preview and Write Off button.

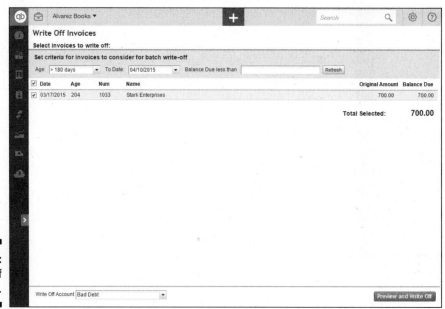

Figure 15-8: Writing off invoices.

QBOA displays the Confirm Write Off dialog box shown in Figure 15-9. If the information in the dialog box is correct, click Write Off. Otherwise, click Cancel.

Closing the books

You use the Close Books command on the Accountant Tools menu to display the Advanced page of the QBO company's Settings dialog box, shown in Figure 15-10. You can click anywhere in the Accounting section to edit the fields in that section, which include the closing date for the books.

You can set a closing date and then allow changes prior to the closing date after QBO issues a warning, or you can require a password to enter changes prior to the closing date.

Reviewing reports

Reports in QBOA work the same way as reports in QBO; see Chapter 10 for details.

But, QBOA contains some reports of particular interest to accountants. If you open a client QBO company and then, from the Accountant Tools menu, click Accountant Reports, the Reports page appears. Below the Profit and Loss graphic, the Accountant Reports tab spotlights the reports available to QBOA users. In Figure 15-11, I hid the Profit and Loss graphic (click the arrow in the lower-right corner of the graphic to hide and display it) so that you can see more of the reports on the Accountant Reports tab. But I still couldn't show all of them; when you're checking out these reports, be sure to scroll down the page.

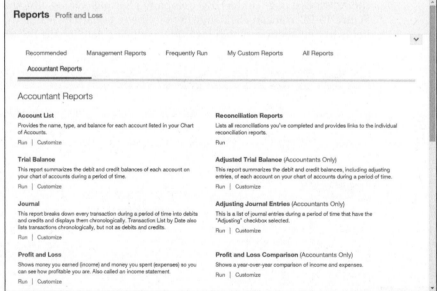

Figure 15-11: Accountant-oriented reports available in QBOA.

If you choose Management Reports from the Accountant Tools menu (or if you click the Management Reports link that appears on the Reports page shown in Figure 15-11), QBOA displays two customized management-style reports: Expanded Company Financials and Basic Company Financials. Both reports display a collection of reports, complete with an elegant cover page and a table of contents.

The Expanded Company Financials report contains the P&L, Balance Sheet, Statement of Cash Flows, and the A/R Aging Detail and A/P Aging Detail reports. The Basic Company Financials report contains all reports except the Aging Detail reports. Using the Edit link in the Action column, you can edit either report to add or delete reports and modify the appearance of pages in the report, including determining whether pages such as the table of contents appear in the report. Using the down arrow that appears in the Action column, you can print these reports, send them via email, export the information to PDF files or DOCX files, and make copies of them so that you can make your own set of management reports.

Copying one of these reports before you change it is a great idea; that way, you keep the original report intact but create your own version of it as well.

If you choose My Custom Reports from the Accountant Tools menu, reports you have customized and saved appear. And you can click Reports Tools on the Accountant Tools menu to set default report dates and accounting basis. You also can see account reconciliation status and view and set company closing date information.

A brief look at other accountant tools

The Accountant Tools menu contains a few other tools that make an accountant's life easier, such as the Reconcile page; from this page, you can opt to reconcile an account you select, or you can review existing reconciliation reports.

Also from the Accountant Tools menu, you can choose Journal Entries to display the Journal Entry window, or Chart of Accounts to display the Chart of Accounts window; I describe working in the Chart of Accounts window in Chapter 13. You also can use the New Window command described in Chapter 14 to quickly open a new window in QBOA.

Part IV
The Part of Tens

Check out the free article at www.dummies.com/extras/quickbooksonline to see keyboard shortcuts you can use to help you work quickly and efficiently in QBO.

In this part . . .

- ✔ Become familiar with the Chrome browser and its features, including the Omnibox, the star, and the Chrome menu.

- ✔ Learn about setting up Chrome users and working with Chrome windows and tabs.

- ✔ Examine the value and the pitfalls of signing into and out of Chrome.

- ✔ Examine Chrome's security and privacy.

- ✔ Learn how to establish a home page and create and use bookmarks.

Chapter 16

Ten Things about the Chrome Browser Interface

Chrome — officially Google Chrome — is the free web browser created by Google, Inc., the American-based multinational corporation that focuses on Internet-related products and services, such as Gmail for email, Google Maps, and Google Docs, just to name a few. But most of Google's profits come from online advertising technologies.

Although QuickBooks Online (QBO) and QuickBooks Online Accountant (QBOA) work in the Chrome, Firefox, Safari, and Internet Explorer browsers, I found that both products work best in Chrome. If you're not familiar with Chrome or haven't worked much in it, this chapter and Chapter 17 are designed to help you become adept at using Chrome with QBO and QBOA. This chapter focuses on helping you become familiar with the Chrome interface and make use of it. Figure 16-1 shows you how Chrome looks shortly after you install and open it; don't forget to refer back to this figure as you read the chapter.

If you don't already have Chrome installed on your computer, you can visit www.google.com/chrome/browser/. From this web page, you can download and install Chrome.

Back and Forward buttons

Current tab

Chrome Menu button

Refresh button   Omnibox

Bookmark This Page button

New Tab button

Current User button

Figure 16-1:
Reviewing the Chrome interface.

Recently visited sites   Buttons used to navigate to various Google apps

Understanding Users

The Current User button in the top-right corner of the screen represents a Chrome user. The icon may appear generically, as you see it in Figure 16-1, or it may display your name or email address. In Chrome, you can set up multiple users, each of whom can have different Chrome settings. In this way, each person using Chrome on a single computer can customize the program, saving his or her own bookmarks, passwords, and more. See Chapter 17 to learn how to create a Chrome user.

Windows and Tabs

You can open Chrome more than once to view multiple web pages — a process called *opening a new window.*

To open a new window, first open Chrome. Then, press Ctrl+N, and a second instance of the Chrome browser appears. In Figure 16-2, I've resized Chrome's second window so that you can see both instances of Chrome. Also notice that two buttons for Chrome appear in the Windows taskbar.

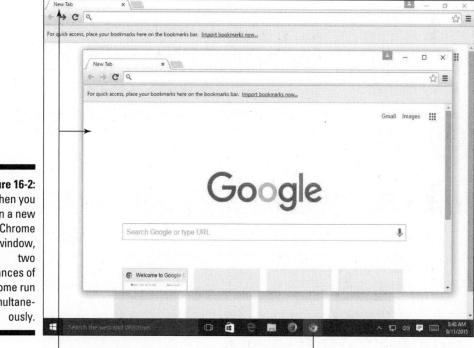

Figure 16-2: When you open a new Chrome window, two instances of Chrome run simultaneously.

Two instances of Chrome   Two Chrome icons appear on the taskbar

But, in most cases, you don't need to open multiple instances of Chrome; you can use Chrome's tabs to display multiple web pages while you work.

Tabs appear at the top of the Chrome window and initially display the same shortcuts you see when you open a new window. You can add a tab by clicking the New Tab button, which appears just beside the last open tab (refer back to Figure 16-1). And, you can close any tab by clicking the X that appears in the tab. You also can reposition tabs in the Chrome window by dragging a tab's title.

In either a new window or a new tab, you navigate to a new website using the Omnibox (read on).

Using the Omnibox to Visit a Web Page

You've probably heard of the *address bar* in other browsers; Chrome refers to the text box at the top of the browser as the *Omnibox* because it's a multi-purpose box.

To visit a web page, type the address of the web page into the Omnibox and either press Enter or click the Refresh button. After you've visited a few websites, you can click the Back and Forward buttons to revisit pages you have recently visited in the order you visited them.

If you right-click or click and hold either the Back button or the Forward button, you can view a historical list of the websites you have visited. You can left-click one to return to it.

Using the Omnibox to Search the Web

Chrome uses the Omnibox to combine the functions of navigating to web-sites and searching the Internet; as you might expect, Chrome uses Google's search engine by default. You can type a search term into the Omnibox, and as you type, suggestions driven by Google's search technology appear. You can then click a suggestion to navigate to the associated Google search page or web page.

A gray icon appears to the left of each suggestion in the Omnibox; the icon indicates the type of suggestion:

- ✔ A piece of paper represents a page you've viewed previously or a web-site related to what you're typing.

- ✔ A magnifying glass indicates that the suggestion is a potential search term.

- ✔ A star identifies a suggestion as one of your existing bookmarks (see the next section, "What's the Star?" for more on bookmarks).

What's the Star?

You can easily save the web address of a site you visit frequently so that you don't have to type the address each time you want to visit the site. In Chrome, saving a web address is called *bookmarking,* and you click the star icon to create a bookmark for the web page you are currently viewing. You can read more about working with bookmarks, including managing bookmarks, in Chapter 17.

Examining the Chrome Menu

You can click the Chrome Menu button (see Figure 16-3) to view a series of commands that help you work in Chrome.

Using options on the Chrome Menu, you can

✔ Work with bookmarks (described in Chapter 17).

✔ Reopen recently closed tabs.

✔ Copy and paste text.

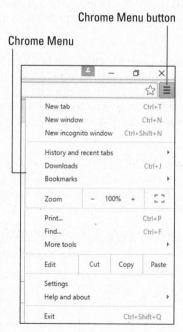

Figure 16-3:
The Google
Chrome
Menu.

✔ Save a web page.

✔ Find text on a web page.

✔ Print a web page.

✔ View files you have downloaded.

✔ Make changes to Chrome's settings.

The options available to you on the Chrome Menu aren't limited to the ones I've listed — there are too many for me to list them all. But, for example, if you want to see how your web browsing affects your computer's use of memory, you can choose Chrome Menu ⇨ More Tools ⇨ Task Manager.

About Signing In to (and Out of) Chrome

I'm going to repeat myself in this section because it's important for you to understand the ramifications of signing in and signing out of Chrome. Let me start by saying — emphasizing, in fact — that you don't have to sign in to use Chrome. In particular, you don't need to sign in to Chrome to use QBO or QBOA.

That said, why sign in? If you sign in, bookmarks and passwords you save, browsing history, and settings are saved to the cloud. You can then sign in to Chrome on a different computer and use all your settings from that computer or any computer.

The act of signing in can result in some negative side effects. Even though you sign out of Chrome, Chrome can still remember some of your information, making it visible to anyone who uses Chrome on the same computer. And, on a public computer, leaving traces of your activity could result in others gaining access to your personal information, email, and saved passwords.

 I strongly urge you to avoid signing in to Chrome if you are using a public computer. Remember, you don't need to sign in to Chrome to use QBO or QBOA. And, I'll be repeating this warning again in this section because it's important to the security of your financial data.

If you want to sign in to Chrome, you need a Google account. If you have a Gmail email address, you already have an account, and you can skip the section, "Creating a Google account."

Creating a Google account

If you don't have a Google account, you can easily create one; creating a Google account automatically creates a Gmail email address and a Google+ profile. Once you have a Google account, you can use Google services such as Gmail, Google Docs, and Google Calendar. Follow these steps to create a Google account:

If you already have a Gmail email address, you already have a Google account. Skip these steps and continue in the next section, "Signing in to Chrome."

1. **Navigate to** www.google.com.

2. **Click the Sign In button in the top-right corner of the page.**

3. **On the page that appears, click the Create Account link.**

   The link appears below the box where you would ordinarily provide your email address.

4. **Provide the requested information.**

   The requested information includes your name, a username, which is a proposed Gmail email address and associated password, birth date, gender, mobile phone number, current email address, and location.

5. **Review Google's Terms of Service and Privacy policies and click Next Step.**

6. **On the Create Your Profile page, you can add a photo to your Google+ profile. If you don't want to set a profile photo at this time, click Next step.**

   Google creates your account.

Signing in to Chrome

If you sign in to the Chrome browser, bookmarks and passwords you save, browsing history, and settings are available to you from any computer.

Avoid signing in to Chrome if you are using a public computer, because signing out might not remove all your information, leaving it visible to anyone who uses Chrome on the computer.

To sign in to Chrome, follow these steps:

1. **Click the User icon in the top-right corner of the browser.**

2. **Click Sign in to Chrome.**

   The sign-in form appears, requesting your Google Account email and password.

3. **Enter your Google account username or Gmail email address and password.**

4. **Click Sign In.**

   A message appears, letting you know you are signed in to Chrome (see Figure 16-4).

5. **Click OK, Got It!**

   The Current User button changes to reflect either your name or your email address — an indication that you are signed in to Chrome.

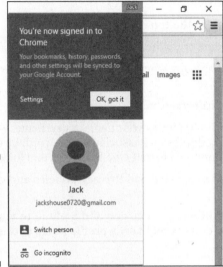

Figure 16-4: Once you've signed in to Chrome, this message appears.

Signing out of Chrome

You should sign out of your Google account when you finish using Chrome, or when you no longer want changes you make on your computer saved to your Google account and synced to Google Chrome on your other devices. Signing out also can help if you think an error with Chrome's synchronization has occurred, and you want to try to fix the error by signing out and then signing in again.

By default, when you sign out of your Google account in the browser window, you leave behind traces of yourself. On a public computer, it's possible that other people might gain access to your personal information, email, and saved passwords.

But, an option appears during the sign-out process that you can select to eliminate all traces of you on the computer. The option deletes saved information on the local computer about the Chrome user who signed in.

On your own private computer, deleting all traces of the user who signed in, including the user profile, might be a bit more drastic than you want. You can opt to clear history separately and less drastically; see Chapter 17 for details on clearing history. But, if you're working on a public computer, you should delete the user as well as the user's settings.

Follow these steps to sign out of Chrome:

1. **Click the Chrome Menu button to open the Chrome Menu.**

2. **Click Settings.**

   The Chrome Settings page appears (see Figure 16-5).

Figure 16-5:
The Sign In section of the Chrome Settings page.

Chrome	Settings
History	Sign in
Extensions	Signed in as jackshouse0720@gmail.com. Manage your synced data on Google Dashboard.
Settings	Disconnect your Google Account... Advanced sync settings...

3. **In the Sign In section at the top of the page, click Disconnect Your Google Account.**

   A confirmation dialog box appears (see Figure 16-6).

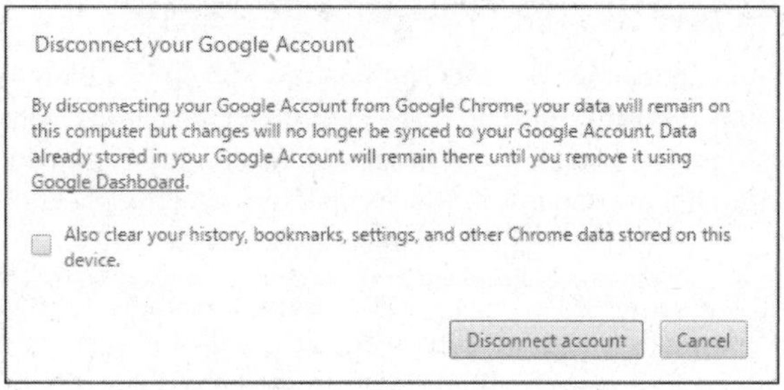

Figure 16-6:
A dialog box appears, asking you to confirm disconnecting from your Google account.

Disconnect your Google Account

By disconnecting your Google Account from Google Chrome, your data will remain on this computer but changes will no longer be synced to your Google Account. Data already stored in your Google Account will remain there until you remove it using Google Dashboard.

☐ Also clear your history, bookmarks, settings, and other Chrome data stored on this device.

Disconnect account   Cancel

4. **Select the Also Clear Your History, Bookmarks, Settings, and Other Chrome Data Stored on This Device check box if you want to eliminate all trace on the computer of the user who signed in to Chrome.**

Checking this box deletes everything on the computer associated with the user — your account history, bookmarks, settings, and other Chrome data saved on the computer. I can't repeat this mantra often enough: If you are working on a public computer, you should safeguard your privacy and check this box. However, if you're working on a private computer, you can safely keep the user and optionally clear history. To keep the user, do not check this box; see Chapter 17 for details on clearing history.

5. **Click Disconnect Account.**

Google signs you out of your Google account and Chrome. The appearance of the Current User button returns to a generic form.

Using the Chrome Web Store

You can enhance the capabilities of Chrome using web apps, plug-ins, and extensions such as calculators, ad blockers, or password managers. These browser-capable enhancers work like software you install on your computer, phone, or tablet, but they typically function within Chrome.

If you plan to use an ad blocker, be aware that you need to configure it properly to work with QBOA. For information about configuring the two most popular ad blockers, AdBlock and AdBlock Plus, see this support article from Intuit: `http://accountants.intuit.com/support/accounting/qboa/document.jsp?product=QBOA&id=HOW22468`.

Web apps and plug-ins and extensions, oh my!

So what exactly is a web app and how does it differ from a plug-in or extension? Honestly, for the purposes of this book, you probably don't care. But, for better or for worse, here are some simple definitions:

✔ Web apps run inside your browser with their own dedicated user interface.

✔ Extensions, unlike web apps, do not typically have a user interface. Instead, they extend the functionality of Chrome and the websites you view using Chrome.

✔ Plug-ins are similar to extensions in that they extend functionality by helping Chrome process special types of web content, but a plug-in affects only the specific web page that contains it.

So, as you can see, each has a technical definition that distinguishes it from the others, but, for most of us, the bottom line is this: All of them enhance the capabilities of a browser by providing some function that the browser does not, inherently, provide.

You can obtain web apps, plug-ins, and extensions from the Chrome Web Store found at `https://chrome.google.com/webstore`. The Chrome Web Store provides tools you can use to search for web apps, plug-ins, and extensions.

Web apps you install should appear on the New Tab page, from which you can launch them. You also can remove a web app by right-clicking it on the New Tab page and then clicking Remove from Chrome.

Extensions run by default when you open Chrome. You can view a list of installed extensions from the Settings page. Choose Chrome Menu⇨Settings. Then, on the left side of the Settings page, click Extensions (see Figure 16-7).

Click here to view installed extensions

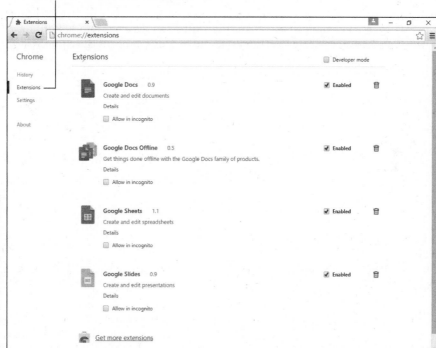

Figure 16-7:
You can view and enable or disable extensions from the Settings page.

You might want to disable an extension if you suspect it is causing a conflict as you work; uncheck the Enabled check box beside the extension. If the extension proves to be the source of your problem, you can delete it by clicking the trash can icon beside it.

Plug-ins enable certain types of web content that browsers can't process. When Chrome encounters a plug-in on a web page, Chrome allows the plug-in to perform its function. Learn more about managing plug-ins in Chapter 17.

Selecting a Theme

You can use *themes* to change the appearance of Chrome. Themes can change the color of the Chrome window, or they can add background pictures to the entire browser.

You can find available themes in the Chrome Web Store; in the navigation pane that runs down the left side of the Chrome Web Store page, click Themes to preview available themes.

If you install a theme and then later change your mind about using it, choose Chrome Menu ⇨ Settings. On the Settings page, in the Appearance section, click Reset to Default Theme.

Chapter 17

Ten Ways to Use Chrome Effectively

Chapter 16 helps you understand and work with the Chrome interface. This chapter introduces some browser tips and tricks that can make using Chrome easier and more effective both in general and specifically with QBO and QBOA.

Setting a Home Page

Many browsers sport an icon that you can click to return to your *Home page* — the page that appears when you open the browser. When you open Chrome, by default, the New Tab page appears. Although Chrome doesn't show the Home icon, you can set a Home page and display the icon that you click to display that Home page. Note that Chrome doesn't open and display the page you set as the Home page; instead, the Home page appears when you click the Home button.

Before you begin the following steps, make sure you know the web address of the page you want to set as your Home page:

1. Choose Chrome Menu ⇨ Settings.

The Settings tab appears.

2. In the Appearance section, click the Show Home Button check box.

The Home button appears between the Refresh button and the Omnibox (see Figure 17-1). By default, Chrome opens the New Tab page whenever you click the Home button.

Home button

Figure 17-1:
Adding the
Home but-
ton and
setting a
Home page.

Show Home Button check box   Click here to set a Home page address

3. Click Change.

The Home page dialog box appears (see Figure 17-2).

Figure 17-2:
Use this
dialog box
to type the
web
address of
your Home
page.

    4. Select the Open This Page option and type a web address.

    5. Click OK.

The Home page appears whenever you click the Home icon beside the Omnibox.

If you open certain sites every time you start Chrome, you can pin each page as a tab. See the section "Duplicating and Pinning Tabs."

Chrome and Security

Chrome includes several tools that help to keep you safe online. As you are no doubt aware, bad things can happen as you browse the Internet. You can run into *phishing* schemes, where someone tries to trick you into sharing personal or sensitive information, usually through a fake website. You also can run into websites that have been hacked and contain *malware* that tries to install itself on your computer, often without your knowledge; malware usually tries to harm you and your computer in some way, including trying to steal information.

Chrome includes technology, enabled by default, that helps protect you from phishing schemes and malware, displaying a warning whenever you visit a potentially dangerous page.

Chrome also uses a technique called *sandboxing* to open websites. Sandboxing isolates computer processes from anything else happening on the machine. If a sandboxed process crashes or becomes infected with malware, the rest of your computer remains unaffected. Each tab in Chrome opens as a separate process, completely independent of other tabs. If a website contains malware, the sandboxing technique isolates the malware to the browser tab; the malware can't jump to another Chrome tab or to your computer. You eliminate the malware threat when you close the infected website's browser tab.

A third method hackers can use to gain access to your computer is by the use of plug-ins. *Plug-ins* are small add-on programs for browsers. Because they are add-on programs, plug-ins can become out-of-date and hackers can use them to try to introduce malware onto your computer. Adobe Flash Player is one of the most popular browser plug-ins; it is used most often to view video content. Out-of-date versions of Adobe Flash Player are also notorious for introducing malware into computers. Chrome reduces the threat that Adobe Flash Player poses by directly integrating it into Chrome. Because of this integration, updates for Adobe Flash Player are included in Chrome updates.

Chrome also regularly checks for the latest security update without any action on your part. By integrating Adobe Flash Player and regularly checking for security updates, Chrome greatly reduces the danger of malware infection.

To view the default security measures, you can follow the next steps:

1. **Choose Chrome Menu ⇨ Settings.**

   Don't change security settings unless you really know what you're doing.

2. **Scroll to the bottom of the page and click Show Advanced Settings.**

   • In the Privacy section, the Enable Phishing and Malware Protection option warns you if Chrome detects that the site you're trying to visit might contain phishing or other malware.

   • From the HTTPS/SSL section, you can manage your SSL certificates and settings.

Chrome and Privacy

Chrome enables you to control the information you share online. For example, you can change your privacy settings, delete your browsing history, and browse in Incognito mode. To adjust privacy settings, follow these steps:

1. **Choose Chrome Menu ⇨ Settings.**

2. **Scroll to the bottom of the Settings page and click Show Advanced Settings.**

3. **In the Privacy section, click Content Settings.**

   From the Content Settings dialog box, you can make a variety of changes. Below, I'm going to list the settings you might be most likely to change. If I don't cover a setting you want to change, you can search for help on that setting at `https://support.google.com/chrome/`.

Handling cookies

You can control how Chrome handles cookies. In most cases, websites you visit place *cookies* on your computer for the purpose of recognizing your specific browser/computer combination if you return to the site. Chrome allows cookies by default, because they are typically harmless, but cookies can allow sites to track your navigation during your visit to those sites.

Third-party cookies are cookies placed on your computer by one website for some other website. To increase privacy, most people block third-party cookies to prevent sharing information with parties not directly associated with the sites they visit.

Chrome and JavaScript

You can control whether Chrome runs JavaScript, which web developers commonly use to make their sites more interactive. If you disable JavaScript, you might find that some sites don't work properly.

Allowing plug-ins

Plug-ins appear on specific websites and are used by website developers to process web content that browsers can't inherently handle. For example, Adobe Flash Player processes content that web browsers don't inherently process. Chrome allows plug-ins to run by default, and, if you disable this feature, various websites might not function as expected.

Working in Incognito mode

If you work in *Incognito mode,* you can browse the web without recording a history of the websites you have visited and without storing cookies. Using Incognito mode doesn't make Chrome more secure; it simply enhances your privacy by preventing Chrome from keeping a record of the sites you have visited during that particular browsing session. Even in Incognito mode, you shouldn't visit websites that you wouldn't feel safe viewing in a regular Chrome window.

To use Incognito mode, choose Chrome Menu ⇨ New Incognito Window. An incognito window like the one shown in Figure 17-3 appears; notice the Incognito icon in the upper-left corner of the browser window, immediately to the left of the New Tab tab. You use an Incognito window the same way that you use the regular Chrome window; while you work, Chrome doesn't record a history of the sites you visit nor does Chrome allow sites to store cookies on your computer.

Incognito icon

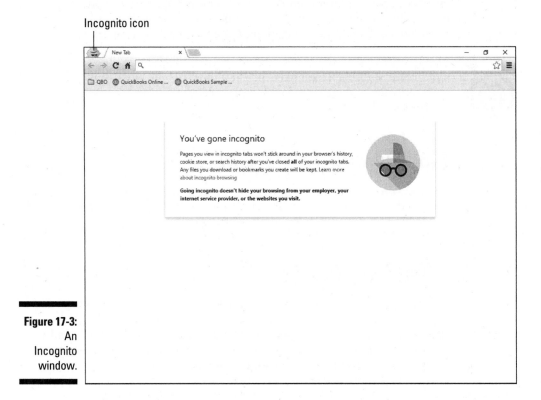

You've gone incognito

Pages you view in incognito tabs won't stick around in your browser's history, cookie store, or search history after you've closed **all** of your incognito tabs. Any files you download or bookmarks you create will be kept. Learn more about incognito browsing

Going incognito doesn't hide your browsing from your employer, your internet service provider, or the websites you visit.

Figure 17-3:
An
Incognito
window.

Deleting browsing history

Like all browsers, if you work in a regular Chrome window (rather than an Incognito window), Chrome keeps track of the websites you have visited during each browsing session. Browsers save your browsing history, among other reasons, to decrease the time you wait to see a web page that you have previously visited. And browser history can help you return to a website you visited previously even though you can't remember the website's address.

To view your browsing history, choose Chrome Menu ⇨ History and Recent Tabs ⇨ History. A page similar to the one shown in Figure 17-4 appears; your browsing history is organized by date and time, with the most recent sites you visited appearing first. You can click any entry to redisplay that web page.

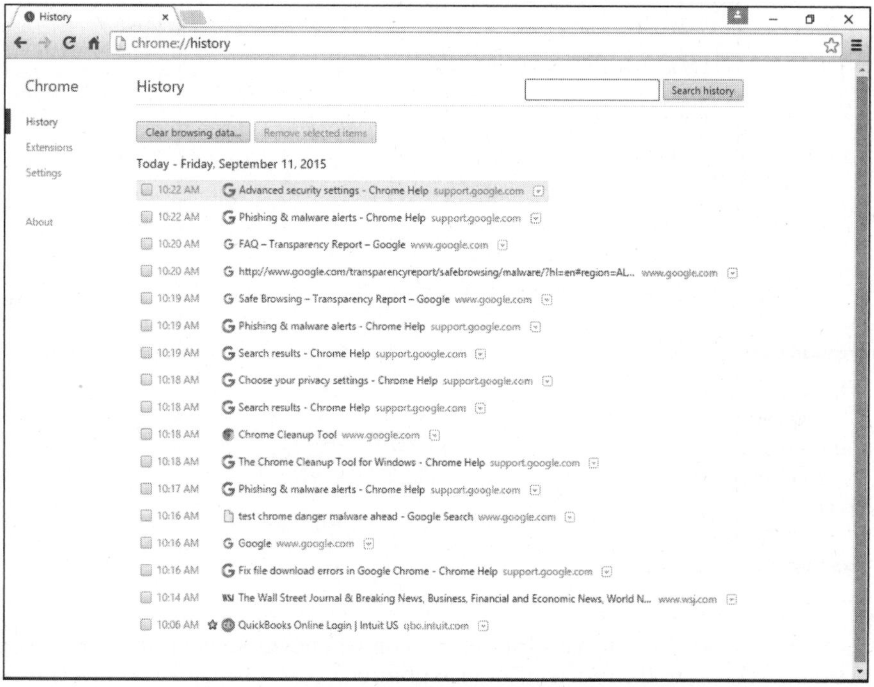

Figure 17-4:
Use your browsing history to revisit a web page you visited previously.

You also can delete all or only part of your browsing history, typically to maintain your privacy. From the History page, click Clear Browsing Data. The dialog box shown in Figure 17-5 appears; you can choose the type of data you want to delete and the time frame over which to delete that data.

To delete a single browsing history entry, display the History page (shown previously in Figure 17-4) and hover the mouse pointer over the entry you want to delete. Select the check box to the left of the entry, and, if appropriate, select additional entries to delete. Then, click the Remove Selected Items button that becomes clickable at the top of the History page.

Reviewing miscellaneous privacy settings

In addition to the settings previously described in this section, you can control the way Chrome handles the following situations; the following descriptions describe Chrome's default behavior:

✔ Chrome asks for permission whenever a website wants to use your location information.

✔ Chrome asks for permission whenever a site wants to automatically show notifications on your computer desktop.

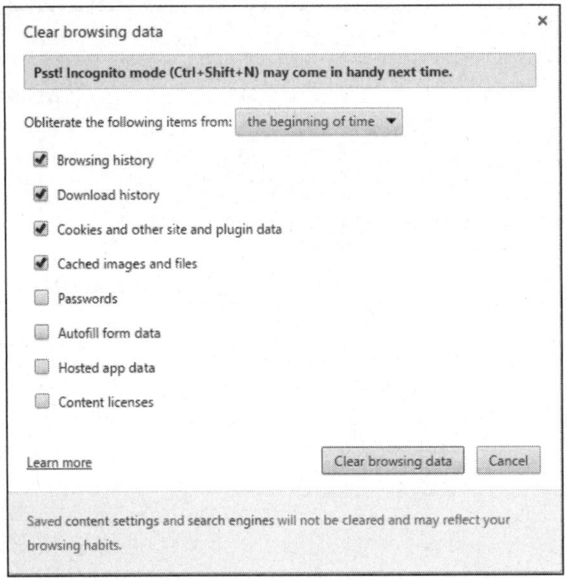

Clear browsing data ×

Psst! Incognito mode (Ctrl+Shift+N) may come in handy next time.

Obliterate the following items from: the beginning of time ▼

☑ Browsing history

☑ Download history

☑ Cookies and other site and plugin data

☑ Cached images and files

☐ Passwords

☐ Autofill form data

☐ Hosted app data

☐ Content licenses

Learn more   [Clear browsing data] [Cancel]

Saved content settings and search engines will not be cleared and may reflect your browsing habits.

Figure 17-5:
Use this
dialog box
to delete
browsing
history.

✔ Chrome asks for permission whenever sites or apps such as games want to disable your mouse pointer.

✔ Chrome asks for permission whenever websites request access to your computer's camera and microphone.

✔ Chrome asks for permission if a website wants to bypass Chrome's sandbox technology and directly access your computer.

✔ Chrome blocks pop-ups from appearing and cluttering your screen.

To use Chrome effectively with QBO and QBOA, you cannot block *all* pop-ups. By default, Chrome blocks all pop-ups. If you try to use QBO or QBOA while pop-ups are blocked, you'll see a screen similar to the one shown in Figure 17-6.

Note the pop-up blocker icon at the right edge of the Omnibox. Click it to display the message shown in Figure 17-6, and then select the first option to allow QBO and QBOA pop-ups.

You can turn on pop-ups selectively for any website. Follow these steps:

1. **Click Chrome Menu ⇨ Settings.**

2. **Click Show Advanced Settings.**

3. **In the Privacy section, click the Content Settings button.**

Click this button to display options for handling
pop-ups on a particular website

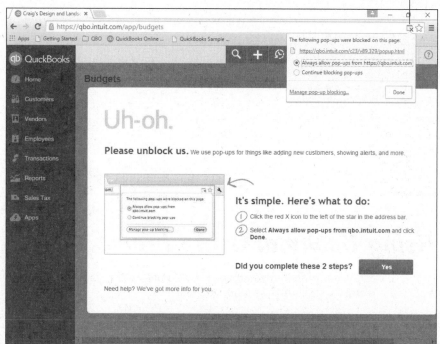

Figure 17-6:
When all
pop-ups are
blocked,
you can't
access QBO
or QBOA.

4. In the Content Settings dialog box, scroll down to the Pop-ups section and click Manage Exceptions (see Figure 17-7).

5. In the Pop-up Exceptions dialog box that appears, type the name of the website for which you want to manage pop-ups.

6. From the Behavior list box beside the web address, choose Allow or Block.

Using Google tools to manage privacy

Although Google can collect a lot of information about you, you can control just how much information Google collects using Google's privacy management tools. Visit www.google.com/goodtoknow/online-safety/security-tools/ from this website, you can, for example, use the Ads Preferences Manager to opt out of targeted ads.

Figure 17-7:
Use the
Manage
Exceptions
button in the
Pop-ups
section to
identify
websites
whose pop-
ups you
want to
allow or
deny.

Using Bookmarks in Chrome

Bookmarks enable you to save a web page address so that you can easily return to it. In this section, you learn to

✔ Create a bookmark.

✔ Use a bookmark to display its associated web page.

✔ Display the Bookmarks bar in Chrome to make bookmarks more accessible.

✔ Organize bookmarks by renaming them, placing them into folders, changing the order in which they appear when you view bookmarks, and deleting bookmarks you no longer need.

Creating a bookmark

Creating a bookmark is easy. First, navigate to the web page you want to bookmark. For example, you might want to bookmark the QBO or QBOA sign-in page. Then click the Bookmark This Page button (the one that looks like a star) at the right edge of the Omnibox, and either press Ctrl+D or choose Chrome Menu ➪ Bookmarks ➪ Bookmark This Page. The Bookmark Added! dialog box appears (see Figure 17-8).

You can change the bookmark's name (I shortened mine) and the folder in which Chrome stores it; you read more about these organizational techniques later in this section. Click Done, and Chrome saves your bookmark.

Figure 17-8:
This dialog
box appears
when you
create a
bookmark.

Bookmark added!

Name: QBO Sign In

Folder: Bookmarks bar

Remove   Edit...   **Done**

Sign in to get your bookmarks everywhere.

Using a bookmark

After you create a bookmark, you can use it to quickly navigate to the bookmark's website. Choose Chrome Menu ➪ Bookmarks. All the bookmarks you've created appear at the bottom of the Bookmarks menu (see Figure 17-9). Just click the bookmark representing the web page you want to view, and Chrome takes you there.

Bookmarks

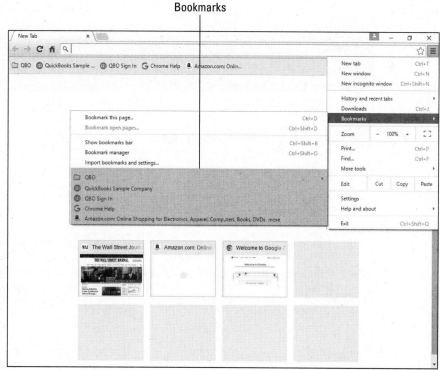

Figure 17-9:
Bookmarks
you've
saved
appear at
the bottom
of the
Bookmarks
menu.

Displaying the Bookmarks bar

By default, Chrome saves your bookmarks to the Bookmarks bar, which appears just below the Omnibox every time you open the New Tab page. The Bookmarks bar makes using bookmarks faster and easier because bookmarks are always visible — you don't need to navigate to the Bookmarks menu to view and use them. You can simply click the appropriate bookmark on the Bookmarks bar.

To take full advantage of the Bookmarks bar, you can display it on all Chrome tabs (instead of just the New Tab tab). Press Ctrl+Shift+B or choose Chrome Menu⇨Bookmarks⇨Show Bookmarks Bar. Chrome displays as many bookmarks as possible on the Bookmarks bar, based on the names you give to your bookmarks: The shorter the name, the more bookmarks Chrome can display. But, you can easily get to the bookmarks you can't see by clicking the small button containing two right-pointing arrows at the right edge of the Bookmarks bar (see Figure 17-10).

Bookmarks bar   Click here to display additional bookmarks

Figure 17-10:
Take advantage of the Bookmarks bar.

Importing bookmarks

If you've been working in a different browser and want to copy your bookmarks from that browser to Chrome, no problem. Choose Chrome Menu⇨Bookmarks⇨Import Bookmarks and Settings. The Import Bookmarks and Settings dialog box appears (see Figure 17-11).

Select or deselect the check boxes beside the items you want to import and, if appropriate, also select the browser from which to import them. Then, click Import, and Chrome imports the information. The imported bookmarks appear in a folder on the Bookmarks bar, and you can use the Bookmark Manager, described in the next section, to reorganize these bookmarks.

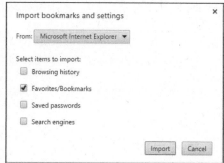

Figure 17-11: Use this dialog box to identify what you want to import.

Managing bookmarks

If you're like me, you'll learn to love bookmarks — perhaps to your detriment. As you accumulate bookmarks, finding them to be able to use them becomes a project. You have a few avenues available to you:

✔ You can organize your bookmarks by repositioning them on the Bookmarks bar and on the list of bookmarks.

✔ You can create folders for your bookmarks and place bookmarks in the appropriate folder.

✔ You can search for a bookmark.

To reposition bookmarks, you can drag them on the Bookmarks bar or on the list of bookmarks (either the list that appears when you click the button at the right edge of the Bookmarks bar, or the list of bookmarks that appears at the bottom of the Bookmarks menu). A black line (vertical if you're dragging on the Bookmarks bar or horizontal if you're dragging on either list of bookmarks) helps you locate the new position for the bookmark; simply release the mouse button when the bookmark appears where you want it to appear.

You also can use the Bookmark Manager to reorder bookmarks; in addition, using the Bookmark Manager, you can create folders and organize bookmarks into those folders, delete bookmarks and folders you no longer need, rename bookmarks, and search for bookmarks.

To open the Bookmark Manager, choose Chrome Menu ➪ Bookmarks ➪ Bookmark Manager. A tab like the one shown in Figure 17-12 appears.

TIP

The Bookmark Manager window works the same way that the Windows Explorer window works; if you're familiar with Windows Explorer, you already know many of the techniques you use to organize bookmarks.

Bookmark Manager Organize menu   Bookmarks search box

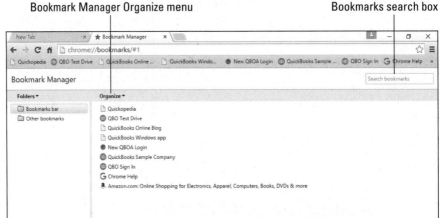

Figure 17-12:
The
Bookmark
Manager.

The left pane displays existing folders, and the right pane shows the book-marks in each folder you select in the left pane. You use the Organize button just above the left pane to make organization changes.

To delete any bookmark or folder except the Bookmarks bar folder and the Other Bookmarks folder, click the bookmark or folder and then press the Delete key on your keyboard. Nope, you can't delete the Bookmarks bar folder or the Other Bookmarks folder.

You can use folders to organize bookmarks; I like to organize my bookmarks by subject. Although you can add new folders to the Other Bookmarks folder at the bottom of the list on the left, I suggest that you confine your organization to the Bookmarks bar folder. You can compare keeping all your book-marks on the Bookmarks bar to owning only one file cabinet. The cabinet has multiple drawers (folders, in this analogy), but you need to search only one cabinet to find what you need. Finding a particular bookmark will be easier if you use only the Bookmarks bar folder.

To create a new folder on the Bookmarks bar, choose Organize ➪ Add Folder. Type a name for the new folder, and press Enter.

When you create a new bookmark that you want to place in this folder, select this folder in the Folder list box of the Bookmark Added dialog box (refer back to Figure 17-8).

To add an existing bookmark to a folder, click the bookmark on the right side of the Bookmark Manager window and drag it to the appropriate folder on the left side of the Bookmark Manager window.

To reorder bookmarks or folders, drag the bookmark or folder up or down in the list on either side of the Bookmark Manager window. That is, you can drag folders in the left side of the window and bookmarks or folders in the right side of the window. A horizontal black line appears as you drag and helps you locate the new position for the bookmark or folder; release the mouse button when the bookmark or folder's black line appears at the correct location in the list.

To rename any folder or bookmark, right-click it and choose Edit from the menu that appears. Then, type a new name and press Enter.

Suppose that, after this wonderful organizing you've done, you can't remember where you put a particular bookmark. No problem. Use the Bookmarks search box (refer to Figure 17-12). Type an address or search term into the Search box and press Enter. Chrome displays any bookmarks that match the address or search term. To cancel the search and redisplay all your bookmarks, click the X that appears in the Search box.

When you finish working in the Bookmark Manager window, click the X that appears in the tab's name.

Duplicating and Pinning Tabs

Chapter 16 describes how to open multiple tabs as you browse in Chrome and how to reposition tabs within the Chrome window.

At times, you might find it useful to duplicate a QuickBooks company tab you've already opened so that you have that tab open twice. To duplicate any tab, right-click the tab and choose Duplicate from the shortcut menu that appears (see Figure 17-13). Chrome automatically opens another tab using the web address of the duplicated tab. You can then work on the tabs independently of each other.

You might also find it useful to *pin* a particular Chrome tab; pinned tabs open automatically whenever you start Chrome. To pin a tab, right-click the tab and choose Pin Tab from the shortcut menu that appears (refer to Figure 17-13).

If you decide you no longer want a pinned tab to appear each time you open Chrome, right-click the pinned tab and click Unpin Tab from the menu that appears. Be aware that the Unpin Tab command appears only if you previously pinned the tab.

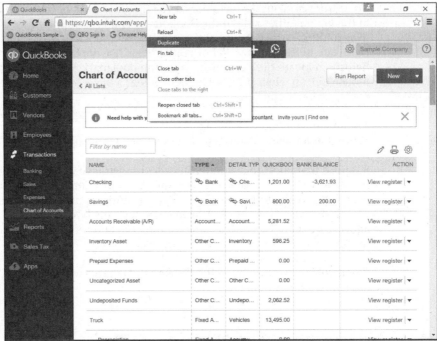

Figure 17-13:
Duplicate a
browser tab
in Chrome.

Using Chrome on Multiple Monitors

Here's another tab-related trick: If you have more than one monitor, you can pull one tab out of the Chrome window and drag it to your other monitor so that you can work in QBO/QBOA on multiple screens. Again, because tabs in Chrome function independently, the work you do in each window is independent of the other.

To pull a tab, click and drag the tab; a preview of the new window appears. Release the mouse button and the tab appears in a new window onscreen. If you didn't drag the tab to a different monitor, no problem. Just drag the new window by its title bar to your second monitor. (Yes, if you have three monitors, you can repeat this process.)

Setting Up Chrome Users

In Chapter 16, I explained that you can set up multiple users, each of whom can have different Chrome settings. At that time, I promised that I'd show you how to set up multiple Chrome users — and, here we are.

If you want to log into two different QBO companies from a single QBO account, you can use different Chrome users. To create a user, choose Chrome Menu ⇨ Settings to display the Settings tab. In the People section, click Add Person to display the Add Person dialog box (see Figure 17-14).

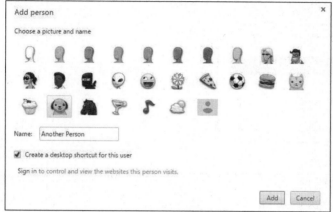

Figure 17-14:
The Add
Person
dialog box.

Select an icon for the new user and enter a name for the user. The name will appear in the Current User button, and the icon will appear when you click the Current User button in the upper-right corner of the Chrome window. Optionally, you can create a desktop shortcut for the user so that the user can quickly and easily open his or her own version of Chrome. Then click Add.

Another instance of Chrome opens, and you'll see two buttons on the Windows taskbar. You can identify the current user by looking at the Current User button in the upper-right corner of the browser, and you can easily switch from one user to another. Let's assume that you have opened only one instance of Chrome, so only one button appears on the Windows taskbar. To switch users, click Current User ⇨ Switch Person, as shown in Figure 17-15.

Chrome displays a window listing the currently defined users (see Figure 17-16); click one or click the Add Person button to go through the process of creating a new user.

Assuming you select an existing user, Chrome opens a new browser window. If you don't maximize Chrome, you can easily see the open windows.

To shortcut the process of switching users, you can right-click the Current User button; a list of available users appears and you can click the one you want.

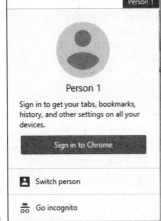

Figure 17-15:
To initiate
switching
users, use
the Current
User button.

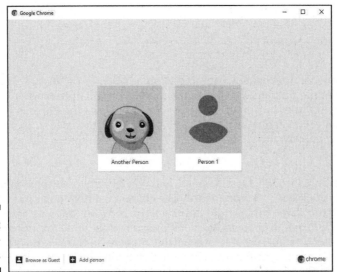

Figure 17-16:
Select a dif-
ferent user.

You can use the menu that appears when you click the Current User button to easily change a user's name or icon. To change a user's icon, click the Current User button and then click the picture currently displayed (see Figure 17-17). Chrome opens the Edit version of the dialog box you saw earlier in Figure 17-14. Just select a different icon. And you can change the user's name here, too.

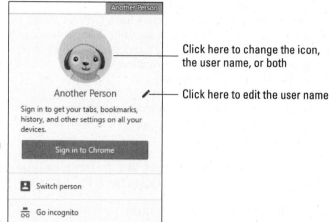

Click here to change the icon, the user name, or both

Click here to edit the user name

To change only the user's name, click the Current User button and slide the mouse cursor over the user's name; a pencil appears (refer to Figure 17-17). Click the pencil, and the text for the user's name becomes editable. Just type a new name and press Enter.

You can delete a user from the Chrome Settings tab.

Zooming In and Out

There are times when tired eyes need help; fortunately, you can zoom in and out of Chrome's windows easily. Press Ctrl++ (plus sign) to make the information in the window larger (known as *zooming in*) and Ctrl+- (minus sign) to reduce the size of the information in the window (known as *zooming out*).

Be aware that, while zooming is great for enlarging text, zooming can also alter how web pages appear, even to the point of hiding content that would otherwise be visible. So, if something seems to be missing, try resetting the zoom factor to 100%.

Downloading Files

Chrome can display many different types of documents, media, and other files, such as PDF and MP3 files. But, you might need to save a file to your computer.

Instead of clicking the file's link — which is always tempting — right-click the link and, from the menu that appears, click Save Link As. Then, in the dialog box that appears, navigate to the folder on your computer where you want to save the file, give the file a name you'll recognize, and click Save. The file downloads, and you can monitor the download progress in the lower-left corner of the Chrome browser window.

If you click a link to a file, it might download automatically or it might open within the Chrome browser. To prevent a file from opening in Chrome, make sure that you right-click the link.

To view and open any of your downloads, use the Downloads tab (see Figure 17-18). Choose Chrome Menu⇨Downloads. From this tab, you can

- Open downloaded files by clicking them.
- Open the Downloads folder by clicking the link on the right side of the screen.
- Search for downloads using the Search box just below the Bookmarks bar.
- Clear the Downloads list using the link at the far right of the window.

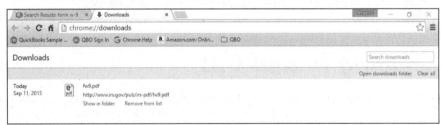

Figure 17-18: The Downloads tab.

Chrome on Mobile Devices

You can use the Chrome browser on mobile devices as well as on desktop computers (of course you can!). Chrome works on both iOS and Android, and the Chrome app is typically preinstalled on Android devices because Android and Chrome are both Google products. Chrome on a mobile device functions pretty much the same way that Chrome on a desktop computer functions.

Index

● *T* ●

About the Author

Elaine Marmel is president of Marmel Enterprises, LLC, an organization that specializes in technical writing and software training. Elaine has an MBA from Cornell University and worked on projects to build financial management systems for New York City and Washington, D.C., and trained more than 600 employees to use these systems. This prior experience provided the foundation for Marmel Enterprises, LLC, to help small businesses implement computerized accounting systems.

Elaine spends most of her time writing: She has authored and co-authored more than 90 books about software products, including Windows, QuickBooks, Quicken for Windows, Quicken for DOS, Microsoft Project, Microsoft Excel, Microsoft Word for Windows, Word for the Mac, 1-2-3 for Windows, and Lotus Notes. From 1994 to 2006, she was also the contributing editor for the monthly publications *Inside Peachtree for Windows, Inside QuickBooks,* and *Inside Timeslips* magazines.

Elaine left her native Chicago for the warmer climes of Arizona (by way of Cincinnati, OH; Jerusalem, Israel; Ithaca, NY; Washington, D.C., and Tampa, FL), where she basks in the sun with her PC and her dog, Jack, and cross-stitches.

Author's Acknowledgments

Because a book is not just the work of the author, I'd like to acknowledge and thank all the folks who made this book possible. Thanks to Katie Mohr for the opportunity to write this book. Thank you, Le' Darien Diaz, for once again being a technical editor extraordinaire, for easing my way as I worked with QBO and QBOA, for ensuring that I "told no lies," and for making the valuable suggestions you offered along the way. Last, but certainly not least, thank you, Susan Pink, for the outstanding job you did guaranteeing that my manuscript was understandable and managing everything involved in this book; you did a great job making my life easy . . . and I really enjoyed the weather reports.

Publisher's Acknowledgments

Senior Acquisitions Editor: Katie Mohr

Project and Copy Editor: Susan Pink

Technical Editor: Le' Darien Diaz

Editorial Assistant: Matthew Lowe

Sr. Editorial Assistant: Cherie Case

Production Editor: Antony Sami

Cover Image: © Comstock Images/Getty Images, Inc.

Apple & Mac

iPad For Dummies,
5th Edition
978-1-118-72306-7

iPhone For Dummies,
7th Edition
978-1-118-69083-3

Macs All-in-One
For Dummies, 4th Edition
978-1-118-82210-4

OS X Mavericks
For Dummies
978-1-118-69188-5

Blogging & Social Media

Facebook For Dummies,
5th Edition
978-1-118-63312-0

Social Media Engagement
For Dummies
978-1-118-53019-1

WordPress For Dummies,
6th Edition
978-1-118-79161-5

Business

Stock Investing
For Dummies, 4th Edition
978-1-118-37678-2

Investing For Dummies,
6th Edition
978-0-470-90545-6

Personal Finance
For Dummies, 7th Edition
978-1-118-11785-9

QuickBooks 2014
For Dummies
978-1-118-72005-9

Small Business Marketing
Kit For Dummies,
3rd Edition
978-1-118-31183-7

Careers

Job Interviews
For Dummies, 4th Edition
978-1-118-11290-8

Job Searching with Social
Media For Dummies,
2nd Edition
978-1-118-67856-5

Personal Branding
For Dummies
978-1-118-11792-7

Resumes For Dummies,
6th Edition
978-0-470-87361-8

Starting an Etsy Business
For Dummies, 2nd Edition
978-1-118-59024-9

Diet & Nutrition

Belly Fat Diet For Dummies
978-1-118-34585-6

Mediterranean Diet
For Dummies
978-1-118-71525-3

Nutrition For Dummies,
5th Edition
978-0-470-93231-5

Digital Photography

Digital SLR Photography
All-in-One For Dummies,
2nd Edition
978-1-118-59082-9

Digital SLR Video &
Filmmaking For Dummies
978-1-118-36598-4

Photoshop Elements 12
For Dummies
978-1-118-72714-0

Gardening

Herb Gardening
For Dummies, 2nd Edition
978-0-470-61778-6

Gardening with Free-Range
Chickens For Dummies
978-1-118-54754-0

Health

Boosting Your Immunity
For Dummies
978-1-118-40200-9

Diabetes For Dummies,
4th Edition
978-1-118-29447-5

Living Paleo For Dummies
978-1-118-29405-5

Big Data

Big Data For Dummies
978-1-118-50422-2

Data Visualization
For Dummies
978-1-118-50289-1

Hadoop For Dummies
978-1-118-60755-8

Language & Foreign Language

500 Spanish Verbs
For Dummies
978-1-118-02382-2

English Grammar
For Dummies, 2nd Edition
978-0-470-54664-2

French All-in-One
For Dummies
978-1-118-22815-9

German Essentials
For Dummies
978-1-118-18422-6

Italian For Dummies,
2nd Edition
978-1-118-00465-4

 **Available in print and e-book formats.**

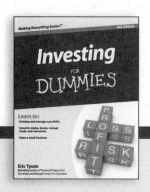   

Available wherever books are sold. **For more information or to order direct visit www.dummies.com**

Math & Science

Algebra I For Dummies,
2nd Edition
978-0-470-55964-2

Anatomy and Physiology
For Dummies, 2nd Edition
978-0-470-92326-9

Astronomy For Dummies,
3rd Edition
978-1-118-37697-3

Biology For Dummies,
2nd Edition
978-0-470-59875-7

Chemistry For Dummies,
2nd Edition
978-1-118-00730-3

1001 Algebra II Practice
Problems For Dummies
978-1-118-44662-1

Microsoft Office

Excel 2013 For Dummies
978-1-118-51012-4

Office 2013 All-in-One
For Dummies
978-1-118-51636-2

PowerPoint 2013
For Dummies
978-1-118-50253-2

Word 2013 For Dummies
978-1-118-49123-2

Music

Blues Harmonica
For Dummies
978-1-118-25269-7

Guitar For Dummies,
3rd Edition
978-1-118-11554-1

iPod & iTunes
For Dummies, 10th Edition
978-1-118-50864-0

Programming

Beginning Programming
with C For Dummies
978-1-118-73763-7

Excel VBA Programming
For Dummies, 3rd Edition
978-1-118-49037-2

Java For Dummies,
6th Edition
978-1-118-40780-6

Religion & Inspiration

The Bible For Dummies
978-0-7645-5296-0

Buddhism For Dummies,
2nd Edition
978-1-118-02379-2

Catholicism For Dummies,
2nd Edition
978-1-118-07778-8

Self-Help & Relationships

Beating Sugar Addiction
For Dummies
978-1-118-54645-1

Meditation For Dummies,
3rd Edition
978-1-118-29144-3

Seniors

Laptops For Seniors
For Dummies, 3rd Edition
978-1-118-71105-7

Computers For Seniors
For Dummies, 3rd Edition
978-1-118-11553-4

iPad For Seniors
For Dummies, 6th Edition
978-1-118-72826-0

Social Security
For Dummies
978-1-118-20573-0

Smartphones & Tablets

Android Phones
For Dummies, 2nd Edition
978-1-118-72030-1

Nexus Tablets
For Dummies
978-1-118-77243-0

Samsung Galaxy S 4
For Dummies
978-1-118-64222-1

Samsung Galaxy Tabs
For Dummies
978-1-118-77294-2

Test Prep

ACT For Dummies,
5th Edition
978-1-118-01259-8

ASVAB For Dummies,
3rd Edition
978-0-470-63760-9

GRE For Dummies,
7th Edition
978-0-470-88921-3

Officer Candidate Tests
For Dummies
978-0-470-59876-4

Physician's Assistant Exam
For Dummies
978-1-118-11556-5

Series 7 Exam For Dummies
978-0-470-09932-2

Windows 8

Windows 8.1 All-in-One
For Dummies
978-1-118-82087-2

Windows 8.1 For Dummies
978-1-118-82121-3

Windows 8.1 For Dummies,
Book + DVD Bundle
978-1-118-82107-7

Available in print and e-book formats.

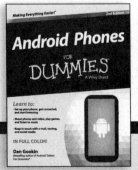

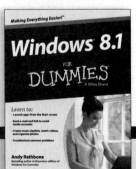

Available wherever books are sold. **For more information or to order direct visit www.dummies.com**

Take Dummies with you everywhere you go!

Whether you are excited about e-books, want more from the web, must have your mobile apps, or are swept up in social media, Dummies makes everything easier.

Leverage the Power

For Dummies is the global leader in the reference category and one of the most trusted and highly regarded brands in the world. No longer just focused on books, customers now have access to the For Dummies content they need in the format they want. Let us help you develop a solution that will fit your brand and help you connect with your customers.

Advertising & Sponsorships

Connect with an engaged audience on a powerful multimedia site, and position your message alongside expert how-to content.

Targeted ads • Video • Email marketing • Microsites • Sweepstakes sponsorship

21 Million Monthly Page Views & 13 Million Unique Visitors